Practical Tourism Forecasting

Practical Tourism Forecasting

Douglas C. Frechtling

Butterworth-Heinemann
Linacre House, Jordan Hill, Oxford OX2 8DP
A division of Reed Educational and Professional Publishing Ltd

A member of the Reed Elsevier plc group

OXFORD   BOSTON   JOHANNESBURG
MELBOURNE   NEW DELHI   SINGAPORE

First published 1996

British Library Cataloguing in Publication Data
Frechtling, Douglas C.
   Practical tourism forecasting
   1.   Tourist trade - Forecasting   2.   Tourist trade - Seasonal
   variations
   I.   Title
   338.4'7'91

ISBN 0 7506 0877 3

Typeset by David Gregson Associates, Beccles, Suffolk
Printed and bound in Great Britain by Biddles Ltd, Guildford and King's
Lynn

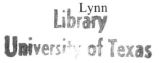

Contents

Tables

Figures

Foreword

Nearly fifty years ago, a wise entrepreneur[1] said, 'We should all be concerned about the future because we will have to spend the rest of our lives there.' The pace of life has accelerated considerably since then, and changes in consumer markets, in ways of serving them, and in technology infrastructures are now so rapid that it often seems we are encountering the future every day.

Hospitality and tourism have, of course, shared in this acceleration of change. Every week brings an announcement of innovations in accommodation services, transportation, travel retailing and myriad ways to serve the traveller away from home. Today, hospitality and tourism leaders must be quick on their feet to recognize new consumer trends, counter competitive challenges and continually exceed customer expectations. Such agility requires future views based on more than emotion and hearsay.

Marriott International believes strongly in the future of global tourism as a growth activity. We are well along the path to our goal of including 2,000 hotels in our global accommodation portfolio by the year 2000. These will all carry forward the traditions of service excellence and value that exceeds price which have proved to be the cornerstones of our success for nearly seventy years.

We would not be investing our resources in this way if we had not carefully gathered the best intelligence on current trends, and employed sound forecasting techniques to discern our prospects. These continuing efforts will profit considerably from Dr Frechtling's authoritative book.

One of the most striking conclusions of this pioneering survey of tourism forecasting is that no single method is best for all situations. Rather, the accomplished forecaster will take management's considered needs into account, along with the data available and the forecast horizon, before choosing the collection of techniques to test.

I trust this book will enable tourism and hospitality managers to think more clearly about their futures and to judge the credibility of forecasts they encounter more shrewdly. This will help ensure that we spend the rest of our lives in a future that we have helped shape, rather than one that just happened to us.

J. Willard Marriott, Jr.
Chairman and Chief Executive Officer
Marriott International
Washington, D.C.

---

[1] Charles F. Kettering was founder of Delco and the Dayton-Wright Airplane Company. The quotation is from his article 'Seed for Thought', 1949.

Preface

My interest in forecasting began while I was working on my Ph.D. dissertation in the U.S. Department of the Treasury during the heady days of macroeconomic fine-tuning and the death of the business cycle in the early 1970s. Large-scale econometric models mimicking the structure of the U.S. economy promised eternal growth and unlimited prosperity if only the politicians would listen.

It was disconcerting even then, however, to note that these monetary and fiscal behemoths spewed out conflicting forecasts more often than not, although the reasons at the time were obscure.

We now know that even the simplest national economy is too complex to be simulated reliably by a system of equations. This is also true for a sector of it, such as the tourism industry. The shelves of corporate business and academe are cluttered with past promises of rosy tourism scenarios turned to dust by a mercilessly unfolding reality.

Yet still we forecast, or accept someone else's forecasts, or reject them and in so doing implicitly project our own views onto the future. And mankind will continue to forecast tourism until the activity and the industry that serves it disappears. (No one forecasts *this* particular outcome with any probability.)

In preparing for a graduate-level workshop on tourism forecasting, I was struck by the clear, broad and unpretentious approach to business forecasting embodied in Thomas W. Moore's *Handbook of Business Forecasting*. He made forecasting tools and issues clear to me that I had difficulty grasping and presenting to a class of sharp and inquiring minds.

In the four years that I have taught this course, I have longed for such a text devoted to tourism as a foundation for exercises and explorations with my students. Encouraged by the foundational studies of alternative tourism demand forecasting methods by Stephen Witt and Christine Witt, I undertook to replicate Tom Moore's clear approach to this arcane topic for a tourism audience.

This book is about applying statistical principles, observation and reason to forecasting tourism demand. It is not designed to be a fully fledged treatise on inferential statistics and forecasting theories; there are few equations in the book. Rather the emphasis is on how various forecasting methods organize information about the past to shed light on the future, their strengths and weaknesses, and the step-by-step process for applying each.

I have employed a time series of demand for commercial lodging in the Washington, D.C. area as an instructional tool. These data suggest the monthly demand for the services of a major sector of the tourism industry.

They also represent visitor demand in a metropolitan area. Finally, this series portrays the trend, seasonal, supra-annual and irregular patterns we often encounter in tourism demand series. In short, this series illustrates the challenges that forecasters will encounter in building forecasting models regardless of the temporal or geographic context they operate in.

I hope this book will illuminate a rather obscure subject for marketing managers and strategic planners in business, transportation planners and economic policy makers in government, and academics who would like to venture forth in futures research. I trust it will also assist students, whether mathematically inclined or not, to understand the characteristics of tourism demand and the principles of evaluating the forecasts of others.

Douglas C. Frechtling
Bethesda, Maryland, U.S.A.
March 1996

Acknowledgements

Many people were kind enough to help me in writing this book. I would particularly like to thank Tom Moore of Tampa Electric Company, Steve Witt of the University of Wales, Swansea, and Darryl Jenkins of the Aviation Foundation for reviewing drafts of this manuscript and offering sagacious and constructive criticisms. Any errors of theory or practice herein remain my own, however.

I appreciate the generosity of Smith Travel Research of Hendersonville, Tennessee, U.S.A. for granting me use of data from its U.S. Lodging Database. Dave Swierenga of the Air Transport Association of America furnished me with historical series on U.S. scheduled air carriers. Kathryn Shaw and Pria Vasan of the U.S. Travel Data Center provided essential information from the Travelometer$_{sm}$ and data from the National Travel Survey. Lynn Franco supplied data from the Conference Board from the Consumer Confidence Survey. I am grateful for their generosity in contributing their time and data to this book.

I also thank Kathryn Grant at Butterworth-Heinemann for her long-suffering and understanding support. Rik Medlik has been a faithful friend and reviewer, as well as a welcome source of wisdom on tourism as a consumer activity, an industry, and a growing presence in the global community.

Finally, I thank my wife, Joy, for her patience and encouragement during what turned out to be an arduous journey from conception to realization.

1 Introduction

Some say that travel and tourism is the 'world's largest industry and generator of quality jobs' (World Travel and Tourism Council 1995, p. 1). They estimate that travel and tourism directly and indirectly contributes more than 10 per cent of the gross world product, the most comprehensive measure of the total value of the goods and services the world's economies produce.

The World Travel and Tourism Council estimated that in 1995 gross world product, both directly and indirectly related to travel and tourism, would total about $3.4 trillion, supporting 212 million jobs, and generating $655 billion in taxes. This activity is supported by $7.0 trillion invested in world plant, equipment and infrastructure related to travel and tourism.

While these numbers are difficult to verify, there is no doubt that tourism activities, encompassing travel away from home for business or pleasure, are a substantial part of lifestyles of the world's residents, or that a very large industry has grown up to serve these travellers.

Futurist John Naisbitt, in his best-selling book *Global Paradox*, subscribes to the concept that tourism will be one of the three industries that will drive the world economy into the twenty-first century. He is also author of the idea that small and medium-sized organizations are growing in importance in the expanding global economy. The managers of these organizations have the agility to act quickly and efficiently to take advantage of trend changes, emerging markets and new business opportunities.

These two realities, the continuing expansion of one of the world's most ubiquitous activities and industries, and the advantages of being small and nimble, place an increasing premium on understanding the shapes of global, national and local futures.

What this book is about

This book is designed to provide the basic and practical understanding of demand forecasting that tourism managers, marketers, planners and researchers will need to thrive in the decade ahead. It can be viewed as an introduction to the range of forecasting methods available to anyone who must forecast future demand for a tourism product. It is also designed to instruct the executive who must evaluate proposals to develop a tourism demand forecasting system, or assess an operating forecasting system and its forecasts for their usefulness in strategic management

There is no distinct set of tourism forecasting methods. Rather, quantitative and qualitative techniques developed to forecast variables of interest to business managers and public planners have been used to forecast phenomena of interest to those interested in tourism.

The present effort is an introduction to a complex issue and not a substitute for the myriad books, reports and articles available on tourism forecasting. Many of these appear as references at the end of the chapters and in the Bibliography. This book is intended to provide a foundation for understanding the various methods available and to encourage the reader to try his or her hand at forecasting some aspect of tourism demand.

It is often remarked that demand forecasting has become a very complex process, basically opaque to managers and other users. The following observation is typical, if more eloquent than most:

> Forecasting often becomes an end in itself, rather than an integral part of the strategic management process, because of the complexity of the methodologies used and the consequent need for specialist analysts to be involved. The analysts, however, have become isolated and detached, and forecasting has become a black box as far as most users are concerned.... Effective integration of tourism demand forecasting with management decision making implies the establishment of a meaningful dialogue between technicians and users. (Faulkner and Valerio 1995, p. 30)

This text is designed to help lift the veil of obscurity from the forecasting process for those who need sound guidance to the shape of the future. It is hoped that it will lead to such a 'meaningful dialogue,' as well as better forecasting and better integration of these forecasts in tourism marketing, planning, development, policy making, and research.

The scope of tourism

While there are many definitions of 'tourism' in use today, the World Tourism Organization (WTO), the affiliate of the United Nations serving as a global forum for tourism policy and issues, is working to standardize tourism terminology and classifications throughout the world. Such standardization will permit comparisons across studies, encourage the accumulation of knowledge about tourism activities, and assist those beginning to study tourism in defining their terms. These standards have been adopted by the United Nations Statistical Commission as well.

In the spirit of encouraging uniformity in tourism data collection and improving world knowledge about tourism behaviour and consequences, the following World Tourism Organization definitions are observed in this book. (The sources of these and further details about them can be found in the World Tourism Organization publications listed at the end of this chapter.)

The **visitor** is the foundational unit in the UN/WTO structure and is defined as any person travelling to a place other than that of his or her usual environment for less than 12 months and whose main purpose of the trip is other than the exercise of an activity remunerated from within the place visited.

Tourism comprises the activities of persons travelling to and staying in places outside their usual environment for not more than one consecutive year for leisure, business and other purposes.

Tourists are visitors who stay at least one night in a collective or private accommodation in a place visited.

The **same-day visitor** is a visitor who does not spend the night in a collective or private accommodation in the place visited. This includes cruise passengers who disembark in a country but spend their nights on board ship.

Tourism expenditure is the total consumption expenditure made by a visitor on behalf of a visitor for and during his or her trip and stay at a destination.

The **tourism industry** is the set of enterprises, establishments and other organizations one of whose principal activities is to provide goods and/or services to tourists.

A term central to this book yet not officially defined by the World Tourism Organization is 'tourism demand'. As employed in this book:

Tourism demand is a measure of visitors' use of a good or service.

'Use' in this case means 'to avail oneself of; apply to one's own purposes'.[1] Such use includes the economists' concept of consumption, as well as the presence of a visitor at a destination, port of entry, or other tourism facility, and on a transport vehicle, regardless of whether an exchange takes place. Consequently, visitor arrivals in a country or local area constitute tourism demand since visitors avail themselves of the services of a destination in arriving there. Tourism demand can be measured in a variety of units, including a national currency, arrivals, nights, days, distance travelled, and passenger-seats occupied.

Archer (1994) aptly describes the objective of tourism demand forecasting as

to predict the *most probable* level of demand that is likely to occur in the light of known circumstances or, when alternative policies are proposed, to show what different levels of demand may be achieved. (p. 105)

The importance of tourism demand forecasting

The tourism industry, and those interested in its success or in its role in contributing to the social and economic welfare of a citizenry, needs to reduce the risk of decisions. One important way to reduce this risk is by discerning certain future events or environments more clearly. One of the most important events is the demand for a tourism product, be it a good, a service, or a bundle of services such as a vacation or what a destination offers.

All industries are interested in such risk reduction. However, this need may be more acute in the tourism industry than for other industries with other products for the following reasons.

1. The tourism product is perishable. Once an airliner has taken off, or a theme park has closed for the day, or morning dawns over a hotel, unsold seats, admissions or sleeping rooms vanish, along with the revenue opportunity associated with them. This puts a premium on shaping demand in the short run, and anticipating it in the long run, to avoid both unsold 'inventory' on the one hand and unfulfilled demand on the other.

2. People are inseparable from the production-consumption process. To a large extent, the production of the tourism product takes place at the same time as its consumption. And much of this production–consumption process involves people interacting as suppliers and consumers, such as hotel staff, waiters and waitresses, flight attendants, and entertainers. This puts a premium on having enough of the right supply personnel available when and where visitors need them.

3. Customer satisfaction depends on complementary services. While a hotelier directly controls only what happens to guests in his or her hotel, the visitor's experience depends on his or her satisfaction with a host of goods and services that make up the visit. A hotel's future demand, therefore, depends on the volume of airline flights and other transport access to its area, the quality of airport services, the friendliness of cab drivers, the quality and cost of entertainment, the availability of recreational opportunities, to name a few of these elements. Forecasting can help ensure these complementary services are available when and where future visitors need them, which will redound to the benefit of the hotel or other individual tourism facility.

4. Leisure tourism demand is extremely sensitive to natural and manmade disasters. Much holiday and vacation travel is stimulated by the desire to seek refuge in venues far from the stress of the everyday environment. Moreover, today there are countless alternatives for spending leisure time pleasantly in most developed nations. As a result, crises such as war, terrorist attacks, disease outbreaks, crime, and extreme weather conditions can easily dissuade leisure travellers from visiting a destination suffering from one of these or from travelling at all. The ability to forecast such events and their projected impact on tourism demand can help minimize the adverse effects of catastrophes on tourism-related sales, income, employment and tax revenue of a place.

5. Tourism supply requires large, long lead-time investments in plant, equipment and infrastructure. A new hotel may take three to five years from concept to opening. A new airport or ski resort may take a decade or so for all planning, approvals, and construction. A new jetliner may take five years from an airline's order to final delivery. Future demand must be anticipated correctly if suppliers are to avoid the heavy costs of excess capacity or the opportunity costs of unfilled demand.

While there are industries that share one or several of these constraints on decision making, the tourism industry appears to be unique in being shackled by all five.

Alternative views of the future

There are two extreme views of any event in the future we need to be aware of. One extreme is that the event is absolutely predictable, that its occurrence has a 100 per cent probability. Of course, there is no future event in the universe that has such a high probability, although the positions of the planets in our solar system, the hours of sunrise and sunset, and many other events studied in the physical sciences come close to this, at least in the medium term.

Certain future events in tourism are a 'sure thing' as well. These include that at least one person in Europe will begin a trip away from home tomorrow, that at least one hotel will be partially occupied, and that at least one government will accrue some revenue as a result of tourism this year.

These nearly certain events have at least two characteristics in common: forecasting them accurately is quite easy, and these forecasts are useless to tourism marketers. They are useless because they are trivial. Furthermore, no action we can take will change these occurrences.

At the other end of the spectrum, as indicated in Figure 1.1, are those future events that are essentially random, that is, each possible occurrence of an event has the same probability. Flipping a coin or choosing a card from a well-shuffled deck are examples. The numbers selected in a lottery are

---

1. The future is totally predictable (i.e. unalterable)

implying

sound forecasts are useless.

2. The future is totally unpredictable (i.e. random)

implying

sound forecasts are impossible.

3. The future is

somewhat predictable and somewhat alterable

implying

sound forecasts are useful and feasible.

Figure 1.1   Three views of the future

designed to be random as well. In tourism, whether the next person to enter a restaurant is male or female is a random event under most circumstances.

These quite uncertain events are, by definition, impossible to forecast with any acceptable degree of accuracy. Consequently, forecasting them is not a worthwhile endeavour.

Fortunately, there is an alternative to these pessimistic views of the future that gives hope to forecasters. That is, future events important to tourism operations are somewhat predictable and somewhat changeable. We can predict events with probabilities significantly greater than zero and markedly less than 100 per cent. And these events can be affected by other events, including our own actions. This is the view adopted in this book.

This is also the hope of marketers: that we can infer enough about the future to choose certain actions to shape it toward our preferences. Some call this 'inventing the future'. We obtain these inferences from reviewing the past. A forecasting method is simply a systematic way of organizing information from the past to infer the occurrence of an event in the future.

The two extreme views suggest a warning. We make a mistake if we invest heavily in trying to achieve a near-perfect forecasting method. If we achieve such, the results will be useless. Rather we must expect that our forecasts are not going to hit the mark each time, and this is good news for those trying to invent the future. The other caveat is that we can find a forecasting method that will tell us something useful about future tourism in most cases. That is, it will increase our probability of making an accurate forecast.

Forecasting definitions

Forecasting is fundamentally the process of organizing information about a phenomenon's past in order to predict a future.

A **phenomenon** is simply 'An occurrence, a circumstance, or a fact that is perceptible by the senses' as *The American Heritage Dictionary*, third edition, defines the word. We can organize information about a phenomenon's past in many ways. One way is to manipulate objective, quantitative data by mathematical rules. Another is to analyse the opinions of experts about the phenomenon, past and future. Both of these classes of forecasting methods are treated in this book.[2]

Many who study the future believe as Herman Kahn did, that there are 'alternative futures, that the future is not a single inevitable state, but change can evolve in strikingly different ways' (Coates and Jarrett 1989, p. xi). In effect we can 'invent' a future by making changes in the present. Forecasting, then, allows us to predict a single future or a set of futures, each associated with a different set of postulated changes.

In summary, at its most basic, forecasting 'takes historical fact and scientific knowledge ... to create images of what may happen in the future.' (Cornish 1977, p. 51). This book describes the realm of scientific knowledge that has been applied to tourism demand in the last two decades; the book also focuses on ways of forecasting the behaviour of tourism markets, that is, demand for some tourism product. This product may be a hotel room, a restaurant meal, a visit to a destination, a day at Walt Disney World, or even a trip away from home. In most cases, we want to know how many consumers there will be, how many units will be sold, how much will be spent on the purchases, or any combination of these.

The term 'tourism demand forecasting' will be used to indicate a process designed to reduce the risks of tourism marketing decisions through the use of forecasting. This is assumed to be synonymous with 'tourism market forecasting'.

Other definitions

There are other terms that are not specifically related to tourism but are basic to understanding and discussing forecasting techniques:

Data point: an individual value in a **time series**.

Data series: same as a **time series**.

Forecast time series: a **time series** of future values produced by some method.

Historical time series: refers to the **time series** of past values.

Observation: same as a **data point**, reminding us that each data point must be observed and measured, introducing the possibility of error.

Time series: an ordered sequence of values of a variable observed at equally spaced time intervals.

Variable: any phenomenon that can be measured; usually refers to all of the **data points** associated with it.

Additional terms will be defined as they arise. The glossary provides a complete listing of important terms and their definitions.

Uses of tourism demand forecasts

Tourism demand forecasts can be helpful to marketers and other managers in reducing the risk of decisions regarding the future. For example, tourism marketers use demand forecasts to:

- set marketing goals, either strategic or for the annual marketing plan
- explore potential markets as to the feasibility of persuading them to buy their product and the anticipated volume of these purchases
- simulate the impact of future events on demand, including alternative marketing programmes as well as uncontrollable developments such as the course of the economy and the actions of competitors.

Managers use tourism demand forecasts to:

- determine operational requirements, such as staffing, supplies, and capacity
- study project feasibility, such as the financial viability of building a new hotel tower, expanding a restaurant, constructing a new theme park, or offering an airline service to a new destination.

Planners and others in public agencies use tourism demand forecasts to:

- predict the economic, social/cultural, and environmental consequences of visitors
- assess the potential impact of regulatory policies, such as price regulation and environmental quality controls
- project public revenues from tourism for the budgeting process
- ensure adequate capacity and infrastructure, including airports and airways, bridges and highways, and energy and water treatment utilities.

In short, sound tourism demand forecasts can reduce the risks of dec and the costs of attracting and serving the travelling public.

Consequences of poor forecasting

Every organization develops either implicit or explicit forecasts about the factors that affect its future success. If no explicit forecasting is done, then the organization's implicit forecasts can often be inferred from its actions. If a hotel hires more housekeeping personnel, then it is probably expecting an increase in its numbers of guests. If an airline lays off flight attendants, then it may well expect passenger demand to decline despite the absence of any formal forecasting process.

Most often, a business may make no change in its marketing or operations, implicitly forecasting no change in demand in the next month, quarter or year. This is a naive approach to the future that may well produce dire consequences. Table 1.1 lists some of these consequences.

Table 1.1 Uses of demand forecasts and consequences of poor forecasting

Uses of demand forecasts	Consequences of poor forecasting
Set marketing goals	Over- or under-budgeting for marketing
Explore potential markets	Marketing to wrong segments, ignoring the right ones
Simulate impacts on demand	Incorrect marketing mix, e.g. setting prices too high
Determine operational requirements	Excess labour, or customer unhappiness with limited service
Examine the feasibility of a major investment in plant or equipment	Wasted financial resources, difficulty in financing interest payments
Predict economic, social and environmental consequences	Environmental and social/cultural degradation; inflation or unemployment
Assess potential impact of regulatory policies	Business losses, unemployment, price inflation
Project public revenue	Budget deficits
Plan for adequate capacity and infrastructure	Traffic congestion, delays and accidents

Special difficulties in tourism demand forecasting

The nature of tourism demand presents a number of special challenges to the forecaster that do not afflict those in other industries.

Historical data are often lacking. Most forecasting methods require a minimum of five or ten years of data for forecasting. Some require more. Yet few cities or other destinations have such series. In the U.S., consistent estimates of foreign visitor expenditures are available only from 1984, while the annual series hotel/motel room-nights sold and revenues at the national and regional levels begins in 1987.

One study found the 1992 edition of the World Tourism Organization's *Compendium of Tourism Statistics* included 166 reporting countries out of 184 nations in the world (Frechtling 1992, p. 20). Of these 166 countries, four did not have a measure of international visitors or tourists. Thirteen countries had no recent measure of international tourism receipts, and 46 did not estimate international travel expenditures. More than one-half had no measure of international departures, and two-thirds did not count visitor nights in all accommodation establishments.

Tourism demand can be volatile. Visitor volumes fluctuate with the seasons and over annual periods, and often produce wide variations. Figure 1.2 shows per cent changes in U.S. international airline passenger-miles monthly over the year-earlier period over the early 1990s. Figure 1.3 presents a similar measure for hotel room-nights sold in Los Angeles for a recent period. Figure 1.4 shows the per cent variation in international visitors to the top four European nation destinations. The more volatility there is in an activity, the more difficult it is to discern patterns that can help us forecast futures.

Tourism demand is sensitive to catastrophic influences. Part of the long-term volatility of tourism demand is due to the variety of shocks to the tourism system from external events. The worldwide petroleum shortages in 1973–4 and 1979–80 depressed international and domestic tourism in many countries. The Chernobyl nuclear accident in 1986 coupled with the U.S.– Libya conflict and resulting terrorism reduced U.S. resident travel to individual European countries by one-quarter to two-thirds during that summer (Witt, Newbould and Watkins 1992, p. 37; Brady and Widdows 1988, p. 10). The Gulf War in 1991 depressed international tourism. Hurricanes, earthquakes, floods and epidemics have devastated visitor volumes in may parts of the world as well.

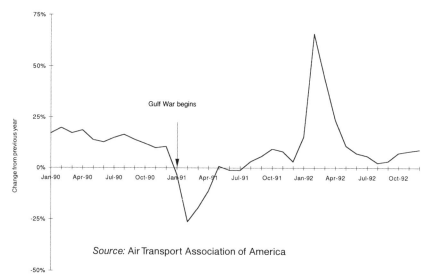

Figure 1.2 U.S. international airline traffic, monthly per cent change, 1990–92

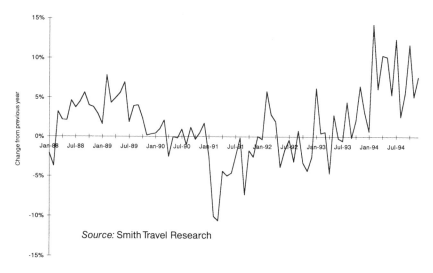

Figure 1.3 Hotel/motel room-night demand in the Los Angeles metropolitan area, monthly per cent change, 1988–94

More recently, reports of crimes against foreign visitors to Florida reduced volumes from Germany and Sweden by one-third in 1994 from the previous year (Florida Department of Commerce 1995, p. 35). And Muslim militants' attacks on foreign visitors in Egypt are credited with depressing tourism receipts by 20 per cent (Holman 1993).

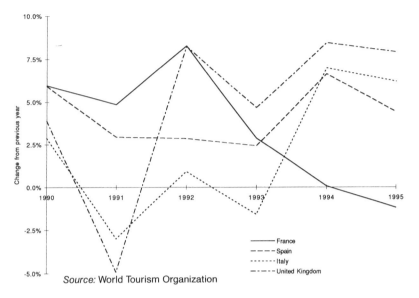

Figure 1.4   Tourist arrivals in the top four European destination countries, annual per cent change, 1990–95

These are sporadic events that are virtually impossible to forecast, and their potential effects on tourism are even more obscure. Yet the forecaster must deal with them all.

Tourism behaviour is complex. Consumers travel for a multitude of reasons: relaxation, visiting friends and relatives, viewing sports, participating in sports, outdoor recreation, sightseeing, health, religious pilgrimages, and more. Business people travel to make sales calls, attend corporate meetings, attend conferences and conventions, inspect plant and equipment, lobby government officials, present press conferences, conduct trade missions, and other purposes. Moreover, the same person travelling for business today can be planning his or her family's vacation trip tomorrow, but with vastly different motives and resources.

Each of these trip purposes may show different patterns over time and be affected by different factors. If all trip purposes are aggregated into a single tourism demand series, the conflicting patterns may prevent determining the best forecasting models and obtaining the most accurate forecasts. For example, a study of various methods of forecasting international visitor arrivals in New Zealand found more accurate results were obtained by distinguishing series of holiday, visit friends/relatives, business and 'other' trip purpose data and independently forecasting them (Turner, Kulendran and Pergat 1995). Witt and Witt (1992) reached a similar conclusion.

However, in many cases, disaggregated tourism demand data may be lacking.

Visitors patronize a myriad of business establishments: airlines, taxicabs, railroads, hotels, bed & breakfast establishments, travel agents, tour operators, amusement parks, museums, spas and other health resorts, performing arts, and gasoline service stations, to name a few. As forecasters, we have no clear concept of the 'travel product' a particular consumer seeks, and how the components affect his or her decisions to purchase complements and substitutes.

Further, there is no consensus on a sound theoretical foundation for tourism demand. We are not even certain how the family makes its vacation travel choices, as complex as they are as to timing, budgets, transport modes, and places visited.

Finally, unlike most consumer products, most sales do not occur in the buyer's home area. Rather, visits to Paris may originate in London, Prague, Montreal, New York city, Tokyo or Martinique. Consequently, we need to consider conditions in a number of widely dispersed areas as they affect demand for a place, an establishment, or a transport service.

There is a wide choice of forecast variables. Automobile industry forecasters must wrestle with hundreds of models from a dozen or so manufacturers. There may be hundreds of retailers of shoes in a country, with hundreds of styles. However, there is no question about the variables to be forecast: either units sold or sales revenue.

The world of tourism demand is not so simple. In attempting a tourism forecast, we must choose from among at least six variables that measure tourism demand, listed in Table 1.2.

It may be self-evident that a hotel company wants to forecast visitor-nights while an airline is interested in passenger-kilometres. Country, city, and other local destinations may focus on visitors, visitor-nights or visitor expenditures. Moreover, terminology changes by user. What are **visitors** to destinations, parks and attractions are **passengers** to transportation companies, **guests** to hotels and resorts, and **customers** to restaurants and rental car companies. This plethora of measures of and terms for tourism demand has constrained the growth of a consistent body of knowledge built upon prior research. For example, forecast models for projecting passenger-miles cannot help most theme park operators very much.

Reviewing 85 international tourism demand forecasting models, Crouch found that nearly two-thirds of them defined demand in terms of arrivals or departures. One-half of them measured demand in terms of expenditures and receipts. Other measures were used quite infrequently (1994a, p. 43). This pattern may not hold in domestic tourism demand models, or those focused on the markets for an individual facility, such as a resort or attraction.

Table 1.2   Alternative measures of tourism activity

Unit of measure	Activity measured
Visitors	Number of people travelling away from home
Visitor parties	Groups of people travelling away from home together
Visitor-nights	Total nights visitors spend away from home
Visitor-miles/kilometres	Distance travelled while away from home
Visitor expenditures	Total money spent purchasing goods and services related to the trip
Market size	Number of people travelling once or more in a year

Witt, Newbould and Watkins found that 'forecasting domestic tourist flows is considerably easier than forecasting international tourist flows' over a one-year horizon (1992, p. 39). They surmise the reasons to be the lack of exchange rate effects and international political upheavals. However, this observation is based on only one application: monthly visitor arrivals in Las Vegas from 1973 to 1988.

Sheldon (1993) maintains that visitor expenditure is the only one of these measures that can directly translate into economic impact (p. 14). However, these are difficult to derive and 'may have a high degree of error' (p. 19). This helps explain why her comparison of eight forecasting methods in simulating international arrivals in six countries produced higher relative errors than similar tests on visitor arrivals data.

Future patterns of any human activity are more or less obscure to those living in the present. But these peculiarities of tourism demand forecasting make discerning the road ahead even more problematic. They require a number of rather difficult decisions to be made before the search for appropriate forecasting methods is begun.

In sum, tourism demand is a ubiquitous and growing phenomenon throughout the world today. Those public and private organizations which seek to serve and manage this demand need to reduce the risk of future failures. This risk is intensified by the special characteristics of tourism demand and supply. The successful manager will seek ways to reduce this risk by organizing knowledge about the past to better discern the future, the essence of tourism demand forecasting.

Organization of this book

Thirteen methods of applied tourism forecasting are discussed in the following pages. Chapter 2 briefly describes these methods and discusses means of evaluating the results of tourism forecasting efforts.

Chapter 3 details the forecasting process that ensures that the forecaster conducts a comprehensive survey of forecasting techniques available and that time and money resources are conserved in the process.

Chapter 4 presents the simplest methods of quantitative forecasting. These 'time series models' do not deal with causes and effects but rather try to simulate historical demand data for extrapolation into the future.

Chapter 5 presents more sophisticated methods for capturing the essence of a tourism demand series' past course. These have proved relatively popular in tourism demand forecasting.

Chapter 6 discusses the Box–Jenkins technique, a complex time series analysis method that has proved quite popular in business and economic forecasting but appears to be little used in tourism.

Chapter 7 explores regression analysis, primarily used to investigate relationships of certain explanatory variables to a tourism demand series. Quantification of these relationships serves to suggest causes of tourism's course, and in equations for producing future values.

Chapter 8 presents an elaborate modelling technique for simulating the complexities of the real world. This has seldom been applied to tourism demand as yet, but may suggest fruitful avenues.

Chapter 9 discusses four qualitative forecasting techniques that have proved useful in forecasting tourism demand in both the short term and the long term.

Finally, Chapter 10 draws the experience of a number of tourism forecasters over the last decade or so to suggest future trends in forecasting this demand.

For further information

Archer, Brian (1994), 'Demand Forecasting and Estimation', *Travel, Tourism, and Hospitality Research, A Handbook for Managers and Researchers*, 2nd edition (J. R. Brent Ritchie and Charles R. Goeldner, eds), pp. 105–114, John Wiley & Sons.

Calantone, Roger J., di Benedetto, C. Anthony and Bojanic, David (1987), 'A Comprehensive Review of the Tourism Forecasting Literature', *Journal of Travel Research*, Vol. XXVI, No. 2 (fall), pp. 28–39.

Coates, Joseph F. and Jarrett, Jennifer (1989), *What Futurists Believe*, Lomond Publications, xiii + 340 pp.

Cornish, Edward (1977), *The Study of the Future*, World Future Society, x + 307 pp.

World Tourism Organization publications

(1995a) *Concepts, Definitions and Classifications for Tourism Statistics: Technical Manual No. 1*, ii + 126 pp.

(1995b) *Collection of Tourism Expenditure Statistics: Technical Manual No. 2*, v + 104 pp.

(1995c) *Collection of Domestic Tourism Statistics: Technical Manual No. 3*, vi + 125 pp.

(1995d) *Collection and Compilation of Tourism Statistics: Technical Manual No. 4*, v + 149 pp.

(1995e) *A Satellite Account for Tourism*, v + 81 pp.

United Nations and World Tourism Organization (1994), *Recommendations on Tourism Statistics*, United Nations Department for Economic and Social Information and Policy Analysis, New York, 1994, v + 77 pp.

Notes

[1] *Random House Unabridged Dictionary*, second edition, 1993.

[2] Forecasting should not be confused with *prophecy*, which is foretelling the future by means of inspired revelation. Prophecy does not depend upon arranging and analysing information about the past. But it is far less accessible to those forcasting tourism demand.

2 Alternative forecasting methods and evaluation

Choosing an appropriate forecasting model is something like fitting a glove. There is some effort involved because one size does not fit all. Most people have five fingers on a hand, but some have more or fewer. Fingers vary in length and circumference. Some find wool linings itchy while others prefer these to any other.

It is relatively easy to tell when a glove fits properly. We can usually determine this before buying a pair. We don't have this luxury with a forecasting model. We cannot completely assess its ability to predict the future until that future has passed and we have had time to measure it. However, we can make some informed judgements at the initial stage of fitting the model to the information about the past at our disposal. Certain evaluation criteria help us weed out inappropriate techniques when considering which methods to begin with and which model to adopt for producing forecasts.

This chapter briefly discusses thirteen forecasting methods that have been applied to forecasting tourism demand. These will be explored in detail in the following chapters. Then, we examine various assessment criteria that, if properly applied and heeded, can save us a lot of headaches as we attempt to model tourism futures.

Types of forecasting methods

Business forecasting methods, and tourism methods among them, fall into two major categories: quantitative and qualitative (see Figure 2.1). **Quantitative methods** organize past information about a phenomenon by mathematical rules. These rules take advantage of underlying patterns and relationships in the data of interest to the forecaster. Objective numerical measurements consistent over some historical period are required in these methods.

There are two major subcategories of quantitative methods: extrapolative and causal. **Extrapolative methods**, also called 'time series methods', assume that the variable's past course is the key to predicting its future. Patterns in the data over the past are used to project or extrapolate future values. Causal relationships are ignored.

The other subcategory of quantitative forecasting methods is **causal methods**. These attempt to mathematically simulate cause and effect relationships. Determining the causal variables that affect the forecast variable and the appropriate mathematical expression of this relationship is the central objective.

These methods have the advantage over time series methods of explicitly portraying cause and effect relationships. This is crucial in certain forecasting situations, such as when management wants to know how much impact on demand an increased advertising budget will have. Likewise, tourism policy forecasting requires causal models. However, these methods are more costly and time consuming to construct than time series models, and are often considerably less accurate.

Qualitative methods are also called 'judgemental methods'. Past information about the forecast variable is organized by experts using their judgement rather than mathematical rules. These are not necessarily cheaper or easier to apply than quantitative methods, but they have the advantage of not requiring historical data series.

Figure 2.1 summarizes these classifications and lists the forecasting methods that are covered in this book.

A. Quantitative methods

   1. Extrapolative methods
      a. Naive
      b. Single moving average
      c. Single exponential smoothing
      d. Double exponential smoothing
      e. Classical decomposition
      f. Autoregression
      g. Box–Jenkins approach.

   2. Causal methods
      a. Regression analysis
      b. Structural models.

B. Qualitative methods

   1. Jury of executive opinion
   2. Subjective probability assessment
   3. Delphi method
   4. Consumer intentions survey.

Figure 2.1   Types of forecasting methods

Forecasting methods and models

It is useful to understanding various approaches to forecasting tourism's future to recognize the distinction between a **forecasting method** and a **forecasting model**.

A forecasting **method** is simply a systematic way of organizing information from the past to infer the occurrence of an event in the future. 'Systematic' means following a distinct set of procedures in a prescribed sequence.

A forecasting **model** is one expression of a forecasting method. More specifically, it is a simplified representation of reality, comprising a set of relationships, historical information on these relationships, and procedures to project these relationships into the future.

In the quantitative applications, a forecasting model may be a single equation or a group of related equations. In applying quantitative forecasting methods, it is the common practice to test several models incorporating the assumptions of a given method in order to find the most accurate one. This will be made clear in the following chapters.

Forecasting model evaluation criteria

Since there are a number of quantitative forecasting methods (e.g. Figure 2.1), and each method can spawn from one to a score or more models, it is essential to have objective criteria by which to evaluate these. The following criteria are useful for evaluating your own models or those of others, and are not listed in order of importance. You will want to determine your own priorities.

- specified structure
- plausible structure
- acceptability
- explanatory power
- robustness
- parsimony
- cost
- accuracy.

Specified structure. Before you can evaluate your own model or someone else's, you must have the model's structure clearly detailed. There is a tendency among some to present forecasts as if derived from a 'black box', with input and output specified but no explanation of how the former are transformed into the latter. Advancement of scientific knowledge depends on replication of research studies. In contrast, the black box approach obfuscates, preventing replication or even evaluation, and should be avoided in forecast modelling.

Plausible structure. Once you examine a model's structure, you can determine whether it is credible or not. A model that does not logically reflect the way the world works is not likely to produce accurate forecasts over significant periods. A common problem in using regression analysis for forecasting is when the relationships in the forecasting model defy common sense, such as when the equation indicates that demand for airline seats increases as fares are raised.

Acceptability. This is a pragmatic criterion. Is the model acceptable to management, or does it violate managers' paradigms or concepts of what constitutes a valid model? There is not much point in applying a forecasting model that management finds unacceptable in its assumptions.

Explanatory power. In some cases, it is essential to explain the important relationships at work in producing the forecast values. When this is a requirement, the question becomes, does the forecasting model under study explain as much as management wants to know?

Robustness. A forecasting model is robust if its forecasts are little affected by the extreme values in the historical series. These extreme values are called 'outliers' because they lie outside of the range of most of the other values. For example, air travel across the north Atlantic was depressed by the Gulf War in January–February 1991. You would want to avoid a forecasting model that magnifies these effects in the forecasts it produces for subsequent months.

Some forecasting models may be extremely sensitive to extreme values, that is, their forecasts change significantly if the outliers are removed. Others, however, are robust and their forecasts are resistant to the presence or absence of extreme historical values.

Parsimony. William of Ockham (1300–49) was a Franciscan cleric and philosopher. He proclaimed a logical principle known as Ockham's Razor: 'What can be done with fewer is done in vain with more' (Van Doren 1991, pp. 126, 209). The parsimony criterion argues for the simpler model over the more complex one when other important criteria are similar between the two. The more complex the model, the more costly it is to operate and the more likely that errors will occur in its construction and use. If you plan to spend time and money resources to develop a complex tourism forecasting model, you should carefully evaluate its anticipated advantages over a simpler one. Ockham's Razor can shave time and money off the forecasting process and may achieve better accuracy as well.

Cost. Since time is always a scarce resource and money usually is, management generally prefers models that require less of both.

Accuracy. If the primary purpose of building a forecasting model is to clearly discern the future of a phenomenon, then the most important criterion of all is how accurately a model does this. That is, how closely do the estimates provided by the model conform to the actual events being forecast. There are at least three dimensions of accuracy: error magnitude accuracy, directional change accuracy, and trend change or turning point accuracy. Moreover, there are at least three time frames where a forecasting model's accuracy can be explored: over all of the past data available when building the model, over the recent past of these data, and over a period beyond the data set used to construct the model. These aspects of accuracy are discussed in the following section.

Forecast measures of accuracy

Tourism demand forecasting is important to the tourism manager and to those that depend on that manager. More accurate forecasts reduce the risks of decisions more than do less accurate ones. In a brief survey of tourism demand forecasters and users of such forecasts, Witt and Witt found 'that accuracy is the most important forecast evaluation criterion' (1992, pp. 154-61).

There are three measures of accuracy commonly found to be useful to tourism managers, and each of these is discussed in turn. (Further discussion of these can be found in Witt and Witt 1992, pp. 124–134.)

- error magnitude
- directional change
- turning point.

Error magnitude accuracy

The most familiar concept of forecasting accuracy is called 'error magnitude accuracy', and relates to forecast error associated with a particular forecasting model. This is defined as:

$$e_t = A_t - F_t \tag{2.1}$$

where
   $t =$ some time period, such as a month, quarter or year
   $e =$ forecast error
   $A =$ actual value of the variable being forecast
   $F =$ forecast value

If the actual value is greater than the forecast value at time, t, then the forecasting error is positive. If less than the forecast value, then the forecasting error is negative.

Any model designed to forecast human behaviour will suffer from forecasting errors. Such errors are due to at least three factors that sometimes interact:

1. Omission of influential variables. No forecasting model can include all of the variables that affect the one being forecast. Moreover, even if such a model could be built, it is quite unlikely the forecaster could accurately estimate the true relationships between these and the forecast variable. Some events that affect visitor flows between England and France, for example, are simply random. These include the weather, transportation equipment failures, and labour strikes, to name a few salient ones.

2. Measurement error. We cannot measure visitor flows or other variables representing tourism demand completely accurately. Moreover, the variables that affect demand may be mis-measured as well. This is because some variables of interest are inherently unmeasurable (e.g. the attractiveness of a destination) and some are difficult to measure due to data collection difficulties (e.g. visitor expenditures).

3. Human indeterminacy. Human beings do not always act in rational ways, or even always in their own best interests. They often ignore budget constraints when planning a vacation. Patterns of behaviour do not last: a couple will visit the same destination every summer for years and then suddenly turn to an alternative. Humans become sick and must cancel planned trips, or schedule new ones to receive health treatments. There is always a degree of randomness in human behaviour and this shows up in forecast errors.

There are quite a few ways to summarize the error magnitude accuracy of a forecasting model. Some of these compute measures of absolute error, and are thus subject to the units and time period over which the model is tested. They are often difficult to interpret and compare across different models.

Mean absolute percentage error

Other error magnitude measures compute percentage errors relative to the values in the historical series. These allow you to compare several different models across different time periods. One of the most useful of these, due to its simplicity and intuitive clarity, is the mean absolute percentage error, or **MAPE:**

$$\text{MAPE} = \frac{1}{n} * \sum \left(\frac{|e_t|}{A_t} \right) * 100 \tag{2.2}$$

where:

n = number of periods
e = forecast error
A = actual value of the variable being forecast
t = some time period

The MAPE is a sum of the absolute errors for each time period divided by the actual value for the period this sum is divided by the number of periods to obtain a mean value. Then, by convention, this is multiplied by 100 to state it in percentage terms. This is a simple measure permitting comparison across different forecasting models with different time periods and numbers of observations, and weighting all percentage error magnitudes the same. Lower MAPE values are preferred to higher ones because they indicate a forecasting model is producing smaller percentage errors.

Moreover, its interpretation is intuitive. The MAPE indicates, on average, the percentage error a given forecasting model produces for a specified period. One author has suggested the following interpretation of MAPE values:

- less than 10 per cent is highly accurate forecasting
- between 10 and 20 per cent is good forecasting
- between 20 and 50 per cent is reasonable forecasting
- greater than 50 per cent is inaccurate forecasting (Lewis 1982, p. 40).

Such a standard can be quite misleading, because it ignores the change characteristics of the time series being forecast. If a time series increases at a mean rate of 2 per cent per year in the past, then a forecasting model with a MAPE of 8 per cent is not very useful and achieving the 'highly accurate' label is irrelevant to the case.

The essence of quantitative forecasting is identifying the particular patterns of a given time series – its personality. Applying forecasting accuracy standards that ignore this personality is tantamount to treating all wild animals as if they were hamsters: you will have severe problems with the tigers.

A better set of standards for assessing the accuracy of a forecasting model in simulating its time series is based on the 'naive' forecasting model. The simple version of this model forecasts the next period's value to be the same as this period's. If your tourism demand series is monthly or quarterly, then its seasonality requires you to set a period's value as equal to the same period one year earlier, the 'seasonal naive model'.

To set the standards for evaluating the MAPE of a forecasting model, compute the MAPE for the naive model, compare the two, and apply the following guidelines:

- a model with a MAPE less than one-half of the naive MAPE indicates a highly accurate forecasting model
- a model MAPE equal to between 50 and 100 per cent of the naive MAPE indicates a reasonably accurate forecasting model
- a model MAPE equal to more than the naive MAPE is a poor forecasting model: you would be better off using the simpler, cheaper naive model and achieving the lower forecasting error.

Root mean square percentage error

Another measure of error magnitude accuracy useful over all time series and quantitative forecasting methods is the root mean square percentage error, or **RMSPE**:

$$\text{RMSPE} = \sqrt{\frac{\Sigma \left(\frac{e_t}{A_t}\right)^2}{n}} * 100 \tag{2.3}$$

where

n = number of periods
e = forecast error
A = actual value of the variable being forecast
t = some time period

This measure also computes an average error in terms of percentages and can be compared to actual rates of change in the historical data series. However, it penalizes larger errors more than small ones. This may be important if you can live with continuing but small errors from your forecasting model but cannot accept several large ones. For example, in staffing a hotel, it may not matter to you if the number of guests checking in on a day exceeds your forecast by 10 per cent because the existing staff can handle this. However, if check-ins occasionally turn out to be 50 per cent more than forecast, your customers and your staff will suffer during such periods. You would prefer the RMSPE measure of forecasting error to choose the model that most avoids these large mistakes.

Figure 2.2 presents a case where these two measures of percentage error magnitude provide divergent signals of forecasting model accuracy. The actual visitor series is artificial for a fictitious destination. It shows a constant trend until 1985, when a major festival doubles the number of visitors.

Two forecast models have been employed to forecast the actual visitor data. Forecast model 1 simulates the trend of visitation quite well, and produces the lower MAPE. However, it completely misses the 1985 visitor spike. Forecast model 2 does not simulate the trend as well. Its MAPE is higher than forecast 1. But it does capture most of the 1985 visitor spike. By

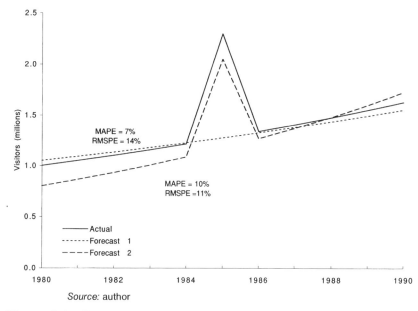

Figure 2.2   Two measures of error magnitude accuracy

the RMSPE measure of error magnitude, it is superior to forecast 1 because the latter is heavily penalized for its 1985 forecast error in the RMSPE calculation.

If you are more interested in capturing the overall trend, forecast model 1 is the better as indicated by its lower MAPE. On the other hand, if you are more interested in avoiding occasional large forecasting errors such as occurred with model 1 in 1985, then the RMSPE indicates model 2 is superior for your purposes.

This author believes the MAPE to be the better all-round indicator of forecasting accuracy than the RMSPE. MAPE is easier to calculate, is easier to understand, and can be used to compare a forecasting method across a number of series. In the latter case, the RMSPE will indicate that a method is less accurate for time series with large values compared to those with small values. Finally, the RMSPE will heavily penalize a method with one very bad forecast caused by a shock such as a catastrophic storm or terrorist attacks on tourist facilities.

Perhaps the choice between MAPE and RMSPE as the best measure of error magnitude accuracy is not critical for most tourism demand series. Witt and Witt found, in a comparison of various methods for forecasting international travel demand among countries, that both measures indicated approximately the same ranking of models (1992, p. 122). However, neither

MAPE nor RMSPE is a useful indicator of the following two concepts of forecasting accuracy.

Directional change accuracy

Sometimes, the most important information we wish about the future is whether there will be more or fewer visitors next year than this year. This can help, for example, in deciding whether or not to increase transport capacity or staffing.

A directional change error, sometimes called 'tracking error', occurs when a forecasting model fails to predict the actual direction of change for a period. Table 2.1 indicates the occasions of such errors, indicated by the ⊠ marks. The diagonal of √ marks indicates occasions when a forecasting model accurately identifies a change in direction.

There is a measure of directional change accuracy that indicates a model's success in forecasting whether a variable will be higher or lower than its previous value. The equation for this measure is

$$DCA = \frac{\sum FD_t}{\sum AD_t} * 100 \qquad (2.4)$$

where
   DCA = directional change accuracy in per cent
   FD = directional change accurately forecast
   AD = directional change actually occurring
   t = some time period

Figure 2.3 shows an application of this measure of directional change accuracy. This chart shows actual annual visitor volume at the John F. Kennedy Center for the Performing Arts in Washington, D.C., and a simple forecast model's values. When a √ appears, the model has correctly forecast the directional movement. Where a ⊠ is shown, the forecast model has failed to predict the next period's change correctly.

Table 2.1 Occasions of forecast model directional change accuracy

Actual data show:	Forecast model predicts:		
	Increase	*No change*	*Decrease*
Increase	√	⊠	⊠
No change	⊠	√	⊠
Decrease	⊠	⊠	√

√ = model accurately forecasts direction of change
⊠ = model does not accurately forecast direction of change

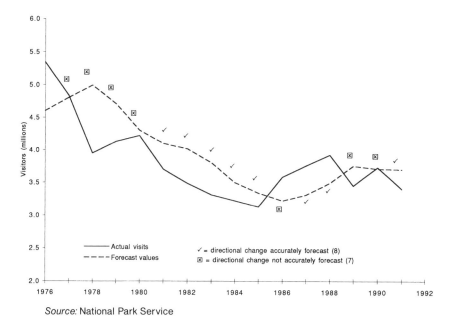

Figure 2.3   Directional change in actual and forecast visitor volume at the John F. Kennedy Center, annually, 1976–91

Altogether, the actual series shows nine periods of decline and the model correctly predicted six of these. The actual series rose six times, and the model forecast two of these. According to equation (2.4), eight movements were correctly forecast out of 15 occurring, for a directional change accuracy of 53 per cent.

Trend change accuracy

Turning point or trend change error is a subset of change of direction error. It occurs when a forecasting model fails to predict a turning point when one occurs, or predicts a turning point when none occurs.

A trend change or **turning point** is defined as at least two periods showing an upward trend over an initial period, and the next period showing a downward change:

$$\text{upward trend} = A_{t-2} < A_{t-1} < A_t$$
$$\text{and turning point} = A_t > A_{t+1}$$
$$\text{or no turning point} = A_t < A_{t+1}$$

or at least two periods showing a downward trend from an initial period and the next period showing an upward change:

$$\text{downward trend} = A_{t-2} > A_{t-1} > A_t$$
$$\text{and turning point} = A_t < A_{t+1}$$
$$\text{or no turning point} = A_t > A_{t+1}$$

Thus, four consecutive data points are required to define turning points and enable us to calculate trend change error. The latter is equal to the percentage of turning points and no turning points forecast accurately. A common practice is to divide the number of turning points and no turning points accurately forecast by the total number of turning points and no turning points actually occurring, and multiplying this quotient by 100 to place it in per cent terms.

In Figure 2.4, the 'TP' symbols indicate a change in trend (i.e. a turning point) in the actual time series. If there is a turning point, it is located at the third point of the four required to identify it. For example, in 1979, after declining through 1976–78 period (three data points), visitor volume increased (i.e. changed direction) in 1979. This created a turning point in 1978. The forecast series failed to do the same, and this is marked by an ⊠. Then visitor volume declined each year until 1986, when it changed direction

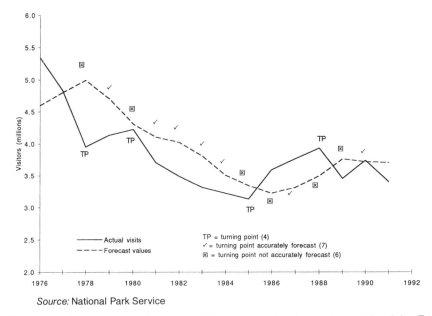

Source: National Park Service

Figure 2.4 Actual and forecast visitor volume turning points at the John F. Kennedy Center, annually, 1976–91

again. The forecast model also failed to identify this 1987 turning point. Finally, after rising over the 1985–88 period, the actual series fell in 1989, creating the last turning point at 1988. The forecast model disregarded this as well, missing all four turning points.

The forecast model correctly predicted seven out of ten of the 'non-turning points' in the series, indicated by ✓ in Figure 2.4. So, this model's overall score in correctly predicting turning points is the sum of zero turning points forecast plus seven non-turning points actually predicted, divided by 13 possible predictions turning points, or 54 per cent.

These turning points can be viewed as the peaks or troughs of cycles. If a tourism manager can forecast these turning points far enough in advance, the company can reduce the risk of major capital investments and other financial decisions. If you discern a downward turn on the horizon after a rising trend in a certain visitor segment, you can reduce resources directed to that segment and use them to attract growing segments.

Value of graphical data displays

It is hard to exaggerate the importance of viewing a data series to forecasting it properly. Each time series has a personality, and displaying the series helps make this explicit as no other method can.

A **time plot** is a graph that displays a time series related to its periods at equally spaced intervals. These may be days, weeks, months, seasons, quarters or years. Figure 2.5 shows a time plot of U.S. domestic airline traffic annually as a line chart. (This is usually preferable to a bar chart because it emphasizes the time sequence of the values.) We can more clearly discern the progress of this series here than by simply viewing a table of the values: after slow growth through 1982, airline traffic accelerated through 1990, declined for a year, and then resumed its upward trend.

Figure 2.5 also includes the eight elements essential to understanding any graphical data display:

- name of the series (chart title)
- periods charted (in this case, calendar years)
- time period covered (1980–94)
- name of the units of the series (vertical axis title)
- series units shown (value labels on the vertical axis)
- time units (value labels on the horizontal axis)
- source of the time series (at bottom left)
- time series values (the line or 'curve' representing the data).

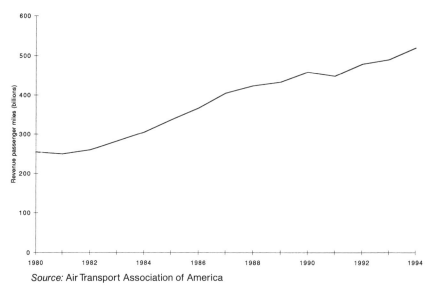

Source: Air Transport Association of America

Figure 2.5   U.S. domestic airline traffic, annually, 1980–94

This information gives a clear understanding of the series charted and where it came from. Moreover, it helps the forecaster to distinguish different series and the same series over different time periods (e.g. months instead of years).

Sometimes, it is helpful to identify the actual values in the curve charted by either including the numbers or horizontal and vertical lines at each value on the horizontal and vertical axes. In addition, the values charted need not be the actual values of the time series. They may be the time series transformed or redefined as changes each period, per cent changes, indexed to some base year, or logarithms of the time series.

Of course, we can show more than one series on a single chart.

The other graphical display most useful in forecasting is the **scatter diagram**, which shows two time series at each point in time as a single point. Figure 2.6 shows the scatter diagram for U.S. real gross domestic product and U.S. airline traffic. Note that each point corresponds to a single year. Note also that there appears to be a clear relationship between the two series: as GDP rises, so does airline traffic. The only exception is the 1981–82 period.

Since the scatter diagram plots two series, the units may not be consistent. These are clearly stated, however, as the horizontal and vertical axis labels. Note also that the origin does not denote zero for either series. This is to avoid a large empty space and compressing the points to fit into a relatively small portion of the chart space.

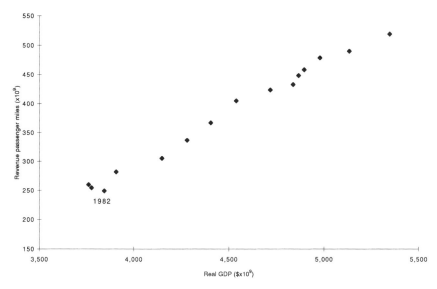

Source: U.S. Department of Commerce, Air Transport Association of America

Figure 2.6   Scatter diagram of real U.S. GDP and U.S. airline traffic, annually, 1980–94

Computer software

The forecasting methods discussed here require the use of a personal computer or a mainframe computer. There are a number of software programs designed for the personal computer that embody the forecasting methods discussed in the following chapters. SPSS and SAS are two of the most widely known, but there are a host of others being released or upgraded monthly. You should check with your computer software resource people for an up-to-date assessment of what is available.

However, be aware that current spreadsheet programs available for the personal computer, such as Microsoft® Excel or Lotus 1-2-3, have built-in statistical programs that suffice for many forecasting applications, such as correlation and linear regression analysis. Since these programs also include graphical display programs, you can enter your time series, chart the data, and explore forecasting methods all on the same computer display screen.

Assessing data quality

Every forecasting model designed to simulate human behaviour will produce forecasting errors. Some of these are due to the difficulty of measuring phenomena accurately, both the activity we wish to forecast and factors that may affect that time series. Before we begin to apply various forecasting methods, we need to assess the quality of our time series. The following discussion applies both to the time series we wish to forecast and to time series we are considering for use in explaining the course of our forecast series in a causal model.

Missing data

We need complete time series over the period we wish to study, that is, there is a data point corresponding to each time unit. Most quantitative forecasting methods will not work on time series with missing data points. If the points are missing at the very beginning of the series, then we can simply deal with the shorter series. If data are missing within the time series, and we do not wish to discard earlier data, then we must replace the missing data with estimates.

One procedure is to search for other time series which are highly correlated with the one we are trying to complete. Then, we regress the longest complete segment in our series on the correlated one to obtain a regression equation that can 'forecast' data points for the missing periods. Another popular method used to supply missing data is the linear time trend regression. Correlation and regression will be discussed more fully in Chapter 7. If the data are seasonal, then you need to use only the same months, quarters, etc., in the years in your regression model.

The simplest method is to interpolate the missing data point. That is, set the missing value equal to the mean of the data points on either side of it in time. If you are dealing with seasonal data, use the same months in adjoining years to interpolate.

Discontinuous series

The U.S. Department of Commerce maintains a time series of U.S. receipts from international travellers from 1964 to 1994. However, as indicated in

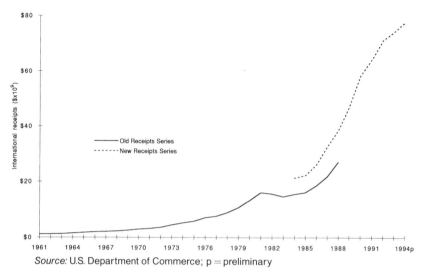

Source: U.S. Department of Commerce; p = preliminary

Figure 2.7 U.S. international travel and passenger fare receipts, old and new annual series, 1961–94

Figure 2.7, a new estimating methodology was instituted in 1987, producing a new time series beginning with 1984.

It is clear that there are two different time series at work here: 1964 to 1987 and 1984 to 1994. Yet it is published as a single time series, with a marked jump in 1984. Using this series for forecasting will incorporate this jump as a change in traveller behaviour rather than a change in estimation methodology.

The careful forecaster has two choices. One is to deal only with the consistent time series of 1984 to the present. The other is to try to 'backcast' from the new series back to earlier years. We should avoid, however, simply shifting the old series up by an amount to splice it in with the new. Such a splicing assumes that the old methodology captured traveller behaviour as well as the new one, an assumption we have no grounds to make.

Data anomalies

An 'anomaly' is a deviation from an established pattern. In time series, these extreme values are commonly called 'outliers'. They are extreme values that deviate unusually far from the pattern established by our time series. The values for January to April 1991, in Figure 1.2 (Chapter 1), are outliers in the international airline traffic series, as are the February and March values in 1992.

You can identify such anomalies through your graphical data displays. They will also be evident when you produce forecasts of your time series and some values fall unusually far from your forecast line.

Most outliers can be explained. Catastrophic events such as unusually harsh weather, wars, and terrorism can depress tourism demand for a short period. Special events such as the quadrennial Olympic Festival can artificially boost visitor volume for two weeks to a month. You should look for such explanations before dealing with outliers.

If there is no explanation, and you suspect the anomalous value is due to measurement error, then you will want to correct the offending value. The technique suggested for filling in missing data above can be used here. However, if there is an explanation, most statistical experts argue against adjusting the outlier in any way. To do so is to eliminate information that is useful in understanding how extreme events affect your time series. Such information can be incorporated in your forecasting model.

Number of data points

Generally, the more observations we have in our time series, the more likely our forecasting method will capture the patterns of the activity we are trying to forecast.

Some forecasters suggest that you need five data points for each one you are trying to forecast. If you want to forecast two years ahead, you need ten years in your time series, according to this rule. If you want to forecast each of twelve months ahead, you need at least five complete years of monthly data to do so adequately. However, this should be viewed as a minimum. Some quantitative forecasting methods require significantly more data points to provide reliable estimates.

Data precision

Most tourism demand data can be stated in terms of thousands or millions of visitors, and millions or thousands of millions of visitor expenditure units. As a practical matter, dealing with data with six or more digits obscures interpretation. We are usually interested in what will happen next year or so, and the changes we are interested in are captured only in the first three or four digits. Moreover, the more digits we are attempting to maintain in a database, the more apt we are to make data entry errors.

On the other hand, if we represent forecast variables in only one or two digits, we limit the amount of variation that will show up in our time series. Quantitative forecasting methods examine such variation for patterns useful in predicting the future.

A useful middle course is to round off your series to four digits. This allows the variability in the series to express itself, keeps the maximum rounding error to five one-hundredths of one per cent, and does not strain our ability to catch data entry errors very much. This minimal loss of precision is not likely to affect the accuracy of your forecasts.

By the four-digits rule, you may round off the number, 1 234 567, to the nearest thousand and enter 1235. But you should avoid rounding off a number such as 678 910 to the nearest thousand, because this would produce the three-digit number 679. (Instead, round it off to 678.9 thousand.) The reason for this is that the maximum rounding error for a three-digit number is nearly one-half of one per cent. If you are forecasting a series where the annual percentage changes are small, this rounding error could significantly distort your forecasts.

Reasonable data

Graphing your time series will indicate whether its course appears reasonable or not. Tourism demand has risen since the Second World War for most countries, and its time series should reflect this. On the other hand, if catastrophes have intervened, declines in the series should be evident.

Most tourism demand fluctuates substantially as seasons change. You should see these changes in monthly or quarterly data. The number of distinctive seasons will vary according to the location of the demand. Some tropical destinations have two seasons, while those in moderate northern and southern latitudes experience four.

If your time series do not appear to follow a reasonable path, you should inquire about measurement errors among those who have collected, compiled, or transcribed the data.

Sound data collection

Tourism demand data can be compiled from administrative reports. Most transportation data are based on such reports of actual counts of tickets sold, passengers carried, etc. Theme parks, museums and other attractions also produce administrative records useful to the tourism forecaster. Commercial lodging places in most countries are required to keep careful records of the number of guests and length of stay. The only questions here are, are the data transcribed properly, and are they complete?

Some tourism demand data are estimated through sample surveys. To be representative of the larger population to which they refer, such surveys must ensure that every member of the population has a known, non-zero chance of being included. For a thorough discussion of the elements of valid tourism surveys, see World Tourism Organization (1995d).

The careful forecaster will inquire into how the data to be used were collected and processed, to understand what measurement anomalies may be present and how much of the variation through time is due to sampling error.

Finally, a technique sometimes used in tourism demand estimation is direct observation. By counting the number of passengers getting off an airline flight, you can develop a time series of the number of passengers carried on the flight. It is common to estimate tourism by personal motor vehicle by counting vehicles and ascribing some average number of passengers per vehicle.

If such observation is used to develop your time series, you should seek to clearly understand how measurement errors may have crept into it. Observer fatigue, limited observation under bad weather conditions, observer carelessness and other events may significantly affect the data reported yet not reflect the behaviour of the phenomenon you are trying to measure.

Summary

There is a substantial history of tourism demand forecast modelling. This suggests that successfully dealing with the special characteristics of tourism demand over time is not a trivial task. Questions of definitions and classifications and the appropriate measure of demand must be resolved first before tackling the art of model building.

There are two main classes of business forecasting models: quantitative and qualitative. Within these, there are a number of viable alternatives the forecaster can use. Fortunately, there are tested criteria for evaluating forecasting models and for testing their accuracy in three areas: error magnitude, directional change and trend change accuracy. Research has indicated that no one tourism demand forecasting method is superior in all of these three accuracy measures.

Accuracy is the most popular single criterion for judging tourism demand forecasting models, and can be measured in several ways. The mean absolute percentage error (MAPE) is the most versatile, self-evident, and simplest to determine of these.

Graphically displaying a time series of the past and future helps immeasurably to model it and evaluate a model's output. Such displays will make problems with past measures evident and suggest ways of dealing with them. Moreover, charts of time series prove quite useful in narrowing the field of potential forecasting methods to try.

For further information

Archer, Brian (1994), 'Demand Forecasting and Estimation', *Travel, Tourism, and Hospitality Research, A Handbook for Managers and Researchers*, 2nd edition (J. R. Brent Ritchie and Charles R. Goeldner, eds), pp. 105–114, John Wiley & Sons.

Calantone, Roger J., di Benedetto, C. Anthony and Bojanic, David (1987), 'A Comprehensive Review of the Tourism Forecasting Literature', *Journal of Travel Research*, Vol. XXVI, No. 2 (fall), pp. 28–39.

Levenbach, Hans and Cleary, James P. (1981), *The Beginning Forecaster: The Forecasting Process Through Data Analysis*, Lifetime Learning Publications, Chapters 1 and 6.

Makridakis, Spyros, Wheelwright, Steven C. and McGee, Victor E. (1983), *Forecasting: Methods and Applications*, 2nd edition, John Wiley & Sons, Chapter 1.

Witt, Stephen F. and Witt, Christine A. (1991), 'Tourism Forecasting: Error Magnitude, Direction of Change Error, and Trend Change Error', *Journal of Travel Research*, Vol. XXX, No. 2 (fall), pp. 26–33.

Witt, Stephen F. and Witt, Christine A. (1992), *Modeling and Forecasting Demand in Tourism*, Academic Press Ltd, Chapters 1, 6 and 8.

3 The tourism forecasting process

Simply put, forecasting is a *process* designed to predict future events. In the realm of tourism demand, an event may be the number of visitors to a destination, the number of room-nights sold in a hotel or a group of hotels, the number of passengers flying between two points, or the number of brochures requested by potential visitors. A valid forecast event has two characteristics: a specific time and a specific outcome. These outcomes are often precise volumes of demand. However, they may be stated as ranges or even qualitative conditions, such as visitor demand is forecast to be greater next year than this year.

This chapter presents the tourism demand forecasting process in its sequential steps, describes the methods and models available to forecasters, and discusses how we can evaluate these models. Since historical data are critical to most forecasting methods; criteria for judging the quality of data available to the forecaster are also discussed.

The forecasting process

We emphasize the term 'process' to make clear that sound forecasting requires a formal structure of sequential steps that lead to a defined objective. Most of this book is about the various tools available to the tourism researcher to forecast futures through the forecasting process.

Figure 3.1 presents the four major phases of the forecasting process.

The **design phase** guides the forecaster in choosing the appropriate forecasting method to use. This phase examines the problem, the resources and the relationships that help determine a preliminary choice of method.

The **specification phase** includes determining the relationships that will comprise the appropriate forecasting model and selecting an appropriate model.

The **implementation phase** comprises employing the selected model to generate forecasts and preparing these forecasts for presentation to management.

1. Design phase.

2. Specification phase.

3. Implementation phase.

4. Evaluation phase.

Figure 3.1   The forecasting process

The **evaluation phase** covers monitoring the forecasts over time to determine if adjustments should be made and making the appropriate adjustments to secure the most accurate series of forecasts.

The following sections detail the steps comprising each of these phases of the forecasting process.

The design phase

This initial stage of the forecasting process guides the forecaster in selecting the appropriate forecasting method to use. A forecasting **method** is an individual technique for projecting future events. This is distinct from a forecasting **model**, which is an individual application of a given method. For example, we might test a number of regression models to determine the most reliable, but we are only examining applications of one method: regression analysis.

The forecasting methods most useful in tourism forecasting are listed in this chapter, and described in detail in Chapters 4 to 9.

Figure 3.2 lists the steps in the design phase. Each of these is discussed below.

The first step in the design phase is to **define the problem**. This will often be done by the forecaster's supervisor or a higher official. The problem should be stated as clearly as possible, avoiding jargon and mathematical language at this stage. And the problem should involve some future event, so that forecasting is the appropriate tool for suggesting solutions.

Figure 3.3 indicates some of the types of problems a tourism forecaster may be asked to resolve.

After defining the problem, the next step is to **determine user needs**. Precisely what information will the manager require to resolve the problem? Over what future period? By what time unit (day, week, month, year, etc.)? Broken out by what market segments or some other classification?

Once you have gathered these views, you can determine the variables to be forecast. You must translate user needs into one or more events that can be

A. Define the problem.

B. Determine user needs.

C. Determine variables to be forecast.

D. Determine resources available.

E. Hypothesize relationships.

F. Determine data availability.

G. List available forecasting methods.

H. Apply preliminary selection criteria.

I. Make a preliminary selection of method.

Figure 3.2   Design phase

A. Feasibility of offering passenger service on a new airline route.

B. Expected hotel room sales for budgeting purposes.

C. Number of restaurant personnel needed during a weekend.

D. Appropriate goals for a theme park's marketing plan.

E. Potential demand from a new market segment.

F. Expected effects of a lodging tax increase on room-nights sold.

G. Anticipated government revenue from a lodging tax increase.

H. Economic, social/cultural, or environmental consequences of increased visitor volume.

I. Adequacy of tourism infrastructure capacity ten years from now.

Figure 3.3   Representative tourism forecasting problems

measured and predicted. If, for example, your hotel's director of sales needs to know by how much business will rise next year, you can translate this into the variables room-nights sold and room revenue.

The next step is to **determine the resources available** to you for your forecast. These resources include money for purchasing data and computer software, and time for completing and presenting the forecast.

Next, you need to **hypothesize relationships**. Staying with the hotel sales example, what are the major factors in the market place that have a strong influence on the hotel's room sales? Such factors might be competitors' room rates, your hotel's room rates, airline service into your area, and the state of the economy in your generating markets. You should write down how each of these factors is expected to influence demand for your product.

For example, if your competitors cut room rates, this would most likely have an adverse impact on your demand. Articles in professional journals and the advice of your colleagues can help you isolate these.

Economic theory can be helpful to you in listing expected relationships. The following economic principles suggest relationships you should consider in your forecasting. Each of these is *ceteris paribus*, that is, all other factors are held constant:

- Raising the price of your product will tend to reduce your demand; lowering the price will increase demand.
- If a competitor increases the price of a product similar to yours, this will tend to increase the demand for your product; the opposite occurs if a competitor reduces the price.
- Increasing the quality of your product, that is, the value as perceived by the consumer, will tend to increase the demand; reducing the quality will reduce demand.
- If a tourism operator increases the price of a product that is usually consumed jointly with yours (called a 'complementary product'), this will tend to reduce the demand for your product (e.g. increasing gasoline prices reduces demand for auto rentals).
- Reducing consumers' cost of obtaining information about your product will tend to increase demand for your product; this is a salutary effect of marketing programmes.
- Reducing consumers' costs of reserving and purchasing your product will increase the demand; efforts to improve distribution are helpful here.
- Rising business or personal income after taxes will tend to increase the demand for most tourism products; falling income after taxes will have the opposite effect.
- An increase in the supply of a product similar to yours will tend to reduce the demand for yours.

Sometimes, you do not need to include any explanatory variable other than time, and there is a collection of forecasting techniques (called 'time series methods') for applying this assumption to your past data. These are discussed in Chapters 4 to 6.

The next step is to **determine data availability**. In forecasting your hotel's room-nights sold next year, you have an in-house historical series of appropriate data. But you may need to include the size of the local market for hotel rooms, average room rates, major special events expected, airline fares, the economic situation in your major generating markets, among others. Chapter 7 discusses these explanatory variables more fully.

Next, you should **list available forecasting methods**. This book presents a number of these used in forecasting tourism demand. (See Figure 2.1 in Chapter 2 for the list.) Your own list would include those for which you have computer software or you feel comfortable applying through computer spreadsheet analysis.

Next, from this list you should **apply preliminary selection criteria** in order to narrow the list of available methods down to a few key approaches likely to produce the most reliable forecasts. These are preliminary in the sense that their ability to forecast accurately within your historical data series while observing the principles, restrictions and assumptions of the method will ultimately determine which method you finally select for use.

One straightforward way first to narrow the choices down to one of four major groups of methods is to follow the guide in Figure 3.4. In the discussion of extrapolation, or time series, methods, additional guidelines will be provided to make advance selection of the methods likely to provide the most reliable forecasts.

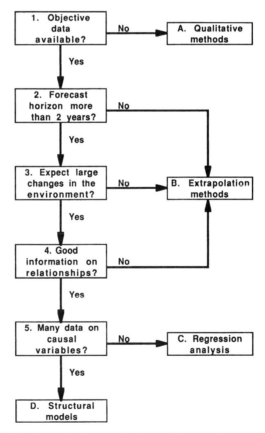

Figure 3.4 Guide to preliminary selection of the most appropriate forecasting method

Objective data (criterion 1 in Figure 3.4) are numerical measures of the activity you are trying to forecast produced by objective measurement techniques rather than someone's opinion or subjective judgement.

The **forecast horizon** (criterion 2) refers to the most distant time period you are trying to forecast. Extrapolative techniques have often proved less successful in providing accurate long-range forecasts than causal methods (i.e. regression analysis and structural models).

Large changes in the environment (criterion 3) denotes future forces likely to change relationships among the forecast variables and the factors that influence them. These include major economic expansions and recessions, tax and regulatory policies, price inflation, availability of key commodities such as petroleum, and terrorist threats and attacks, among others.

Good information on relationships (criterion 4) refers to how much is known about which variables affect the variable you are trying to forecast, and how they do so. For example, price and income are two variables that often explain changes in visitor flows from one country to another. Economic theory suggests that as prices (air fares, hotel rates, exchange rates, etc.) rise, the flow slackens or declines. And as income rises, the flow increases or accelerates. Our knowledge of this theory encourages us to use a forecasting method that embodies these relationships.

It is important to note here that part of this answer is whether we need to explain what is causing changes in the variable we are trying to forecast. In policy forecasting, for example, it is important to understand the process that is producing changes in visitor demand. In this case, we cannot rely on extrapolation methods (method B), because they, by definition, do not include any causal factors.

Finally, **many data on causal variables** (criterion 5) refers to how long the time series are on the factors that influence your forecast variable. A rule of thumb often proposed for causal methods such as regression analysis and structural models is that you need at least five historical data points for every period ahead you plan to forecast. For example, if you plan to forecast tourism arrivals in your country from abroad for each of the next three years, you need at least fifteen years of historical data on these arrivals.

You have now enough information to **make a preliminary selection of forecasting method**. The major decision is whether to choose a **qualitative** forecasting method (as discussed in Chapter 9) or a **quantitative** method, including extrapolation methods (method B in Figure 3.4), regression analysis (method C) and structural models (method D). Once you have done this, you proceed to the second phase of the forecasting process.

The specification phase

The next stage in the forecasting process is the specification phase. The objective here is to determine the best forecasting *model* based upon historical data patterns and relationships. We begin by detailing the specification of a quantitative method, as outlined in Figure 3.5.

If you have chosen to use one of the causal quantitative methods (regression analysis or structural models), the first step in the specification phase is to **specify relationships** between the variable you wish to forecast and the variables that you believe affect it. For example, economic theory and research suggests that the cost of airline tickets inversely affects the demand for airline travel. As ticket costs rise, air travel demand declines. This is a relationship you may want to investigate in this phase.

Sometimes the explanatory variables affecting your activity may affect one another. For example, for airlines and hotels, the amount of capacity available tends to inversely affect fares and rates. Fares and rates, in turn, affect the demand for your service. Consequently, you need to investigate these complex relationships in selecting your best forecasting model.

The next step is to **collect, prepare and verify input data**. You may need to purchase one or more time series. If so, try to obtain them in an electronic medium that you can directly read into your computer. If you can obtain data only in paper copy form, someone must then enter these into a computer. Make sure you verify that these data have been entered correctly.

Next, **select the starting model and program it**. This model is the one that appears *a priori* to provide the best forecasts. Program it into your computer software by following the rules of your particular statistical program or spreadsheet.

> A. Specify relationships if a causal method.
>
> B. Collect, prepare and verify input data.
>
> C. Select the starting model and program it.
>
> D. Estimate model parameters.
>
> E. Verify their reasonableness.
>
> F. Determine the model's accuracy in the past.
>
> G. Test other models.
>
> H. Compare their accuracies and choose the best model.
>
> I. Document results to date.

Figure 3.5 Quantitative method specification phase

Next, **estimate the model parameters**. **Parameters** in this use are factors that define the actual relationships in the equation or equations that comprise your forecasting model. A given set of parameters constitutes a specific forecasting model.

You must now **verify the reasonableness** of these parameters, that is, verify that the parameters in your forecasting equation are sensible or logical. If you find, for example, that your price variable is positively correlated with the demand you are trying to forecast, this is not reasonable. It suggests that as you increase room rates, your demand for rooms increases. Economic theory argues against this relationship, except in rare cases.

Or you might find that your price and income variables have relatively small parameters, indicating each of these has little impact on visitor demand. This does not appear reasonable given the preponderance of research indicating these are important variables in most tourism demand forecasting situations.

If you are using regression analysis, another aspect of this verification is checking the validity of your model. This is discussed more fully in Chapter 7.

If your model does not produce reasonable or valid parameters, then you must discard it and try another.

Once you are satisfied with the parameter values, you should **determine the model's accuracy in the past**. Here, you use the model to forecast values over the period for which you have actual values for the forecast variable, and compare the model's estimates with these actual values. This is called 'backcasting', or making 'within-sample predictions'. Optimally, you want a forecasting model that accurately simulates the past. If it does not, then it is difficult to have much confidence in its ability to forecast the future.

There are several ways to assess a forecasting model's success in backcasting. Here, you employ the measures of accuracy discussed in Chapter 2, such as the mean absolute percentage error (MAPE) or the root mean square percentage error (RMSPE). You may also assess the model's success in predicting turning points or changes in trend.

Once you have tested your initial model, try a different model, following the same steps. And when you have tested a set of models, you can **compare their accuracies and choose the best model** based on this comparison. This is rather straightforward. You want to use the model that most accurately forecasts the actual values you have in your historical series.

The final step in the specification phase is to **document the results to date**. Write down the details on all of the models you tested and why you chose the one that you did for actual forecasting use. This documentation will prevent you from wasting time testing models you have already reviewed, and answering questions from your managers about potential forecasting models.

A. Specify the method to be implemented.

B. Detail how the experts will be selected.

C. Indicate what phenomena will be covered.

D. Document the plan.

Figure 3.6   Qualitative method specification phase

Qualitative forecasting methods utilize experts to provide forecasts. Figure 3.6 outlines the specification phase of this set of forecasting methods.

The first step is to **specify the method to be implemented**. Four qualitative forecasting methods are described in Chapter 9. All of these require that a panel of experts be composed.

Next, **detail how the experts will be selected**. As explained in Chapter 9, these experts may be business colleagues, other professionals and managers, or consumers.

The third step is to **indicate what phenomena will be covered**. These topics must be turned into carefully worded questions that will elicit reasoned responses from the experts.

Finally, **document the plan** by writing down in detail the procedures to be followed. Review these carefully to avoid allowing researcher opinions to bias the results.

The implementation phase

Implementation is the third phase in the forecasting process, as outlined in Figure 3.7. Here, the forecast is actually produced, documented and presented.

The first step is to **obtain the forecast**. If using a quantitative method, you input values into your model that are necessary for reaching your forecast-

---

A. Obtain the forecast.

B. Make subjective adjustments, if necessary.

C. Document the model and its results.

D. Present the forecast to management.

Figure 3.7   Implementation phase

ing horizon. If using a qualitative method, you develop the forecast out of the responses received from your experts.

The next step is to **make subjective adjustments, if necessary** in the forecast. For example, the last several values of your historical series may all be lower than your forecast model results for these periods. To present your forecast values for the future without adjustment is to guarantee they will be inaccurate. Appendix 3 presents a technique for modifying your model's results to reflect recent history accurately.

The third step in the implementation phase is to **document the model and its results**. Here you write up how you carried out the design phase, specification phase and implementation phase of the forecasting process. This should include models that were tested and rejected and the reasons why, as well as any subjective adjustments made. Having complete documentation can prevent you from testing models again you have already examined and rejected.

Finally, the forecaster **presents the results to management**.

The evaluation phase

The final stage in the forecasting process is the evaluation phase, as outlined in Figure 3.8.

The evaluation phase begins with the step to **monitor forecast accuracy**, that is, track the relationship between actual values as the future unfolds, and forecast values. A popular method for tracking forecasts against actual values is presented in Chapter 10. If your model does not simulate future values relatively accurately as time unfolds, the next step is to **determine the causes for any deviations**. If your review of causes indicates that your forecast values are likely to over- or under-estimate future values of your variable, then you may choose to **revise the forecast**.

A. Monitor forecast accuracy.

B. Determine the causes for any deviations.

C. Revise the forecast, if warranted.

D. Determine if parameters have changed.

E. Generate a new forecast from existing model or develop a new model.

Figure 3.8 Evaluation phase

Or you may find evidence that the trend or causal relationships have changed and you then must **determine if your parameters have changed**. That is, whether the coefficients or equations no longer reflect what is actually happening as the future unfolds.

Finally, after considering all the evidence, you may decide to **generate a new forecast from the existing model or, alternatively, develop a new model**.

Summary

Like all serious attempts to discern futures, the tourism demand forecasting process should follow four sequential steps:

1. design
2. specification
3. implementation
4. evaluation.

The design phase guides you in choosing the appropriate forecasting method to use. The diagram in Figure 3.4 can help you make a preliminary selection of the most fruitful forecasting method to follow. These methods are detailed in the chapters that follow.

The specification phase includes determining the relationships that will comprise the appropriate forecasting model and selecting an appropriate model. The implementation phase comprises employing the selected model to generate forecasts and preparing these forecasts for presentation to management. Finally, the evaluation phase covers monitoring the forecasts over time to determine if adjustments should be made, and making the appropriate adjustments to secure the most accurate forecasts.

Following these steps may seem tedious to the new forecaster, but they will help ensure you do not waste time and money in determining the shapes of the tourism futures you are interested in.

For further information

Armstrong, J. Scott (1985), *Long-range Forecasting: From Crystal Ball to Computer*, 2nd edition, John Wiley & Sons, Chapter 3.

Levenbach, Hans and Cleary, James P. (1981), *The Beginning Forecaster, The Forecasting Process Through Data Analysis*, Lifetime Learning Publications, pp. 1–40.

Makridakis, Spyros, Wheelwright, Steven C. and McGee, Victor E. (1983), *Forecasting: Methods and Applications*, 2nd edition, John Wiley & Sons, Chapter 16.

Moore, Thomas W. (1989), *Handbook of Business Forecasting*, Harper & Row, Chapters 1 and 2.

Saunders, John A., Sharp, John A. and Witt, Stephen F. (1987), *Practical Business Forecasting*, Gower Publishing Company, Chapter 1.

4 Basic extrapolative models and decomposition

Extrapolative or time series forecasting methods use only past patterns in a data series to extrapolate the future from the past. These implicitly assume that the course of a variable, such as tourism demand, over time is the product of a substantial number of unknown forces that give the series a momentum. This momentum can be captured in a model reflecting one of several time series methods.

> A **time series forecasting model** relates the values of a time series to previous values of that time series or values derived from the previous values. (Makridakis, Wheelwright and McGee 1983, p. 912)

The advantage of time series methods is that they are, for the most part, relatively simple to apply, requiring no more than a data series and a computer spreadsheet program. The exception is the Box–Jenkins approach, which requires a computer program specifically designed to prepare the analyses.

In this chapter, we examine the following basic time series methods:

- naive
- single moving average.

In addition, we will explore an approach to dealing with time series with recurring seasonal patterns.

In Chapter 5, the following time series forecasting methods are discussed:

- single exponential smoothing
- double exponential smoothing
- autoregression.

Chapter 6 presents the most sophisticated process for developing a quality forecasting model using time series methods: the Box–Jenkins approach.

Since forecasts derived from such methods depend so heavily on past patterns in the data, a premium is placed on examining the shape of the historical data series to be forecast. Graphical presentation is indispensable to this process. Through portraying the course of the time series over the past, we can tentatively determine the best extrapolative method to apply (the design phase). Then we test different models and determine the best one for forecasting our future (the specification phase).

Patterns in time series

There are five data patterns to look for in building time series forecasting models. Identifying the type of time series we have helps us make an initial choice as to best extrapolative method to use in the design phase of our forecasting process:

- seasonality
- stationarity
- linear trend
- non-linear trend
- stepped series.

Each of these patterns will be discussed in turn. Figures 4.1 to 4.6 display each of these patterns in tourism data.

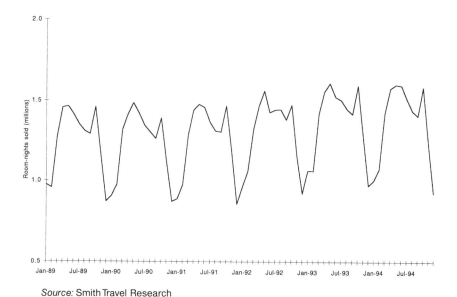

Source: Smith Travel Research

Figure 4.1 Seasonal series of hotel/motel room demand in the Washington, D.C. metropolitan area, monthly, 1989–94

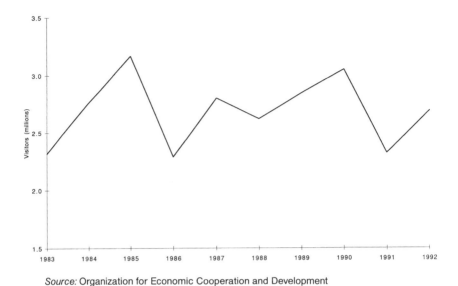

Source: Organization for Economic Cooperation and Development

Figure 4.2   Stationary series: U.S. visitors to the United Kingdom, annually, 1983–92

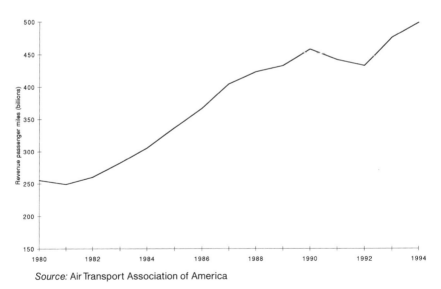

Source: Air Transport Association of America

Figure 4.3   Upward linear trend: U.S. scheduled airline traffic, annually, 1980–94

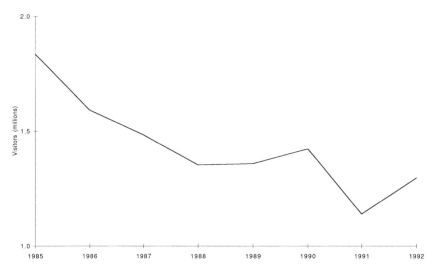

Source: Organization for Economic Cooperation and Development

Figure 4.4   Downward linear trend: U.S. visitors to Italy, annually, 1985–92

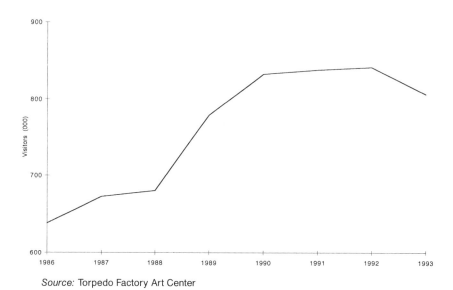

Source: Torpedo Factory Art Center

Figure 4.5   Non-linear trend: Torpedo Factory Art Center visitors, annually, 1986–93

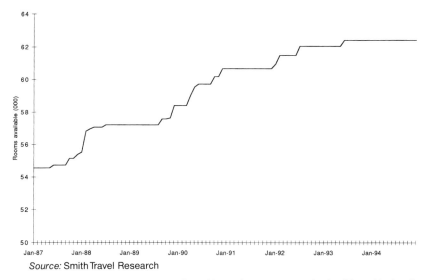

Figure 4.6 Stepped series: hotel/motel room supply in New York city, monthly, 1987–94

Seasonal patterns

The first data pattern we look for in a historical series of our data is the seasonal pattern or 'seasonality'.

> **Seasonality** refers to movements in a time series during a particular time of year that recur similarly each year. (Moore 1989, p. 49)

The seasonal pattern is due to climate and weather, social customs and holidays, business customs, and the calendar. Those that relate specifically to tourism demand are shown in Table 4.1.

Calendar effects are significant in assessing tourism's seasonality. The fact that February usually only has 28 days makes it the low month in many tourism series.

These seasonal patterns occur regularly and often obscure the underlying trends we are trying to forecast. Consequently, it is wise to remove seasonality from a weekly, monthly, quarterly or any other sub-annual series. This produces a 'seasonally adjusted' series which is better suited for forecasting. However, once you are satisfied with a forecast of your seasonally adjusted series, then you add seasonality back into the series, since most managers are interested in what values will actually occur in a future month or quarter.

There are also certain events that do not occur regularly every year, but recur regularly over a period of years. Such periodic events that produce

Table 4.1   Causes of seasonality in tourism demand

Cause of seasonality	Tourism examples
Climate/weather	Summer vacations, snow skiing, fall foliage tours, popularity of tropical destinations in the winter, cruise line departures, ocean resort demand
Social customs/holidays	Christmas/New Year holidays, school breaks, travel to visit friends and relatives, fairs and festivals, religious observances, pilgrimages
Business customs	Conventions and trade shows, government assemblies, political campaign tours, sports events
Calendar effects	Number of days in the month; number of weekends in the month, quarter, season or year

regular increases in tourism demand for certain destinations include the U.S. Presidential Inauguration in Washington, D.C. (January of each year after a year evenly divisible by 4, i.e. 1981, 1985, 1989, 1993), and the Passion Play at Oberammergau, Germany (years ending in zero). Methods for dealing with such regular 'super-annual' events are discussed in Appendix 2.

The fact that February has 29 days every fourth year will add a small increase to that month's tourism figures. (This increase should average about $1 \div 28 = 0.035$ per cent.) Moreover, much leisure travel is centred on weekends and these are not distributed equally among the months or among years. The normal pattern is for a month to have four complete weekends, and two or three months in a year will have five weekends. However, the following years have four months with five weekends, an unusual event: 1995, 2003, 2005, and 2011. The year 2000 will be nearly unique in that it will include *five* months with five complete weekends, for a total of 53 complete weekends. The last time this happened was 1972, and it will not happen again until 2028.

The regularity of the impact of such super-annual recurrent events on tourism demand should be taken into account in tourism forecasting. Ways to do this in the different methods are presented below.

Figure 4.1 shows the monthly demand for hotel/motel rooms in terms of room-nights sold in the Washington, D.C. metropolitan area over six recent years. It is clear that there are seasonal patterns in the data: May and October usually vie for peak month, while December, January and February compete for the trough. The series rises from this low each year throughout the spring to its May peak, and then falls gradually during the summer to a trough in September. Hotel/motel demand rises sharply in October (a big month for meetings and conventions) and then declines steadily to December.

If it exists, seasonality is easily recognizable from a graph of sub-annual data. Another, more quantitative, way of identifying seasonality is to examine the autocorrelation function for a period up to one year's worth of sub-annual periods (e.g. 12 periods for monthly data). This technique is beyond the scope of the present discussion, but details are provided in Saunders, Sharp and Witt (1987, pp. 71–2) and Makridakis, Wheelwright and McGee (1983, pp. 384–8).

We will discuss techniques for dealing with this seasonality later in this chapter.

Other data patterns

Stationarity means a time series fluctuates rather evenly around a horizontal level. In statisticians' parlance, it is **stationary** in its mean, that is, the mean of the series is constant over time. Figure 4.2 presents such a tourism demand series. This is the easiest data pattern to deal with in forecasting.

Linear trend is illustrated in Figures 4.3 and 4.4. These show time series rising or falling at a rather steady rate each period. Many tourism demand series follow a rising linear trend.

Non-linear trend has a rate of increase that varies in a regular way over the time series. Figure 4.5 shows a series that appears to follow an S shape, a familiar pattern in forecasting and represented by the logistic curve or Gompertz's equation. This pattern shows rapid growth at the beginning of the series, levels off to a saturation point, and then declines.

Stepped series are unusual in tourism demand. A stepped series occurs when there is a saturation point, such as a capacity constraint, that is periodically adjusted. For example, the number of cruise visitors allowed to disembark in Bermuda would be a constraint on such tourism. Whenever the government changes this limit, the series would rise (or fall) to another plateau, assuming the island remains as popular with cruise lines as it is currently. Figure 4.6 displays the rooms available in the New York city metropolitan area and reflects new lodging properties opening for business and hotel construction pauses 1989–1994. This, of course, is not a tourism demand series; rather, it represents tourism supply. If demand for New York city hotel/motel rooms were at capacity over a period of years, then a stepped demand series would result.

These four basic data patterns suggest the appropriate time series forecasting methods to employ on a seasonally adjusted series.

Time series forecasting methods

In the balance of this chapter and in the next two chapters, we examine seven different extrapolation methods for forecasting time series, in order of their complexity, beginning with the simplest.

The naive forecasting method

The naive forecasting method simply states that the value for the period to be forecast is equal to the actual value of the last period available. More formally,

$$F_t = A_{t-1} \qquad (4.1)$$

where

F = forecast value
A = actual value
t = some time period

Equation (4.1) is also called the 'random walk model', because it embodies the idea that a series is random, that is, exhibits no discernible trend or other pattern. So the last value is the best forecast of the next value.

This is the simplest forecasting model. As such, it is frequently used as a benchmark to compare other forecast models against. It is not unusual for more elaborate models to produce higher MAPEs than the naive model, and are thus not worth the time and money to operate. Witt and Witt (1992, pp. 99–123) present a number of these situations among international tourism demand series and conclude that more complex forecasting models are less accurate than the naive model for many series.

There are two other versions of the naive concept that are sometimes used as a benchmark forecast. We can define the 'Naive 2' forecast value as the current value multiplied by the growth rate between the current value and the previous value. This might be a useful benchmark for a series that trends upward or downward. 'Seasonal naive' can be used with seasonal data and postulates that the next period's value is equal to the value of the same period in the previous year. So, for example, the seasonal naive value for July 1995 is equal to the actual value for July 1994.

Single moving average

Sometimes the last value does not seem 'typical' of our time series. We might obtain a better forecast for the next period by averaging the last several values. This is the single moving average (SMA) method of extrapolation and is second in simplicity only to the naive method.

We can average any number of periods to produce a forecast through the SMA model. The general equation for the single moving average is:

$$F_t = \frac{A_{t-1} + A_{t-2} + \cdots + A_{t-n}}{n} \qquad (4.2)$$

where

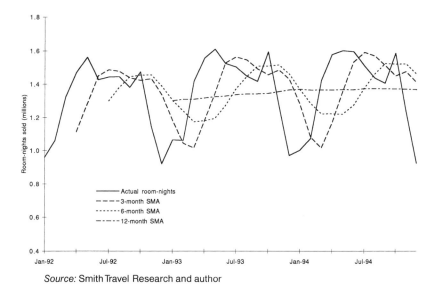

Source: Smith Travel Research and author

Figure 4.7   Single moving averages of Washington, D.C., hotel/motel room demand, monthly, 1992–94

F = forecast value
A = actual value
t = some time period
n = number of past periods

The SMA method allows some past values to determine forecast values, and all have the same influence on the forecast value. For example, we might use the average of the previous three values to serve as our forecast for the next period. Or we might use the previous four values or six values or any number than can be accommodated by our time series.

Figure 4.7 shows single moving averages for three, six and twelve periods on the seasonal series of hotel/motel room demand in the Washington, D.C. metropolitan area. It is clear that the more past values included in the single moving average, the smoother it becomes. This is because the more values (the higher *n* is), the less influence any one value has on the average; rather, the values tend to offset each other to provide a smooth forecast series.

If a time series shows wide variations around a trend, then the longer single moving average the better it will pick up the trend. In Figure 4.7, for example, the 12-month SMA clearly shows the series trend, while the shorter SMAs do not. However, long SMAs are slow to pick up recent changes in trend because so many past values are affecting it. The SMA method is more accurate in forecasting a series with very little variation around its trend than one with significant seasonality or extreme variations.

Table 4.2 Comparison of accuracies of naive and single moving averages in forecasting Washington, D.C. hotel/motel room demand, monthly, 1992–94

Method/model	*MAPE*
Naive	
Naive 1	11%
Naive 2	13%
Seasonal naive	4.0%
Single moving average	
3-month	15%
6-month	18%
12-month	16%

Table 4.2 compares the accuracy of the three naive models and three single moving average models for forecasting hotel/motel room demand in Washington, D.C. We assess the relative accuracy of these forecasting models by comparing how low each model's mean absolute percentage error is.

It is clear the SMA models are not good forecasting models. Neither are the Naive 1 and Naive 2 models. The seasonal naive model, however, produces relatively accurate forecasts, but still misses the actual value by 4 per cent on average. Any other model we develop should be compared to the seasonal naive model, to see if it can improve on that model's accuracy.

The room demand series in Figure 4.1 contains a pattern that appears to repeat itself every year: **seasonality**. Many forecasting methods have difficulty simulating this regularity. It is far better for the forecaster to take advantage of the regular seasonal pattern by building a forecasting model to simulate it and using this to remove seasonality from the data series we wish to forecast.

One straightforward method of systematically dealing with seasonality and forecasting is the **classical decomposition** approach. This uses a single moving average to remove seasonality from a series we wish to forecast and then considers a number of methods for forecasting the remaining series. There are other ways to deal with seasonality which will be discussed in the context of specific forecasting methods.

Decomposition

The classical decomposition approach attempts to decompose a time series into four constituent parts: trend, cycle, seasonal, and an irregular component. These are defined, as follows:

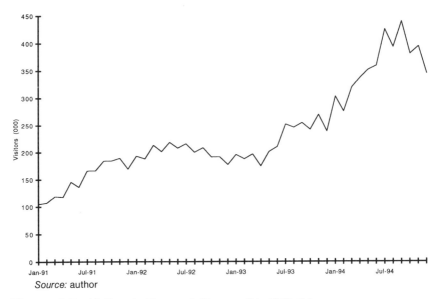

Source: author

Figure 4.8   Visitors to Pleasantville, monthly, 1991–94

- the **trend component** is the long-term movement of the time series and is often linear
- the **cyclical component** is a wave-like movement around the long-term trend that varies in amplitude and duration, but normally lasts for several years or more from a peak to the following peak
- the **seasonal component** represents patterns in a time series that are repeated over fixed intervals of time up to a year in length
- the **irregular component** is the error term and is usually assumed to be random with a constant variance.

Figure 4.8 charts an artificial time series of the number of monthly visitors to 'Pleasantville', an imaginary destination. The series appears to follow a weak upward trend until April 1993, and then a stronger trend thereafter. Seasonality is not evident, nor is a cyclical pattern clear.

However, Figure 4.8 is actually the product of the trend, cycle, seasonal and irregular components shown in Figures 4.9 to 4.12. Classical decomposition decomposes a time series such as monthly visitor volumes in Pleasantville (Figure 4.8) into its component parts (shown in Figures 4.9 to 4.12).

While there are several possible ways to apply decomposition, the method presented here has been widely used and is called the 'ratio-to-moving-averages classical decomposition method'. It assumes a multiplicative relationship among the components as follows:

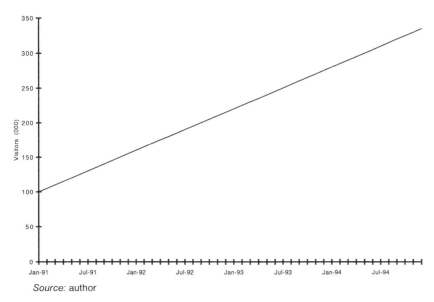

Source: author

Figure 4.9   Visitors to Pleasantville – trend

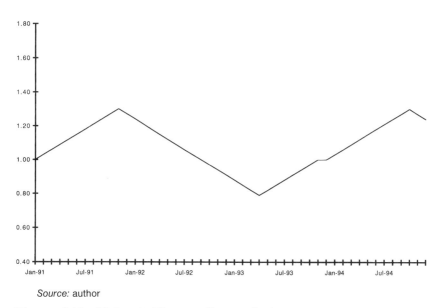

Source: author

Figure 4.10   Visitors to Pleasantville – cyclical pattern

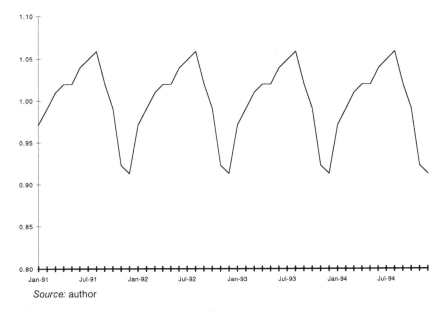

Figure 4.11   Visitors to Pleasantville – seasonal pattern

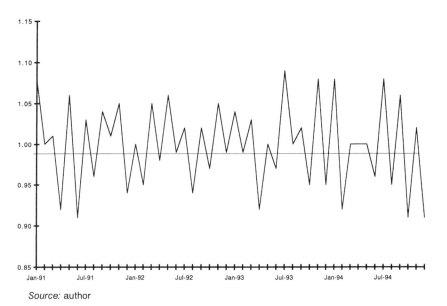

Figure 4.12   Visitors to Pleasantville – irregular pattern

$$A_t = T_t \times C_t \times S_t \times I_t \qquad (4.3)$$

where

A = actual value in the time series
T = the trend component
C = the cyclical component
S = the seasonal component
I = the irregular component
t = some time period less than one year (usually a month or quarter)

The challenge of decomposition is to distinguish these components, develop forecasts for each, and then recombine them to produce forecasts of the actual values useful to managers.

The first step in this decomposition method is to isolate the seasonal and irregular factors through the ratio-to-moving-averages method. We begin by developing a moving average series as long as the number of data points our time series has in a year. For example, if we are examining a monthly series, then we would compute a 12-month moving average. If we are dealing with quarterly data, then we would produce a 4-quarter moving average.

Such moving averages represent the trend-cycle ($T_t \times C_t$) components of equation (4.3) because they contain no seasonal effects by definition, and little or no randomness since the irregular component period tends to cancel itself out when averaged over a number of periods. We will employ monthly data in this exercise, so a 12-month moving average represents the trend-cycle components of the time series.

The following example demonstrates the steps in this decomposition method.

Figure 4.13 shows monthly hotel/motel room-nights sold in the Washington, D.C. metropolitan area for the years 1991 to 1994.[1]

It is clear that there is a seasonal pattern in these data. This is highlighted in Figure 4.14, which simply stacks the monthly data by years.

The seasonal patterns are rather consistent over these years. An exception appears in January 1993, which shows higher room demand than the following February. This is due to the presidential inauguration that year which boosted hotel occupancies toward their limit for a week to ten days. It is wise to deal with such a periodic 'super-annual' event before quantifying the seasonality of a time series. Procedures for doing so are discussed in Appendix 2.

To quantify the seasonal pattern, we set up a spreadsheet as in Table 4.3, with the periods identified in the first column and the data points in the second. Next, compute the 12-month moving average: this begins in December 1991, at the end of the first 12-month period. For example, the average of the first 12 months is 1249, which is placed in the Dec-91 cell in the third column.

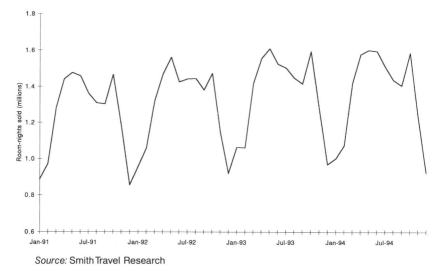

Source: Smith Travel Research

Figure 4.13   Hotel/motel room demand in the Washington, D.C. metropolitan area, monthly, 1991–94

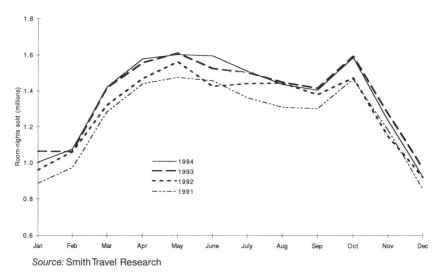

Source: Smith Travel Research

Figure 4.14   Seasonality of hotel/motel room demand in Washington, D.C., monthly, 1991–94

Table 4.3 Hotel/motel room demand in Washington, D.C. and seasonal ratios, 1991–94

1. Month-year	2. Room-nights sold (000)	3. 12-month moving average	4. Centred 12-month moving average (T × C)	5. Seasonal ratios (S × I)
Jan-91	885			
Feb-91	971			
Mar-91	1283			
Apr-91	1440			
May-91	1476			
Jun-91	1457			
Jul-91	1362		1252	1.088
Aug-91	1309		1259	1.040
Sep-91	1303		1264	1.030
Oct-91	1466		1267	1.157
Nov-91	1182		1272	0.929
Dec-91	855	1249	1274	0.671
Jan-92	959	1255	1276	0.752
Feb-92	1059	1263	1285	0.824
Mar-92	1321	1266	1294	1.021
Apr-92	1468	1268	1297	1.132
May-92	1562	1275	1296	1.205
Jun-92	1426	1273	1297	1.099
Jul-92	1442	1279	1305	1.105
Aug-92	1444	1291	1309	1.103
Sep-92	1380	1297	1313	1.051
Oct-92	1473	1298	1321	1.116
Nov-92	1147	1295	1326	0.865
Dec-92	920	1300	1332	0.690
Jan-93	1063	1309	1339	0.794
Feb-93	1061	1309	1342	0.791
Mar-93	1417	1317	1343	1.055
Apr-93	1556	1324	1350	1.153
May-93	1609	1328	1360	1.183
Jun-93	1524	1336	1368	1.115
Jul-93	1503	1342	1367	1.100
Aug-93	1448	1342	1365	1.061
Sep-93	1416	1345	1366	1.037
Oct-93	1594	1355	1367	1.166
Nov-93	1274	1366	1367	0.932
Dec-93	969	1370	1370	0.708
Jan-94	1002	1365	1373	0.729
Feb-94	1073	1366	1373	0.782
Mar-94	1421	1366	1372	1.036
Apr-94	1577	1368	1371	1.150
May-94	1601	1367	1369	1.169
Jun-94	1594	1373	1366	1.168
Jul-94	1510	1373		
Aug-94	1436	1372		
Sep-94	1405	1371		
Oct-94	1585	1371		
Nov-94	1235	1367		
Dec-94	923	1364		

This moving average ends at the data point shown in the third column. We need to transform this moving average so that each monthly value is at its centre. That is, for example, the 12-month moving average for January 1992 has that month as its centre. Unfortunately, the centre of 12 values is half-way between the sixth and the seventh values. This is half way between June and July for the first 12-month moving average.

Fortunately, there is a simple way of centring the moving average on an actual month. The centre of the first 12 months of data (January to December 1991) is half way between June and July 1991. The centre of the next 12-month moving average (February 1991 to January 1992) is half way between July and August 1991. The average of these two values would be centred on July 1991.

Consequently, the first value in the fourth column of Table 4.5 is the average of the first two values in the third column. This two-month moving average is repeated for each of the data points available. The result is a centred 12-month moving average for July 1991 to June 1994.

Returning to equation (4.3), we can see what we have accomplished. If we divide each actual data point by the centred 12-month moving average, we have:

$$\frac{A_t}{T_t \times C_t} = S_t \times I_t \tag{4.4}$$

where
  A = actual value in the time series
  T = the trend component
  C = the cyclical component
  S = the seasonal component
  I = the irregular component
  t = some time period less than one year

That is, by dividing each value by the 12-month centred moving average, we isolate the seasonal-irregular ($S_t \times I_t$) component. This is the series in the last column of Table 4.3 entitled '5. Seasonal ratios ($S \times I$)'.

These seasonal ratios are arrayed in Part B of Table 4.4 by month. Their average for each month is shown in the sixth column entitled 'Raw seasonal factors'. These ratios represent the seasonality pattern of the monthly data. For example, hotel/motel room-nights sold in January are, on average, only 75.8 per cent of the average monthly rooms sold for a year. February is almost 80 per cent. September is the month that comes closest to representing average monthly room demand at only 4 per cent above the monthly average for a full year. December is the lowest month for room demand (69.0 per cent of the average) while May is the highest month (18.6 per cent above the average).

These seasonal ratios are 'raw' in the sense that they do necessarily sum to an even 12. They must or they will add an upward boost or downward drag

Table 4.4 Producing a seasonally adjusted series of hotel/motel room demand in Washington, D.C.

A. Hotel/motel room-nights sold in Washington, D.C. (000)

	1991	1992	1993	1994
Jan	885	959	1063	1002
Feb	971	1059	1061	1073
Mar	1283	1321	1417	1421
Apr	1440	1468	1556	1577
May	1476	1562	1609	1601
Jun	1457	1426	1524	1594
Jul	1362	1442	1503	1510
Aug	1309	1444	1448	1436
Sep	1303	1380	1416	1405
Oct	1466	1473	1594	1585
Nov	1182	1147	1274	1235
Dec	855	920	969	923

B. Seasonal ratios and seasonal factors

1. Month	Seasonal factors				6. Raw seasonal factors	7. Adjusted seasonal factors
	1991	1992	1993	1994		
Jan		0.752	0.794	0.729	0.758	0.758
Feb		0.824	0.791	0.782	0.799	0.799
Mar		1.021	1.055	1.036	1.037	1.037
Apr		1.132	1.153	1.150	1.145	1.145
May		1.205	1.183	1.169	1.186	1.185
Jun		1.099	1.115	1.168	1.127	1.127
Jul	1.088	1.105	1.100		1.098	1.097
Aug	1.040	1.103	1.061		1.068	1.068
Sep	1.030	1.051	1.037		1.040	1.039
Oct	1.157	1.116	1.166		1.146	1.146
Nov	0.929	0.865	0.932		0.909	0.909
Dec	0.671	0.690	0.708		0.690	0.690

Total 12.002 12.000

Adjustment factor 0.9998

C. Seasonally adjusted hotel/motel room-nights sold (000)

	1991	1992	1993	1994
Jan	1168	1265	1402	1321
Feb	1216	1326	1328	1344
Mar	1236	1274	1367	1370
Apr	1258	1283	1359	1378
May	1245	1317	1357	1351
Jun	1293	1265	1353	1415
Jul	1241	1314	1370	1376
Aug	1226	1352	1356	1345
Sep	1253	1328	1363	1342
Oct	1279	1286	1390	1383
Nov	1301	1262	1403	1359
Dec	1239	1334	1406	1339

to the forecast series. We force them to sum to 12 by dividing their raw sum into 12 and multiplying the resulting 'adjustment factor' by each of the raw seasonal factors. This produces the final column of '7. Adjusted seasonal factors'. In this case, the adjustment made small reductions in the May, July, and September factors.

By averaging the seasonal ratios in Part B of Table 4.4, we not only isolate the seasonal pattern, we dispose of the irregular component as well. Since this component is assumed to be random, its mean is zero. In averaging the seasonal ratios, we assume the irregular pattern approximates this mean.

The next step is to produce a seasonally adjusted series. Part A of Table 4.4 recounts the actual room-nights sold from Table 4.3, arrayed by month for ease of explanation. By dividing each of these monthly values by the appropriate adjusted seasonal factors in column 7 of Part B, we obtain a series stripped of its seasonal component shown in Part C as described in equation (4.4).

Consequently, each of the values in Part C can be interpreted as embodying the trend-cycle component of the series. This series is shown in Figure 4.15 compared to the actual series with seasonality included. The seasonally adjusted series of room-nights sold shows no seasonal pattern. It appears to indicate a weak upward trend, which is confirmed by examining the positions of the monthly room-night curves in Figure 4.14. Each successive year sits a little bit higher than the previous one, with the exception of 1994, which appears to be about the same level as 1993.

This information is useful for the next step: developing a forecasting model for the trend-cycle series. We could attempt to distinguish the trend from the cyclical components of this series, but this would do us little practical good. While it is relatively simple to develop a good forecasting model for a time series trend, cyclical patterns are very difficult to forecast well due to their varying amplitude and duration (for a discussion of this problem, see Makridakis 1990, pp. 71–72)

Consequently, the next step is to forecast the trend-cycle series. There are a number of time series methods discussed in this chapter and the next, all of which may be used to forecast the seasonally adjusted (i.e. trend-cycle) series. In addition, regression methods may be used as well (Chapter 7). For the present, we will use the simple moving average (SMA) method as an example of applying the decomposition process. In practice, you would experiment with more complex forecasting methods to find the one that best tracks your time series.

Table 4.5 contains several SMA forecasts of the historical time series of hotel/motel room-nights sold in the Washington, D.C. area, along with forecasts for January 1995, the first future period. Note that a single moving average forecast appears the next period after the time span of the SMA. For example, the three-month SMA forecast for Apr-91 is the three-month average for January to March 1991, not February to April, although this

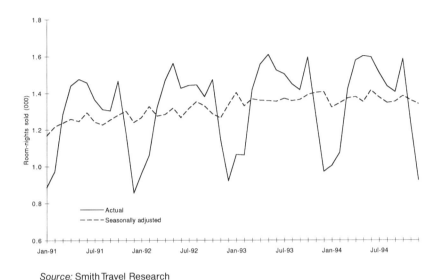

Source: Smith Travel Research

Figure 4.15   Actual and seasonally adjusted hotel/motel room demand in Washington, D.C., monthly, 1991–94

exists. Using the SMA as a forecast requires us to compute it for the latest months we have and then appoint it the forecast for the first future month.

Table 4.5 includes the MAPEs for each of these series. They do not differ very much, and are moderate compared to the compound monthly percentage change (2.43 per cent over this period). However, they are all better than our best naive model, which was seasonal naive with an MAPE of 4.0 per cent (from Table 4.2).

Figure 4.16 charts these forecast series, along with the original seasonally adjusted series of room demand. None of the series captures directional change well, and turning points are not captured at all.

We will test other models on this series in the next chapter, to see if we can obtain more accurate forecasts. However, to continue our decomposition example, we need to choose a 'best' SMA model and return seasonality to the forecasts of this model. The six-month SMA model shows the smallest MAPE in Table 4.5, so this is chosen.

Table 4.6 shows how seasonality is returned to our forecast of the seasonally adjusted series of hotel/motel room demand in Washington, D.C. The '2. Seasonal factors' column contains the adjusted seasonal factors displayed in column 7, in Part B of Table 4.4. They are repeated every 12 months (i.e. all the January factors are the same, all the February factors are the same, etc.) because they are assumed to remain constant.

Table 4.5 Hotel/motel room demand in Washington, D.C., seasonally adjusted actual and forecast series, monthly, 1991–94

	2. Actual	Simple moving average forecasts			
1. Month-year	series	3-month	4-month	6-month	12-month
Jan-91	1168				
Feb-91	1216				
Mar-91	1236				
Apr-91	1258	1207			
May-91	1245	1237	1219		
Jun-91	1293	1246	1239		
Jul-91	1241	1265	1258	1236	
Aug-91	1226	1260	1259	1248	
Sep-91	1253	1253	1251	1250	
Oct-91	1279	1240	1253	1253	
Nov-91	1301	1253	1250	1256	
Dec-91	1239	1278	1265	1266	
Jan-92	1265	1273	1268	1257	1246
Feb-92	1326	1269	1271	1261	1255
Mar-92	1274	1277	1283	1277	1264
Apr-92	1283	1288	1276	1281	1267
May-92	1317	1294	1287	1281	1269
Jun-92	1265	1291	1300	1284	1275
Jul-92	1314	1289	1285	1288	1273
Aug-92	1352	1299	1295	1297	1279
Sep-92	1328	1311	1312	1301	1289
Oct-92	1286	1331	1315	1310	1295
Nov-92	1262	1322	1320	1310	1296
Dec-92	1334	1292	1307	1301	1293
Jan-93	1402	1294	1303	1313	1301
Feb-93	1328	1333	1321	1327	1312
Mar-93	1367	1355	1332	1323	1312
Apr-93	1359	1366	1358	1330	1320
May-93	1357	1351	1364	1342	1326
Jun-93	1353	1361	1353	1358	1330
Jul-93	1370	1356	1359	1361	1337
Aug-93	1356	1360	1360	1356	1342
Sep-93	1363	1360	1359	1360	1342
Oct-93	1390	1363	1360	1360	1345
Nov-93	1403	1370	1370	1365	1354
Dec-93	1406	1385	1378	1372	1365
Jan-94	1321	1400	1390	1381	1371
Feb-94	1344	1377	1380	1373	1364
Mar-94	1370	1357	1368	1371	1366
Apr-94	1378	1345	1360	1372	1366
May-94	1351	1364	1353	1370	1368
Jun-94	1415	1366	1361	1362	1367
Jul-94	1376	1381	1378	1363	1372
Aug-94	1345	1381	1380	1372	1373
Sep-94	1352	1379	1372	1372	1372
Oct-94	1383	1358	1372	1369	1371
Nov-94	1359	1360	1364	1370	1370
Dec-94	1339	1365	1360	1372	1367
	MAPE	2.08%	1.92%	1.89%	2.34%

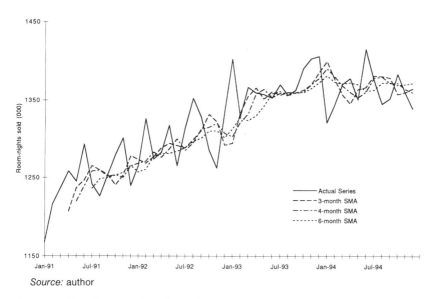

Figure 4.16   Seasonally adjusted hotel/motel room demand in Washington, D.C. and simple moving average forecasts, monthly, 1991–94

The third column of Table 4.6 contains the 6-month SMA forecasts from the fifth column of Table 4.5. They begin with July 1991 because the first six months of the year are used up in the moving average model. To return appropriate seasonality to our forecast series, we multiply the forecasts in column 3 by the seasonal factors in column 2 to obtain the seasonal forecast series in column 4. The last column of Table 4.6 is the actual time series of room demand in Washington, D.C.

Figure 4.17 compares our forecast series to the actual time series of Washington, D.C. room demand. For the most part, our forecast tracks the original series well. It does, however, miss direction changes in July and August 1992, and February 1993. Overall, the SMA model correctly forecasts 38 out of 41 possible directional movements in the actual series, for directional change accuracy of 92 per cent.

There is one last point to consider before moving on to more complex extrapolative models. This is whether we should compare the MAPEs of competing models on the seasonally adjusted series or on the original series with seasonality included.

It is this latter series that we are trying to forecast, so the most prudent approach is to perform our error magnitude accuracy analysis on all forecast models with seasonality returned. This is true whether we are using MAPE, or RMSPE or some other measure of accuracy.

Table 4.6 Computation of SMA seasonal forecast series and actual series of hotel/motel room demand in Washington, D.C., monthly, 1991–94

1. Month-year	2. Seasonal factors	3. 6-month SMA forecasts	4. Seasonal forecast	5. Actual series
Jul-91	1.097	1236	1356	1362
Aug-91	1.068	1248	1333	1309
Sep-91	1.039	1250	1299	1303
Oct-91	1.146	1253	1436	1466
Nov-91	0.909	1256	1141	1182
Dec-91	0.690	1266	873	855
Jan-92	0.758	1257	953	959
Feb-92	0.799	1261	1007	1059
Mar-92	1.037	1277	1325	1321
Apr-92	1.145	1281	1466	1468
May-92	1.185	1281	1519	1562
Jun-92	1.127	1284	1447	1426
Jul-92	1.097	1288	1414	1442
Aug-92	1.068	1297	1385	1444
Sep-92	1.039	1301	1352	1380
Oct-92	1.146	1310	1501	1473
Nov-92	0.909	1310	1191	1147
Dec-92	0.690	1301	897	920
Jan-93	0.758	1313	996	1063
Feb-93	0.799	1327	1060	1061
Mar-93	1.037	1323	1373	1417
Apr-93	1.145	1330	1522	1556
May-93	1.185	1342	1591	1609
Jun-93	1.127	1358	1530	1524
Jul-93	1.097	1361	1494	1503
Aug-93	1.068	1356	1448	1448
Sep-93	1.039	1360	1414	1416
Oct-93	1.146	1360	1558	1594
Nov-93	0.909	1365	1240	1274
Dec-93	0.690	1372	946	969
Jan-94	0.758	1381	1047	1002
Feb-94	0.799	1373	1097	1073
Mar-94	1.037	1371	1422	1421
Apr-94	1.145	1372	1571	1577
May-94	1.185	1370	1624	1601
Jun-94	1.127	1362	1534	1594
Jul-94	1.097	1363	1496	1510
Aug-94	1.068	1372	1465	1436
Sep-94	1.039	1372	1426	1405
Oct-94	1.146	1369	1569	1585
Nov-94	0.909	1370	1245	1235
Dec-94	0.690	1372	946	923

MAPE = 1.89%

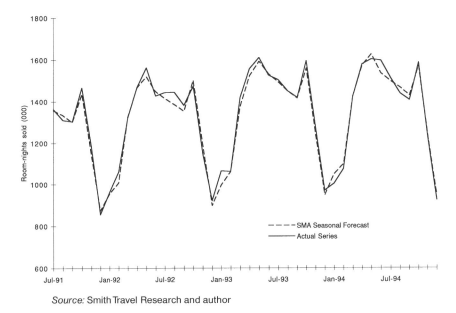

Source: Smith Travel Research and author

Figure 4.17   Hotel/motel room demand in Washington, D.C., actual and forecast series, monthly, 1991–94

When the seasonal pattern is quite regular, however, the MAPEs will not differ for a model between the seasonally adjusted and the original series with seasonality. This is true in the present case of Washington, D.C. hotel/motel room demand. The seasonality in this series is so regular that we can compute the MAPE of the seasonally adjusted series and be confident this will indicate the most accurate model on this criterion on the seasonal series as well. This has the additional advantage of saving time: we do not need to go the extra step of adding seasonality back into our forecast series before comparing error magnitude accuracies.

Applications

Miller, McCahon and Miller (1991) found that single moving average and single exponential smoothing models could accurately forecast daily meals ('covers') served in two restaurants. The models worked better when the seasonal patterns were first removed, and for forecasting the most popular menu items as a group.

Conclusion

The simplest extrapolative forecasting methods are the naive method and the single moving average method. These are seldom used on their own to produce forecasts of tourism demand, but rather are the foundation for developing and applying more sophisticated models. The naive models are especially useful as benchmarks for evaluating our more complex techniques.

Classical decomposition is a straightforward approach to distinguishing the seasonal, cycle-trend, and irregular components of a time series in order to develop reasonable forecasts. The advent of powerful spreadsheets on personal computers has made this method especially easy to apply. Figure 4.18 provides a summary of the steps in this forecasting method.

---

1. Isolate the seasonal component and nullify the irregular component
    a. Compute the 12-month or 4-quarter moving average ending at each observation in the time series for the final period of the first year and each successive period
    b. Centre this series on each value possible
    c. Compute the ratio of each period's value to its moving average
    d. Average these ratios and force the resulting seasonal factors to sum to 12 (monthly series) or 4 (quarterly)
    e. Compute seasonally adjusted values for each period.
2. Forecast the cycle/trend series over the historical series using various methods and choose the best model based on:
    a. error magnitude accuracy, or
    b. directional change accuracy, or
    c. turning point accuracy, or
    d. some combination of these.
3. Use the best model to forecast the future periods of interest.
4. Return seasonality to the forecsst series.

Figure 4.18 Steps in applying the classical decomposition forecasting approach

For further information

Cunningham, Stephen (1991), *Data Analysis in Hotel & Catering Management*, Butterworth-Heinemann, pp. 184–201.

Clifton, Peter, Nguyen, Hai and Nutt, Susan (1992), *Market Research: Using Forecasting in Business*, Butterworth-Heinemann, pp. 223–249.

Levenbach, Hans and Cleary, James P. (1981), *The Beginning Forecaster: The Forecasting Process through Data Analysis*, Lifetime Learning Publications, Chapter 8.

Makridakis, Spyros, Wheelwright, Steven C. and McGee, Victor E. (1983), *Forecasting: Methods and Applications*, 2nd edition, John Wiley & Sons, Chapters 3 and 4.

Moore, Thomas W. (1989), *Handbook of Business Forecasting*, Gower Publishing Company, Chapters 3 and 4.

Saunders, John A., Sharp, John A. and Witt, Stephen F. (1987), *Practical Business Forecasting*, Gower Publishing Company, Chapter 3.

Note

[1] It is best to use all of the time series we have in forecast modelling, which, in this case, goes back to January 1987. However, in the interests of clear exposition and space economy, this series has been shortened to cover only the monthly periods of 1991 to 1994.

5 Intermediate extrapolative methods

In Chapter 4, we introduced the extrapolative or time series methods of forecasting. We explored the use of the most basic extrapolative models: the naive and its variations, and single moving average (SMA) models. We then examined seasonality and took advantage of the regularity of this pattern over years through the classical decomposition approach.

Decomposition estimates the average magnitude of seasonal patterns, removes them from the time series, and provides us with a trend-cycle, or seasonally adjusted series. We can then test a number of alternative quantitative forecasting models on this series, including extrapolative methods. We look for the model that best simulates our data series, using the criterion of error magnitude, directional change, turning point, or some combination of these. This should be the best candidate for forecasting future periods.

Once we have determined this model, we can then produce the forecasts we need and return seasonality to the forecast series.

In this chapter, we will look at intermediate extrapolative forecasting methods, specifically:

- single exponential smoothing
- double exponential smoothing
- autoregression.

These methods are intermediate in their complexity among times series forecasting methods. Single exponential smoothing deals best with stationary time series, while double exponential smoothing is designed for series showing a linear trend. Autoregression uses regression analysis to model a stationary trend. A new technique for producing such a trend, even from seasonal data, will be introduced.

Intermediate time series methods are somewhat more complex than their basic brethren, but can still be handled in modern computer spreadsheets. However, as complexity rises, more data are required in the time series models to obtain satisfactory results. Consequently, we will use the complete time series available to us of hotel/motel room demand for the Washington, D.C. metropolitan area, that is, monthly data from January 1987 to December 1994.

Single exponential smoothing

In trying to forecast a future period, the single moving average method gives equal weight to all of the past values included in it. For example, each of the values in a three-month moving average model has a weight of one-third in determining the forecast. On the other hand, those values excluded from a SMA model (in this case, values four periods or more back) do not have any effect on the forecast at all. The single exponential smoothing (SES) method allows us to vary the importance of recent values to the forecast and includes all of the information past values can provide us.

The logic of the SES is evident in its general equation:

$$F_t = F_{t-1} + \alpha(A_{t-1} - F_{t-1}) \tag{5.1}$$

where

F = forecast value
α = a smoothing constant between 0 and 1
A = actual value
t = some time period

Equation (5.1) says that the forecast for the period, t, is equal to the forecast for the previous period $(t - 1)$ plus a portion of the error the forecasting model produced for that previous period (remember that error is defined as the actual value for a period less the forecast value for that period: see equation (2.1) in Chapter 2).

The portion of the previous period's error to be included in next period's forecast is set by the forecaster and is called the 'smoothing constant'. By convention, the Greek letter alpha (α) is used to represent this constant. The smoothing constant must take a value between zero and one. If it equals zero, then the SES model always forecasts the same value: the initial forecast value. If the smoothing constant equals one, then the SES model reverts to the naive model, because the error on the right-hand side of equation (5.1) is multiplied by zero.

The practice in SES modelling is to try the range of possible values for the smoothing constant in one-tenth or 50 one-hundredths increments to find the one that minimizes the mean absolute percentage error (MAPE) or some other measure of forecasting error over the past series. This minimum error model is the best SES model for the series. Bear in mind that the higher the smoothing constant, the more weight it gives to the last value. The lower this constant, the more weight it gives to all of the values previous to the last one, which are summarized in the F_{t-1} term in equation (5.1).

To aid computation, we can rearrange equation (5.1) to produce:

$$F_t = \alpha A_{t-1} + (1 - \alpha)F_{t-1} \tag{5.2}$$

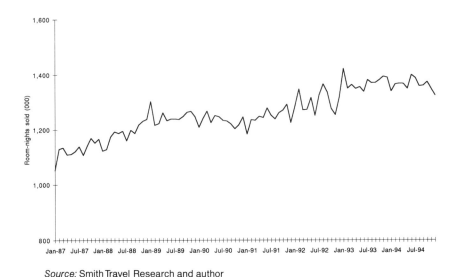

Source: Smith Travel Research and author

Figure 5.1 Hotel/motel room demand in Washington, D.C., seasonally adjusted, monthly, 1987–94

We can place these F_t forecast values in the third column of a spreadsheet, with the dates in the first column and the time series itself in the second.

SES will only work on stationary series with no seasonality. Consequently, you should consider it for dealing with annual data, or monthly or quarterly time series where seasonality has been removed. Figure 5.1 shows the seasonally adjusted series of hotel/motel room demand in the Washington, D.C. metropolitan area developed by the ratio-to-moving-averages method discussed in Chapter 4's treatment of classical decomposition. While there is no seasonal pattern left, it is clear that the series in Figure 5.1 trends upwards. That is, it is not stationary in its mean.

We can achieve stationarity of a trended series by differencing it. Figure 5.2 shows the first differences of our seasonally adjusted room demand series (the solid line). It appears stationary, and thus can provide a satisfactory SES forecast series.

There is one issue left to resolve: how to start the SES forecast series. Each period's forecast requires a forecast for the previous period. However, the first period in the series does not have a forecast value associated with it.

The process of providing a forecast value for the first period is called 'initialization'. Initialization is an important consideration in SES modelling. In some time series, especially one with a large variance around its (stationary) mean, the forecast value chosen for the first period of the SES series will influence all future period forecasts significantly. This is especially true if the smoothing constant is small.

Source: Smith Travel Research and author

Figure 5.2 Hotel/motel room demand in Washington, D.C., monthly first differences, 1987–94

A number of initialization processes have been proposed. None of the alternatives has a superior theoretical foundation, so the principle of parsimony can be applied here with impunity.

The simplest value for the first F_{t-1} is the first **actual** value we have: an application of the naive forecasting method. The next simplest is to average the first three or four values in the series to obtain the initial forecast: an application of the simple moving average method.

Based on experience, the best approach to initialization appears to be the steps shown in Figure 5.3. This assumes you have set up your SES forecast model to produce forecasts based on varying values of the smoothing constant, with the MAPE or some other measure of error magnitude programmed to vary with the constant as well (the MAPE is assumed to be the error magnitude measure in the figure).

Employing this differenced series of the seasonally adjusted room-nights sold by Washington, D.C. hotels and motels, we achieved the lowest MAPE (14.2 per cent) with a smoothing constant of 0.35 and initialized by the average of the differenced series' first four values. The SES forecast series is shown in Figure 5.2. It has indeed smoothed the series of first differences. It produces a forecast for January 1995 of −14. Table 5.1 illustrates how this forecast of first differences is used to obtain a forecast of the actual value for January.

---

1. Use the first actual value as the forecast value for the first period.
2. Vary your smoothing constant between zero and one in one-tenth or 50 one-hundredth increments to find the value with the smallest MAPE, and record the constant and MAPE.
3. Change the initial forecast value to be the moving average of the first three periods.
4. Vary the smoothing constant to see if you can achieve a smaller MAPE, and record it and your constant if you do.
5. Change the initial forecast value to be the four-period moving average.
6. Vary your smoothing constant to see if you can achieve a smaller MAPE than found in step 4.
7. Choose the initial forecast value and smoothing constant combination that achieves the lowest MAPE: this is your best SES model.

Figure 5.3   Steps in obtaining the best SES model by varying the smoothing

Table 5.1   Turning the single exponential smoothing (SES) model forecast of January 1995 first difference into a final forecast

		January 1995		
	Seasonally adjusted series			
1. December 1994	*2. SES forecast first difference*	*3. Seasonally adjusted forecast*	*4. Seasonal factor*	*5. Seasonalized forecast*
1323	−14	1310	0.748	980

Column one contains the last value in the seasonally adjusted historical series of hotel/motel room demand in thousands. The second column contains the SES forecast first difference for January 1995. The third column is simply the sum of the first two columns: the forecast first difference is added to the previous actual value to obtain a forecast of the seasonally adjusted series for January 1995.

Column four shows the seasonal adjustment factor for January for hotel/motel room demand from Table 4.4, Part B, column 7. Column five is the product of this factor and the seasonally adjusted forecast in column 3. It is our best SES forecast of hotel/motel room-nights sold in January 1995.

1. Make sure there is no seasonality in the series to be forecast; remove seasonality by decomposition, if necessary.

2. Confirm by sight that it is stationary; achieve stationarity by first or second differencing, if necessary.

3. Set up a spreadsheet with the time period in the first column and the non-seasonal, stationary historical data in the second column.

4. Program the SES equation in the third column, with the smoothing constant in a separate cell at the top.

5. Program computation of the absolute percentage errors in the fourth column, with the MAPE as the mean of the column.

6. Apply the steps to choosing the optimum smoothing constant and initial value is presented in Figure 5.3.

7. If a smoothing constant of one produces the minimum MAPE, adopt the naive forecasting method instead.

8. Using the best SES model, produce a forecast for the next period.

9. Add non-stationarity to this estimate, if necessary.

10. Return the seasonality to the forecast series, if necessary.

Figure 5.4   Steps in using a single exponential smoothing model to forecast

Figure 5.4 recounts the steps in applying the single exponential smoothing model as detailed above.

The advantages of the SES are its simplicity and ability to fit stationary time series well. Its disadvantages are that it cannot deal with series showing any sort of trend or seasonality. Moreover, achieving stationarity in the mean may be a difficult chore with some time series. Finally, the SES can only forecast one period ahead of the time series. Fortunately, we have another time series method that offers more flexibility in dealing with series without seasonality: double exponential smoothing.

Double exponential smoothing

Second order or double exponential smoothing (DES) was developed to deal with time series showing a linear trend over time, such as the seasonally adjusted series of hotel/motel room demand in Washington, D.C. shown in

Figure 5.1. In essence, a DES model first develops an SES series and then applies exponential smoothing to this series to incorporate the trend.

A number of DES models have been proposed but the simplest and one of the most successful is Brown's one-parameter adaptive method.

The equations for this DES model are:

$$\text{SES}_t = \text{SES}_{t-1} + \alpha(A_{t-1} - \text{SES}_{t-1}) \tag{5.3}$$

$$\text{DES}_t = \text{DES}_{t-1} + \alpha(\text{SES}_t - \text{DES}_{t-1}) \tag{5.4}$$

$$C_t = \text{SES}_t + (\text{SES}_t - \text{DES}_t) \tag{5.5}$$

$$T_t = \frac{\alpha}{1 - \alpha} * (\text{SES}_t - \text{DES}_t) \tag{5.6}$$

$$F_{t+h} = C_t + hT_t \tag{5.7}$$

where

SES = single exponential smoothing series

α = a smoothing constant between 0 and 1

A = actual value

DES = double exponential smoothing series

C = the intercept of the DES forecast series

T = the slope of the DES forecast series

F = forecast value

h = the number of time periods ahead

t = some time period

Equation (5.3) computes the SES series, and is the same as equation (5.2) except for the terminology: we are not producing an SES forecast here but an SES series. Equation (5.4) computes a second smoothed line, the DES series, from the SES series.

Equation (5.5) calculates C, which is the intercept of the DES forecast series, while equation (5.6) computes T, which is the slope. These two values determine the DES forecast values, as shown in the DES forecast equation (5.7).

The DES forecast equation (5.7) is used in two ways. If you are simulating your historical series, you simply compute the F_{t+h} value with $h = 1$. On the other hand, if you are forecasting, say, three periods beyond your historical time series, then $h = 3$ in equation (5.7).

Table 5.2 shows the detailed steps for computing a DES forecast for hotel/motel room demand for February 1988. The data for January 1988, developed according to the SES steps in Figure 5.4, are required to begin the process. In an actual spreadsheet, you would embody equations (5.3) to (5.7) in columns rather than the rows shown in Table 5.2. Values used in producing the F_{t+h} forecast are shown in **bold**.

You should note that a smoothing constant of one will not produce a naive forecast series but rather, through equation (5.6), will produce no solution at all.

Table 5.2 Example of the computation of the double exponential smoothing forecast for hotel/motel room demand in Washington, D.C., for February 1988

Smoothing constant (alpha) = 0.2

	Time period	Actual	SES	DES	DES forecast
Jan-88	$t-1$	1123	1137	1111	1169
$SES_t =$	$SES_{t-1}+$	alpha ×	(Actual$_{t-1}$−	$SES_{t-1}) =$	SES_t
$SES_t =$	$1138+$	$0.2 \times$	$(1123-$	$1137) =$	**1134**
$DES_t =$	$DES_{t-1}+$	alpha ×	$(SES_t-$	$DES_{t-1}) =$	DES_t
$DES_t =$	$1111+$	$0.2 \times$	$(1134-$	$1111) =$	**1115**
$C_t =$	SES_t+	$(SES_t-$	$DES_t) =$		C_t
$C_t =$	$1134+$	$(1134-$	$1115) =$		**1152**
$T_t =$	(alpha/	1 − alpha) ×	$(SES_t-$	$DES_t) =$	T_t
$T_t =$	$(0.2/$	$0.8) \times$	$(1134-$	$1115) =$	**4.64**
$F_{t+h} =$	C_t+	$hT_t =$	DES forecast		
$F_{t+1} =$	$1152+$	$4.64 =$	**1157**		

Summary

	Time period	Actual	SES	DES	DES forecast
Feb-88	t	1128	1134	1115	1157

In summary, the advantages of the DES method are that it is relatively simple, captures linear trends up or down well, and can forecast several periods ahead (unlike the SES method). Its disadvantages are that it cannot track non-linear trends well and fails to simulate a stepped series well. Finally, in common with all time series methods, it does not incorporate any causal relationships which may be important to management.

Figure 5.5 summarizes the steps in a DES forecasting model.

Applications of DES

Sheldon (1993) tested eight models for forecasting international visitor expenditures in six developed countries and found that double exponential smoothing was the second most accurate model in terms of MAPE. The most accurate model was the naive 1 model of no change from the previous year.

Martin and Witt (1989) compared the accuracy of seven forecasting methods for simulating visitor flows among 24 origin-destination pairs and, like Sheldon, found that exponential smoothing was the second most accurate model in terms of MAPE, after naive 1.

1. Make sure there is no seasonality in the series to be forecast; remove seasonality by decomposition, if necessary.
2. Confirm by sight that the series follows a linear trend; if it does not, the DES method will not produce acceptable accuracy.
3. Set up a spreadsheet with the time period in the first column and the historical data in the second column.
4. Program the SES equation (5.3) in the third column, with the smoothing constant in a separate cell at the top.
5. Program the DES equation (5.4) in the fourth column, referring to the same smoothing constant.
6. Program the intercept equation (5.5) in the fifth column.
7. Program the slope equation (5.6) in the sixth column, referring to the same smoothing constant.
8. Program the DES forecast equation (5.7) in the seventh column.
9. Program computation of the absolute percentage errors for each period in the eighth column, with the MAPE as the mean of this column.
10. Apply the steps to choosing the optimum smoothing constant and initial value in Figure 5.3, but focus on the MAPE of the DES series (column 8).
11. Choose the DES model with the minimum MAPE.
12. Using this DES model produce forecasts for future periods.
13. Return seasonality to this forecast series.

Figure 5.5 Steps in developing and applying a double exponential smoothing forecasting model

The autoregressive method

It is not unusual for a tourism series to show a strong relationship between the current period's value and the observation for the previous period's or those for several previous periods. Autoregressive models attempt to exploit this momentum effect, and they have the flexibility of being able to follow non-linear trends. 'Autoregressive' refers to the fact that the current period's value is regressed on some collection of past values from the same time series, usually no more than four or five. Regression analysis is discussed in detail in Chapter 7, and refers to developing a mathematical expression of the relationship of one dependent variable to one or more independent variables.

An autoregressive model follows the form:

$$F_t = a + b_1 A_{t-1} + b_2 A_{t-2} + \cdots + b_n A_{t-n} \tag{5.8}$$

where

F = forecast value
a = estimated constant
b = estimated coefficient
A = actual value in the time series
t = some time period
n = number of past values included

The constant and coefficients as well as which past values to be included are determined by stepwise regression. This is an application of regression analysis (Chapter 7) where independent variables are added to the forecast equation one at a time and retained if they increase the equation's explanatory power (measured by MAPE, the F-statistic or the coefficient of determination) and have coefficients that are significantly different from zero (measured by the t-statistic).

Autoregression is best applied to a seasonally adjusted series. If you are dealing with sub-annual (e.g. monthly or quarterly) data, the first step is to produce such a series from the time series you have, as explained in the decomposition method (Chapter 4). Next, program regression analysis in your spreadsheet. Make sure it produces a measure of explanatory power for each set of variables included (MAPE, F-statistic, etc.).

To program this in a computer spreadsheet, enter your time periods and time series in the first and second columns, respectively. In the third column, enter the time series but lagged one period. That is, the value next to February 1987 should be the original time series value for January 1987. Copy these lagged data through the rest of the column.

Similarly, the fourth column should have the column two time series lagged by two periods: the original January data point would appear in the March 1987 position. Repeat this by column for as many lagged variables as you want to test in your autoregression models. Then, when you run the spreadsheet regression program, you can easily identify the combination of explanatory variables you wish to include.

In our case of modelling hotel/motel room demand in the Washington, D.C. areas, there are seven possible combinations of the time series lagged one, two and three months (e.g. first lagged value only, first and second lagged values, all three lagged values, first and third lagged values). Three of these models indicated all of the coefficients were significantly different from zero. The other four produced insignificant coefficients, indicating the associated independent variable was not significant and the equation was misspecified (discussed further in Chapter 7).

Table 5.3 Comparison of autoregressive models significant at 0.05 on the F-test

Explanatory variables	Adjusted R^2	MAPE
A_{t-1}, A_{t-2}	0.220	1.80%
A_{t-1}	0.080	2.00%
A_{t-2}	0.066	2.05%

The models with significant coefficients are listed in Table 5.3 by their independent variables, along with their MAPEs. Regressing the differenced seasonally adjusted series of hotel/motel room demand on values one period earlier and two periods earlier produced the largest coefficient of determination (R^2) adjusted for degrees of freedom, a common measure of the fit of a regression equation (see Chapter 7 for more details). It also produced the lowest measure of error magnitude, but not significantly lower than the other two autoregressive models with significant regression equations.

In summary, the autoregressive model exploits the idea that the last several values of a time series may be a good basis for forecasting the next value. Since it can produce non-linear trend estimates, it is well suited for any series with a trend. However, since it is based on a set of previous values it can only forecast a few periods after the time series ends before it starts relying on its own forecast values as independent variables. This often degenerates into a horizontal trend after several periods and magnifies any errors in the early forecasts as well.

Figure 5.6 relates the steps in developing an autoregressive tourism forecasting model, as detailed above.

Comparing alternative time series models

At this point, we have examined five time series forecast methods:

1. naive
2. single moving average
3. single exponential smoothing
4. double exponential smoothing
5. autoregressive.

Figure 5.7 shows the actual seasonally adjusted series and those produced by our three best forecast models based on minimum MAPEs.

Table 5.4 summarizes the accuracy of the best models from each of the four extrapolative forecasting methods used on the hotel/motel room

1. If necessary, remove seasonality from the historical time series.
2. Regress the seasonally adjusted series against earlier values in a stepwise fashion
   a. Regress the actual values against combinations of the past four or five values
   b. Examine coefficients for significance by their *t*-statistics
   c. Assess all models where all coefficients are significantly different from zero by examining their MAPEs over the historical series
   d. Choose the model with the lowest MAPE as the forecast mode.
3. Forecast the seasonally adjusted series over the future periods of interest.
4. Return seasonality to the forecast series.

Figure 5.6 Steps in developing and applying an autoregressive forecasting model

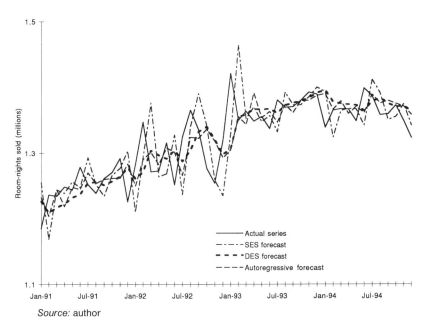

Source: author

Figure 5.7 Extrapolative model forecasts of hotel/motel room demand in Washington, D.C., seasonally adjusted, monthly, 1991–94

Table 5.4   Comparison of time series models forecasting hotel/motel room demand in Washington, D.C., monthly seasonally adjusted, 1987–94

Method	Characteristics	MAPE	Jan-95 forecast	Forecast error
Naive 1	simple	2.13%	1323	2.9%
Single moving average	3-month	2.48%	1323	2.9%
Single exponential smoothing	$\alpha = 0.35$	1.88%	1310	3.9%
Double exponential smoothing	$\alpha = 0.2$	1.88%	1363	0.0%
Autoregressive	A_{t-1}, A_{t-2}	1.80%	1323	3.0%

Actual value for Jan-95 = 1363

demand seasonally adjusted time series. The table also shows relevant characteristics of the best models and their forecasts for January 1995, the first period after the time series.

We can compare the results of the best model for each of these methods in forecasting our seasonally adjusted series of hotel/motel room demand in Washington, D.C. by both picture and number.

This comparison indicates that it is possible to use a relatively straightforward extrapolative model to improve on the naive model for forecasting this

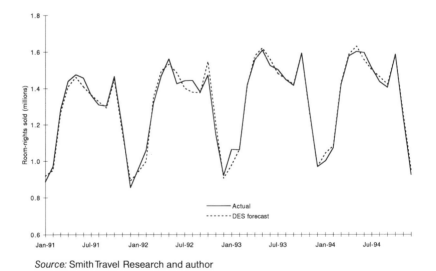

Source: Smith Travel Research and author

Figure 5.8   Actual and DES forecast series of hotel/motel room demand in Washington, D.C., monthly, 1991–94

series. The two exponential smoothing models and the best autoregressive model all produced series with lower MAPEs than the naive model. The best single moving average model did not.

The MAPEs of the three best models are hardly distinguishable. Yet they produced forecasts that varied up to nearly 4 per cent from the actual value for January. Only the DES forecasting model produced the precise value for the forecast period.

But how can we objectively determine this accuracy before the forecast period? One solution is to average the forecasts of the three models with indistinguishable MAPEs. This would have produced a forecast of 1332 thousand room-nights sold for January, 2.3 per cent from the actual number.

Figure 5.8 shows the forecasts from the DES model with seasonality returned along with the actual hotel/motel room demand time series. It is clear the DES series tracks the actual data rather well, except for July–August, 1992.

Choosing a time series method

We have discussed six different time series methods for forecasting tourism demand. Each has advantages and disadvantages in dealing with particular time series. It is useful to have some guidance at the beginning of the forecasting project as to what method to employ first. The following Tables 5.5 to 5.8 can help you in this process. They are an adaptation of ones found in Saunders, Sharp and Witt (1987). These four tables correspond to the four common patterns in time series discussed in Chapter 4 (shown in Figures 4.1 to 4.6):

1. stationary
2. linear trend
3. non-linear trend
4. stepped series.

To make use of these tables, begin by viewing a chart of your series, such as the actual series in Figure 5.8 showing our familiar monthly room demand in the Washington, D.C. metropolitan area. In this case, we can reach the following conclusions:

● type of series: linear trend
● pattern: annual seasonality
● series length: 96 observations.

In addition, assume we must forecast each of the first six months of 1995.

Table 5.5 Decision table for choosing time series methods – stationary data

	1	2	3	4	5	6	7	8	9	10
PATTERN										
Annual seasonality	N	N	N	Y/N	Y/N	Y/N	Y	Y	N	N
Non-annual seasonality	N	N	N	Y/N	Y/N	Y/N	N	N	Y	Y
FORECAST HORIZON										
1 to 3 periods	Y	Y	N	Y/N	Y	N	Y	N	Y	N
4 to 12 periods	N	N	Y/N	Y/N	N	Y/N	N	Y/N	N	Y/N
13 or more periods	N	N	Y/N	XXX	N	Y/N	N	Y/N	N	Y/N
SERIES LENGTH										
< 10 points or 1 season	Y	N	Y/N	Y	N	N	N	N	N	N
< 20 points or 2 seasons	N	Y/N	Y/N	N	Y/N	Y/N	N	N	N	N
< 30 points or 3 seasons	N	Y/N	Y/N	N	Y/N	Y/N	N	N	N	N
> 30 points or 3 seasons	N	Y/N	Y/N	N	N	N	Y	Y	Y	Y
Naive	NS	NS	NS	NA	NA	NA	NA	NA	NA	NA
Classical decomposition	NA	NA	NA	NA	NA	NA	FC	FC	NA	NA
Single exponential smoothing	FC	FC	FC	NA	NA	NA	NA	NA	NA	NA
SES + seasonal differencing	NA	NA	NA	NA	FC	FC	FC	FC	FC	FC
Double exponential smoothing	NR	NR	NR	NA	NA	NA	NA	NA	NA	NA
Autoregressive	SU	NR	NA	NA	NA	NA	NA	NA	NA	NA
Autoregressive + seasonal differencing	NA	NA	NA	NA	SU	NR	SU	NR	SU	NR

KEY TO CODES
Y = yes
N = no
Y/N = yes or no

Y to one implies N to others

XXX = unwise to attempt

FC = first choice

NA = not appropriate

NR = not recommended

NS = normally satisfactory

SU = sometimes useful

After Saunders, John A., Sharp, John A. and Witt, Stephen F. (1987), *Practical Business Forecasting*, p. 100. Used with permission.

Table 5.6 Decision table for choosing time series methods – data with linear trend

	1	2	3	4	5	6	7	8	9	10
PATTERN										
Annual seasonality	N	N	N	Y/N	Y/N	Y/N	Y	Y	N	N
Non-annual seasonality	N	N	N	Y/N	Y/N	Y/N	N	N	Y	Y
FORECAST HORIZON										
1 to 3 periods	Y	Y	N	Y/N	Y	N	Y	N	Y	N
4 to 12 periods	N	N	Y/N	Y/N	N	Y/N	N	Y/N	N	Y/N
13 or more periods	N	N	Y/N	XXX	N	Y/N	N	Y/N	N	Y/N
SERIES LENGTH										
< 10 points or 1 season	Y	N	Y/N	Y	N	N	N	N	N	N
< 20 points or 2 seasons	N	Y/N	Y/N	N	Y/N	Y/N	N	N	N	N
< 30 points or 3 seasons	N	Y/N	Y/N	N	Y/N	Y/N	N	N	N	N
> 30 points or 3 seasons	N	Y/N	Y/N	N	N	N	Y	Y	Y	Y
Naive	NR	NR	NA	NA	NA	NA	NA	NA	NA	NA
Classical decomposition	NA	NA	NA	NA	NA	NA	FC	FC	NA	NA
Single exponential smoothing	NA	NA	NA	NA	NA	NA	NA	NA	NA	NA
SES + seasonal differencing	NA	NA	NA	NA	FC	FC	FC	FC	FC	FC
Double exponential smoothing	FC	FC	FC	NA	NA	NA	NA	NA	NA	NA
Autoregressive	SU	NS	NR	NA	NA	NA	NA	NA	NA	NA
Autoregressive + seasonal differencing	NA	NA	NA	NA	NS	NR	NS	NR	NS	NR

KEY TO CODES
Y = yes
N = no
Y/N = yes or no

Y to one implies N to others

XXX = unwise to attempt
FC = first choice
NA = not appropriate
NR = not recommended
NS = normally satisfactory
SU = sometimes useful

After Saunders, John A., Sharp, John A. and Witt, Stephen F. (1987), *Practical Business Forecasting*, p. 102. Used with permission.

Table 5.7 Decision table for choosing time series methods – data with non-linear trend

	1	*2*	*3*	*4*	*5*	*6*	*7*	*8*	*9*	*10*
PATTERN										
Annual seasonality	N	N	N	Y/N	Y/N	Y/N	Y	Y	N	N
Non-annual seasonality	N	N	N	Y/N	Y/N	Y/N	N	N	Y	Y
FORECAST HORIZON										
1 to 3 periods	Y	Y	N	Y/N	Y	N	Y	N	Y	N
4 to 12 periods	N	N	Y/N	Y/N	N	Y/N	N	Y/N	N	Y/N
13 or more periods	N	N	Y/N	XXX	N	Y/N	N	Y/N	N	Y/N
SERIES LENGTH										
< 10 points or 1 season	Y	N	Y/N	Y	N	N	N	N	N	N
< 20 points or 2 seasons	N	Y/N	Y/N	N	Y/N	Y/N	N	N	N	N
< 30 points or 3 seasons	N	Y/N	Y/N	N	Y/N	Y/N	N	N	N	N
> 30 points or 3 seasons	N	Y/N	Y/N	N	N	N	Y	Y	Y	Y
Naive	NR	NR	NA	NA	NA	NA	NA	NA	NA	NA
Classical decomposition	NA	NA	NA	NA	NA	NA	FC	FC	NA	NA
Single exponential smoothing	NA	NA	NA	NA	NA	NA	NA	NA	NA	NA
SES + seasonal differencing	NA	NA	NA	NA	FC	FC	FC	FC	FC	FC
Double exponential smoothing	FC	FC	FC	NA	NA	NA	NA	NA	NA	NA
Autoregressive	SU	NS	NR	NA	NA	NA	NA	NA	NA	NA
Autoregressive + seasonal differencing	NA	NA	NA	NA	NS	NR	NS	NR	NS	NR

KEY TO CODES
Y = yes
N = no
Y/N = yes or no

Y to one implies N to others

XXX = unwise to attempt

FC = first choice
NA = not appropriate
NR = not recommended
NS = normally satisfactory
SU = sometimes useful

After Saunders, John A., Sharp, John A. and Witt, Stephen F. (1987), *Practical Business Forecasting*, p. 103. Used with permission.

Table 5.8 Decision table for choosing time series methods – stepped data

	1	2	3	4	5	6	7	8	9	10
PATTERN										
Annual seasonality	N	N	N	Y/N	Y/N	Y/N	Y	Y	N	N
Non-annual seasonality	N	N	N	Y/N	Y/N	Y/N	N	N	Y	Y
FORECAST HORIZON										
1 to 3 periods	Y	Y	N	Y/N	Y	N	Y	N	Y	N
4 to 12 periods	N	N	Y/N	Y/N	N	Y/N	N	Y/N	N	Y/N
13 or more periods	N	N	Y/N	XXX	N	Y/N	N	Y/N	N	Y/N
SERIES LENGTH										
< 10 points or 1 season	Y	N	Y/N	Y	N	N	N	N	N	N
< 20 points or 2 seasons	N	Y/N	Y/N	N	Y/N	Y/N	N	N	N	N
< 30 points or 3 seasons	N	Y/N	Y/N	N	Y/N	Y/N	N	N	N	N
> 30 points or 3 seasons	N	Y/N	Y/N	N	N	N	Y	Y	Y	Y
Naive	NS	NS	NS	NA	NA	NA	NA	NA	NA	NA
Classical decomposition	NA	NA	NA	NA	NA	NA	NA	NA	NA	NA
Single exponential smoothing	NA	NA	NA	NA	NA	NA	NA	NA	NA	NA
SES + seasonal differencing	NA	NA	NA	NA	NS	NS	NS	NS	NS	NS
Double exponential smoothing	SU	SU	SU	NA	NA	NA	NA	NA	NA	NA
Autoregressive	NA	NA	NA	NA	NA	NR	NA	NA	NA	NA
Autoregressive + seasonal differencing	NA	NA	NA	NA	NA	NR	NA	NA	NA	NA

KEY TO CODES

Y = yes

N = no

Y/N = yes or no

Y to one implies N to others

XXX = unwise to attempt

FC = first choice

NA = not appropriate

NR = not recommended

NS = normally satisfactory

SU = sometimes useful

After Saunders, John A., Sharp, John A. and Witt, Stephen F. (1987), *Practical Business Forecasting*, p. 101. Used with permission.

Since we have a linear trend, we go to Table 5.6: 'Data with linear trend'. Next, we look across the 'Annual seasonality' line under 'Pattern' and ignore all columns with an 'N', since we do have annual seasonality. This eliminates the first three columns and the last two from consideration because they all assume no annual seasonality.

A point about terminology here may be appropriate. For most tourism uses, 'Non-annual seasonality' refers to weekly series where we focus on daily movements. For example, it is common for guest arrivals to peak on certain days of most weeks. For downtown hotels which cater to business travellers, this is likely to be Monday to Thursday, with fewer check-ins on Friday to Sunday. For resort hotels appealing to the leisure visitor, the peak days for arrivals are likely to be Friday and Saturday, with low periods Tuesday to Thursday. These are patterns that are repeated in a kind of seasonality, but which is not annual. Restaurants, airlines, rental car companies, and attractions tend to show such non-annual seasonality as well. However, our series is a monthly, annual seasonality one.

Focusing on the remaining columns 4 to 8, we next move to 'Forecast horizon'. This has been set at six periods, so we look for columns with 'Y' in the middle line, '4 to 12 periods'. Columns 4, 6 and 8 qualify, while columns 5 and 7 drop out.

Finally, we move to the 'Series length' section. Our series is eight years long and we are working with monthly data, so we have 96 data points. This is the last row in the section ' > 30 points or 3 seasons'. Of columns 4, 6 and 8, only 8 has a 'Y' in it. Consequently, we read down this column to determine which are the methods most likely to produce a quality forecasting model. This suggests that classical decomposition and single exponential smoothing with seasonal differencing are first choices. We might also consider an autoregressive model with seasonal differencing as well.

Summary

The basic and intermediate time series methods discussed here have broad applications in tourism. They are quick, simple and cheap to operate and can account for trends and seasonality. They lend themselves to easy re-estimation as new data become available, and can be operated with little statistical training.

According to Witt, Newbould and Watkins, exponential smoothing tourism forecasting models

> ... tend to perform well, with accuracy levels comparable to more complex and statistically sophisticated forecasting methods which require considerable user understanding to employ them successfully. (1992, p. 38)

They further maintain that while this method is not prominent in forecasting literature, in actual practice it, along with the moving average method, is the most popular.

The major disadvantage of these methods is that they cannot take into account factors affecting the series other than its past values. They do not explain the relationships between such factors and the series of interest. Should events occur that can radically change tourism behaviour, such as pestilence, terrorism, entertainment mega-events or natural disasters, time series methods fail. However, they can indicate the values that should have been achieved in the absence of these catastrophes, and thus measure the magnitude of their impact on tourism.

For further information

Clifton, Peter, Nguyen, Hai and Nutt, Susan (1992), *Market Research: Using Forecasting in Business*, Butterworth-Heinemann, pp. 223–249.

Levenback, Hans and Cleary, James P. (1981), *The Beginning Forecaster, The Forecasting Process through Data Analysis*, Lifetime Learning Publications, Chapter 8.

Makridakis, Spyros (1990), *Forecasting, Planning and Strategy for the 21st Century*, The Free Press, Chapter 3.

Makridakis, Spyros, Wheelwright, Steven C. and McGee, Victor E. (1983), *Forecasting: Methods and Applications*, 2nd edition, John Wiley & Sons, xvii + 926 pp.

Martin, Christine A. and Witt, Stephen F. (1989), 'Accuracy of econometric forecasts of tourism', *Annals of Tourism Research*, pp. 407–428.

Saunders, John A., Sharp, John A. and Witt, Stephen F. (1987), *Practical Business Forecasting*, Gower Publishing Company, Chapter 3.

Shim, Jae K., Siegel, Joel G. and Liew, C. J. (1994), *Strategic Business Forecasting*, Probus Publishing Company, Chapter 6.

Moore, Thomas W. (1989), *Handbook of Business Forecasting*, Harper & Row, Chapters 3 and 4

6 An advanced extrapolative method

In the previous two chapters, we discussed simple and intermediate time series methods. These are readily constructed in spreadsheets and require the grasp of relatively simple mathematical concepts. They are not, however, suited for dealing with the widest range of tourism demand time series. For example, they have difficulty capturing non-linear trends and cannot simulate cycles very well.

This chapter describes the most popular advanced extrapolative method. This method can handle a wider range of time series effectively and is growing in popularity in tourism demand forecasting.

The Box–Jenkins approach

While most of this book is a discussion of individual time series methods of tourism forecasting and specific expressions of these methods in models, we now turn to a process of forecasting called the Box–Jenkins approach after its creators George Box and Gwilym Jenkins of Great Britain. This has become a popular approach due to its ability to handle any time series, its strong theoretical foundations, and its operational success.

The Box–Jenkins approach searches for the combination of two forecasting methods and their parameters that minimizes the error in simulating the past series. It then statistically checks this combination for validity. If the combination passes this test, it can be used in forecasting the series.

The two methods are **autoregression** and **moving average** (note: the latter is different from the single moving average method discussed in Chapter 4). The Box–Jenkins approach is a process that makes use of these two methods to suggest the most appropriate form of the forecasting model and then tests this model's validity. The acronym ARMA is used to identify the auto-regressive/moving average combined method.

ARMA models can only deal with time series stationary in their means and variances. When approaching a time series that is not, differencing is used to achieve stationarity. That is, a first difference is computed by subtracting the first historical value in the time series from the second, and the second from the third, etc., and the resulting series examined for a stationary mean. If this does not appear, then the first differenced series is differenced again, and the resulting series inspected for stationarity.

The number of times a series must be differenced to achieve stationarity is indicated by its 'integration' index. For example, if the second series (of second differences) described above achieves stationarity, then its integration factor is 2. When this approach is used to develop a series to which an ARMA model can be applied, then the integration factor is included in the description of the model, and it is labelled an 'ARIMA' model for autoregressive/integrated/moving average model. We will deal more simply with the stationarity problem here and not discuss the full ARIMA model process. However, the ARMA process captures the important aspects of the Box–Jenkins approach.

The Box–Jenkins approach is appropriate for forecasting horizons of 12 to 18 months and when at least fifty observations are available. It is not appropriate if there are repeated outliers at the end of the historical series. It is a complex and tedious process that does not lend itself to spreadsheet analysis. Rather, you should use a statistical package, such as Statistica[TM],[1] that performs the analysis.

There are five phases in applying the Box–Jenkins approach:

1. preparation (achieving stationarity, removing seasonality)
2. identification (examining autocorrelations, select model)
3. estimation
4. diagnostic checking
5. forecasting.

Preparation phase

The first step is to examine the series for stationarity and seasonality. The Box–Jenkins approach requires that the series to be forecast be stationary in its mean and variance, that is, its mean should not drift up or down as it does in series exhibiting linear trends, non-linear trends and steps.

Stationarity of the mean

Figure 6.1 shows the annual room-nights sold in the Washington, D.C. metropolitan area and the mean of this series as it progresses. Here, the mean is the moving average of all available data points at each period. For example, in 1988, the mean is the average of the values for 1987 and 1988, and for 1989, the mean is the average of the values for 1987 through 1989. It is clear that the mean trends upward and is not stationary.

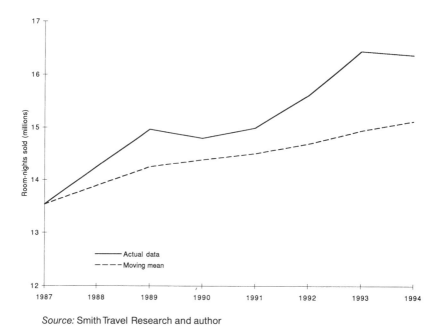

Source: Smith Travel Research and author

Figure 6.1   Hotel/motel room demand in Washington, D.C., annually, 1987–94

Table 6.1 provides the actual data and the moving mean for Figure 6.1. The data here also indicate that this series is not stationary in the mean. This is confirmed by a t-test of the means of the first half of the period (1987 through 1990) and the last half (1991 through 1994). This shows that we can be 95 per cent certain that the difference of the means of these two series is not due to chance. To achieve stationarity in the mean, as we must for applying the Box–Jenkins approach, the series is 'first-differenced', that is, a

Table 6.1   Actual series, moving mean and first differences of Washington, D.C., hotel/motel room demand, annually, 1987–94 (millions)

1. Year	2. Actual series	3. Moving mean	4. First difference	5. Moving mean
1987	13.53	13.53		
1988	14.24	13.89	0.71	0.71
1989	14.96	14.25	0.72	0.72
1990	14.79	14.38	−0.17	0.42
1991	14.99	14.50	0.20	0.36
1992	15.60	14.69	0.61	0.41
1993	16.44	14.94	0.83	0.48
1994	16.36	15.12	−0.07	0.40

new series is created which is the difference between successive values of the original series.[2]

Table 6.1 shows the first differences and their moving mean in columns 4 and 5, respectively. It is clear that, after the first few periods, this achieves stationarity in the mean. It is this series that would be simulated by the Box–Jenkins approach and then forecast. If the first differenced series does not achieve a stationary mean, the remedy is to difference this series again to obtain a second-differenced series. In most cases, you never need go beyond second-differencing to achieve a stable mean.

Stationarity of the variance

Some series are not stationary in their variance. That is, the size of their fluctuations grow over time, even if their mean is stationary. This is often true of long time series that grow at a significant rate. The fluctuations at the later data points tend to be larger than those at the early points. Many tourism time series fit this pattern, reflecting the dramatic increase in travel away from home throughout most of the world since the Second World War.

Figure 6.2 shows such series: U.S. scheduled airline traffic for the years 1960 to 1994. It is evident to the eye that the absolute fluctuations later in

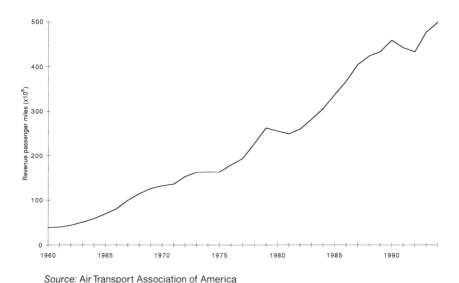

Source: Air Transport Association of America

Figure 6.2   U.S. scheduled airline traffic, annually, 1960–94

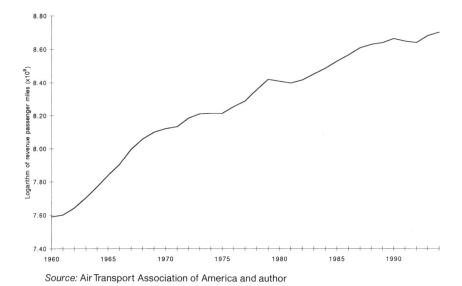

Source: Air Transport Association of America and author

Figure 6.3 Logarithmic transformation of U.S. scheduled airline traffic, annually, 1960–94

the series are greater than earlier. This is confirmed by an F-test of the ratio of the variance of the first 17 years to that of the last 18: there is a difference between the variances of the two series at the 0.05 level of significance.[3]

A common solution to non-stationarity in variance is to transform the series into logarithms. Figure 6.3 shows the logarithms of U.S. scheduled airline traffic over the same period.

The logarithmic transformation is most useful when the variance of the series is proportional to the mean level of the series and this mean increases or decreases at a constant percentage rate. This is not the case here. As a result, this transformation overcorrects the variance by moving it earlier in the series. The fluctuations from 1960 through 1970 are absolutely greater than those later in the logarithmic series. The F-test of the variances of the first and second halves of the time series confirms that the variances are not equal in this transformed series.

If the logarithmic transformation does not stabilize the series variance, then try transforming the original series into its square roots. The square root transformation of the airline traffic series is shown in Figure 6.4. It appears that the variance around the moving mean is constant over the period. This is confirmed by the F-test of the variances of the first and second halves of the series: there is no difference at the 0.05 level of significance.

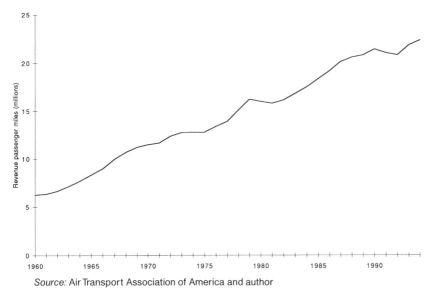

Source: Air Transport Association of America and author

Figure 6.4 Square root transformation of U.S. scheduled airline traffic, annually, 1960–94

An F-test of the variances of the Washington, D.C. hotel/motel demand series indicates the series is stable in its variance. Therefore, no transformation was needed to achieve stationarity of this series' variance.

In summary, check for stationarity of the variance of your series first. If this is lacking, transform the original series into logarithms or square roots to stabilize its variance. Then examine this transformed series for stability of its mean. If the mean is not stable (i.e. the transformed series indicates a trend), resolve this through first or second differencing of your transformed series. Make sure you address non-stationarity in the variance first, however. You want to complete your logarithmic or square root transformation before any differencing. This is because differencing frequently produces negative values, and you cannot transform a negative number into a logarithm or square root.

Seasonality

The autoregressive and moving average processes at the heart of the Box–Jenkins approach cannot work with seasonal data series such as most monthly or quarterly series of tourism demand. After the series has been transformed to achieve stationarity in both mean and variance, you should look for seasonal patterns in the resulting series. Identifying seasonality and dealing with it differ in the Box–Jenkins approach from that used in classical decomposition discussed in Chapter 4.

Identifying seasonality in the series to be forecast is done by examining the **autocorrelation coefficients**. Autocorrelation coefficients are similar to the coefficients estimated in the autoregressive method discussed in Chapter 5. But instead of regressing the current value of a series on a group of its past values, you compute the **correlations** for each relationship.

Formally, the autocorrelation coefficient, r, for any A_t and A_{t-n}, where n is the number of time periods previous you are interested in, is equal to:

$$r_{A_t, A_{t-n}} = \frac{\sum (A_t - \bar{A})(A_{t-n} - \bar{A})}{\sum (A_t - \bar{A})^2} \tag{6.1}$$

where

r = correlation coefficient
A = value in the time series
$\bar{A}$ = the mean of the time series
t = any time period
n = number of time periods to t

For example, if n equals 1, then you are correlating each value with its immediate predecessor. If n equals 12, then you are correlating each value with its counterpart 12 periods earlier, or 'lagged' 12 periods.

The correlation coefficient, r, will vary between -1 and $+1$. The closer it is to the ends of this range (that is, the farther it is from zero), the higher the correlation between the two values. If the correlation coefficient is nearly $+1$, then the two series move together: when one is much larger than its mean, the other one will tend to be larger than its mean. When one is far below its mean, then the other series will tend to be also.

The closer r is to -1, the more the two series move in opposite directions. If one series is much higher than its mean, then the other will be much lower, and vice versa.

Seasonality is identified in a sub-annual time series when there is significant autocorrelation at points $n = 4, 8, 12$, etc., for quarterly series, and $n = 12, 24, 36$, etc. for monthly series. Figure 6.5 shows the correlation coefficients for the Washington, D.C. hotel/motel room demand monthly series for $n = 1$ through 25 months.

An individual autocorrelation between data points at any given distance apart, such as any one shown in Figure 6.5, is deemed significant at the 95 per cent confidence level if its value falls outside of the following range:

$$-\frac{1.96}{\sqrt{n}} < r < \frac{1.96}{\sqrt{n}} \tag{6.2}$$

where

n = number of data points or observations
r = autocorrelation value

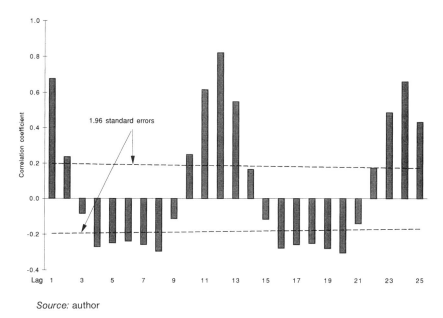

Source: author

Figure 6.5 Autocorrelations of hotel/motel room demand in Washington, D.C., lagged one to 25 periods

The dashed horizontal lines indicate 1.96 standard errors on either side of zero. Thus, vertical bars that do not exceed these lines are not significantly different from zero at the 95 per cent confidence level (or 0.05 level of significance). Those autocorrelations that break these lines (as most of them do) are significantly different from zero.

It is clear that the highest correlations in this figure are at $n = 12$ and 24. This indicates there is monthly seasonality. (We ignore the high correlation at a one-month lag: this is a common characteristic of monthly time series indicating that adjoining months share seasonal and trend characteristics.) There are also significant correlations for 'runs' of successive monthly spans, such as four to eight months. This suggests the series is not stationary in its mean, i.e. the data show a trend.

Many tourism demand series will show both seasonality and trend. Indeed, a series without inherent seasonality will appear to be seasonal if it has a significant trend: e.g. December's values will always be greater than the previous January's. It is suggested, therefore, first to remove the trend by first differencing before tackling the seasonal pattern.

Figure 6.6 shows the autocorrelations for the first-differenced series of Washington, D.C. room-nights sold. This has removed the runs of four or more months of significant autocorrelations. However, the transformed

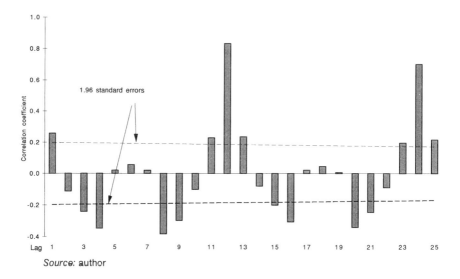

Source: author

Figure 6.6 Autocorrelations of hotel/motel room demand in Washington, D.C., one-span differences

series emphasizes the seasonality of hotel/motel room demand by the high correlations at 12 and 24 previous months. The autocorrelation at 12 months exceeds 0.8, not far from a perfect correlation of 1.0.

Once seasonality is identified, it is removed by again differencing the first-differenced series. With monthly seasonality, 'seasonal differences' (sometimes called 'long differences', or '12-span differences') are computed, where a new series is constructed of the difference of a current period's value and the value lagged 12 periods. Table 6.2 shows the computation for monthly Washington, D.C. hotel/motel demand for 1994. Note that a seasonal pattern remains after the first differencing: the largest absolute values in column 3 remain in the spring and fall. But the 12-span differencing in column 5 appears to be a random pattern.

Figure 6.7 shows the first-differenced series of rooms nights from Figure 6.6 differenced again: this time, a span of 12 periods. This has removed all significant autocorrelations except for three lags: one month, two months, and twelve months.

It is not uncommon for autocorrelations to remain significant for the first one or two periods even after significant differencing. This recognizes that a monthly value is likely to be close to values for the first and second preceding months because they all embody some of the same seasonal and trend patterns. Such information is used to suggesting the form of the autoregressive, moving average model.

For a series to be stationary, it is necessary for the autocorrelations to drop quickly into insignificance as the number of lags increases. This is true

Table 6.2 Computation of seasonal differences of first-differenced Washington, D.C. hotel/motel room demand, monthly, 1994

		Room-nights sold (000)		
1. Month-year	2. Actual (A_t)	3. First differences ($A_t - A_{t-1}$) = FD_t	4. Year earlier first differences ($A_{t-12} - A_{t-11}$) = FD_t	5. Seasonal second differences ($FD_t - FD_{t-12}$)
Dec-93	969			
Jan-94	1002	33	143	−110
Feb-94	1073	71	−2	73
Mar-94	1421	348	356	−8
Apr-94	1577	156	139	17
May-94	1601	34	53	−19
Jun-94	1594	−7	−85	78
Jul-94	1510	−84	−21	−63
Aug-94	1436	−74	−55	−19
Sep-94	1405	−31	−32	1
Oct-94	1585	180	177	3
Nov-94	1235	−350	−319	31
Dec-94	923	−312	−305	−7

Source: Smith Travel Research (see Appendix 1)

Source: author

Figure 6.7 Autocorrelations of hotel/motel room demand in Washington, D.C., 12-span differences of one-span differences

of our short- and long-differenced series in Figure 6.6: the autocorrelations drop below the 1.96 standard error bounds after the second lag.

There is still a significant autocorrelation at the 12 months span in the long-differenced series. However, it is now negative, and has declined to a value of 0.4. Further short and long differencing cannot improve on the autocorrelation series shown in Figure 6.7. We will not let this moderate autocorrelation trouble us, since we cannot get rid of it by differencing. Furthermore, since we are testing the significance of autocorrelations at the 0.05 level of significance, we could expect to find at least one significant autocorrelation in 20 consecutive lagged values even of a truly random series. That is, in one case out of 20, an autocorrelation may appear to be significant when it is really not significant.

Consequently, we will use the series shown in Figure 6.7 to identify the most appropriate form of our ARMA model.

Identification phase

In this stage, the combination of two forecasting processes producing the best simulation of the historical series is tentatively identified. The two methods are autoregression, as discussed in Chapter 5, and a moving average process which is completely different from the concept of moving averages we discussed at the outset of Chapter 4.

Autoregressive models

Recall the form of the autoregression equation discussed in Chapter 5:

$$A_t = a + b_1 A_{t-1} + b_2 A_{t-2} + \cdots + b_n A_{t-n} \tag{6.3}$$

where

A = actual value in the time series

a = a constant identified through computational iteration

b = coefficient identified through computational iteration, called the 'autocorrelation'

t = some time period

n = number of past values included

'Computational iteration' indicates that from a set initial value of the constant or a coefficient, a computer program tries different values to improve the ability of the equation to simulate the time series, that is, reduce the squared error (or some other measure of error) of the forecast series compared to the actual time series.

The number of past values included on the right side of the autoregressive equation (i.e. the value of n) identifies the model's **order**. If, for example, we include only one past value (A_t), then it is a first order autoregressive model. If we include three past values (A_{t-1}, A_{t-2}, and A_{t-3}), then we have a third order autoregressive model. Of course, the number of autocorrelations equals the number of terms on the right hand side and the order of the model.

Moving average models

Unfortunately, the term 'moving average', has been adopted in this context to refer to a type of model that has no relationship to the moving average models discussed in Chapter 4. Here, 'moving average' refers to a relationship between actual values in our time series and successive error terms (the actual values minus the forecast values). The general form of the moving average model is:

$$A_t = c - b_1 e_{t-1} - b_2 e_{t-2} - \cdots - b_m e_{t-m} \tag{6.4}$$

where

A = actual value
c = a constant identified through computational iteration
b = coefficient identified through computational iteration
e = error term
t = some time period
m = number of past error values included

As for the autoregressive model, the order of the moving average model is indicated by the number of error terms included in the equation (i.e. the value of m).

The Box–Jenkins approach combines these two models (called an autoregressive moving average, or ARMA, model) in order to produce the best simulation of the time series. The general equation of such a combined model is:

$$A_t = d + a_1 A_{t-1} + \cdots + a_n A_{t-n} - b_1 e_{t-1} - \cdots - b_m e_{t-m} \qquad (6.5)$$

where

A = actual value
d = a constant identified through computational iteration
a = coefficient identified through computational iteration
b = coefficient identified through computational iteration
e = error term
t = some time period
n = number of past actual values included
m = number of past error values included

Procedures for identifying the appropriate model

There are a large number of autoregressive models we might use to best represent our time series for forecasting purposes. There are also a large number of moving average models we might use as well. And there are an even larger number of ARMA models available to us. One of the distinctive features of the Box–Jenkins approach is the process of examining certain data in order to provisionally identify the appropriate ARMA model in advance for forecasting.

The data examined are the autocorrelations and the partial autocorrelations. The autocorrelations are the same correlation coefficients we discussed with regard to identifying trend or seasonality in our time series. We compute these coefficients for a number of past values individually and chart them similarly to Figure 6.6.

It is helpful to examine 20 or so autocorrelations for certain patterns that suggest the appropriate model. Computing twenty equations similar to equation (6.3) is tedious and prone to error in a spreadsheet program. Rather, you should use a statistical package, such as Statistica^{TM} that performs the relevant analyses for you to examine.

Partial autocorrelations represent the degree of association between A_t and any A_{t-n} after the effects of interim lagged values have been partialled out. For example, consider the following equation:

$$A_t = r_{t,t-1}A_{t-1} + r_{t,t-2}A_{t-2} + r_{t,t-3}A_{t-3} \qquad (6.6)$$

where

A = actual values
t = some time period
r = correlation coefficient

Equation (6.6) is an autocorrelation equation, that is, the forecast for the current period is dependent on the previous three values of the time series. The third partial autocorrelation coefficient is $r_{t,t-3}$. Generally, for similar equations with n terms on the right-hand side, the partial autocorrelation coefficient for the nth term or lagged value is the last autocorrelation coefficient.

It is customary to examine twenty or so partial autocorrelation coefficients to discern certain patterns. If, for example, you wanted to compute twenty partial autocorrelation coefficients, you would have to compute twenty equations similar to (6.6). This is tedious to say the least, and underlines the importance of using a statistical package to conduct the Box–Jenkins analysis.

Table 6.3 is a decision matrix for identifying the appropriate form of the ARMA model. The order of the autoregressive or moving average model is suggested by the pattern of the autocorrelations and partial autocorrelations. To 'cut off' means to drop immediately to statistical insignificance, while to 'tail off' is to decline over time into insignificance.

Figures 6.8 to 6.12 present examples that illustrate the decision matrix. Figure 6.8 shows autocorrelations and partial autocorrelations for the autoregressive models of order 1: that is, models containing one past value or one past value on the right-hand side. The dashed horizontal lines indicate the 1.96 standard error threshold for a 95 per cent confidence level. In both cases, the first autocorrelations are substantial, but they tail off in an exponential fashion to zero. It is the pattern of the partial autocorrelations that indicates whether the autocorrelation model should include one past

Table 6.3 ARMA models suggested by time series autocorrelations and partial autocorrelations

Model (order)	Autocorrelations	Partial autocorrelations
Autoregressive (p)	Tail off	Cut off after lag p
Moving average (q)	Cut off after lag q	Tail off
ARMA(1, 1)	Tail off	Tail off

Source: Vandaele 1983, p. 94

Source: author
Figure 6.8   Autoregressive models of order 1

value, or two. This is indicated by the number of significant partial autocorrelations. For an autoregressive model of order one, there should be only one partial autocorrelation significant at the 95 per cent confidence level.

Figure 6.9 indicates that the autocorrelation model of order 2 also shows autocorrelations tailing off to zero rather quickly. However, two partial autocorrelations are significantly different from zero, rather than only one as in the order 1 model.

Figures 6.10 and 6.11 display the salient characteristics of moving average models of orders 1 and 2, respectively. Moving average models show partial autocorrelations declining to zero rapidly. It is the number of significant partial autocorrelations that determine whether the moving average model is of order 1 or 2.

Finally, Figure 6.12 shows the patterns suggesting an autoregressive moving average model of order 1, 1: that is, including one lagged variable and one error term. Patterns of more complex ARMA models are beyond the scope of this text.

Identifying the appropriate room-demand ARMA model

Figure 6.13 shows the autocorrelations and partial autocorrelations for hotel/motel room demand in Washington, D.C. (the autocorrelations chart

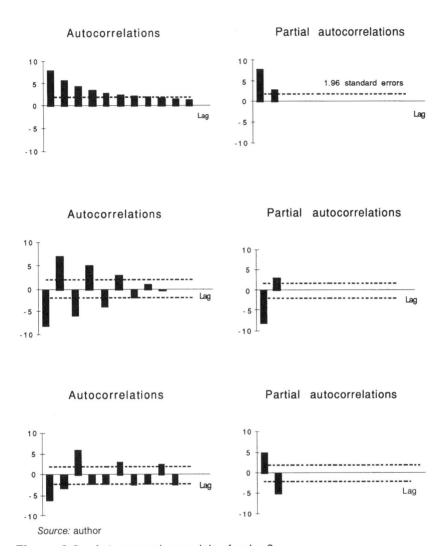

Figure 6.9   Autoregressive models of order 2

is a repeat of Figure 6.7). The partial autocorrelations tail off to insignificance, suggesting a moving average model. The fact that the first two autocorrelations are significant indicates that the order of this model is 2: the current and past value of the error terms should be included. Consequently, a moving average model of order (MA(2)) is our first choice. We will test the validity of this model. It is important to have backup models we can turn to if this first choice model proves invalid through diagnostic checking. It seems appropriate to include ARMA models incorporating autoregressive processes of orders 1 and 2 along with the order 2 moving

Source: author

Figure 6.10   Moving average models of order 1

average process. This is usually represented by ARMA(1, 2) and ARMA(2, 2). These will be tested if our MA(2) models fails its diagnostic checking.

Identification phase summary

In the identification phase of the Box-Jenkins approach, we examine the autocorrelations and the partial autocorrelations to determine which of three methods to test for developing a good forecasting model: the autoregressive method, the moving average method, or the autoregressive moving average method.

- If the autocorrelations decay exponentially and there is one significant partial autocorrelation, then the autoregressive model of order 1 [AR(1)] is suggested.
- If the partial autocorrelations decay exponentially and there is one significant autocorrelation, than the moving average model of order 1 [MA(1)] is suggested.
- If both the autocorrelations and the partial autocorrelations decay exponentially, then the ARMA model is suggested [ARMA(1, 1)].

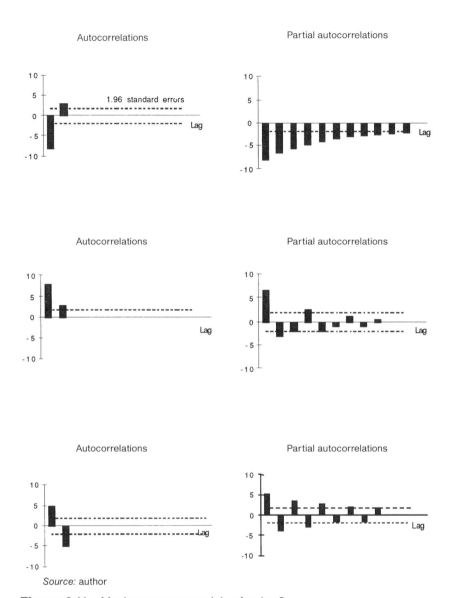

Figure 6.11   Moving average models of order 2

- If the autocorrelations show a decaying sine wave pattern, and there are two significant partial autocorrelations then an AR(2) model is indicated.
- If the partial autocorrelations indicate a decaying sine wave pattern, then an MA(2) model is suggested.

It is seldom useful to proceed beyond these models into higher order ones.

Figure 6.12   Autoregressive moving average models of order 1,1

Estimation phase

We have identified the most appropriate model and two backup models. However, before we estimate the parameters of the preferred model, we need to make one additional choice: whether to include a constant in the model or

Autocorrelations

Partial autocorrelations

Source: author

Figure 6.13 Hotel/motel room demand in Washington, D.C., 12-span differences of one-span differences

not. Recall that we are forecasting a series that has been differenced once by a span of one period and again by a span of twelve periods. Theory does indicate whether a constant is appropriate for such a series or not. Consequently, we can estimate the model twice: once with a constant and second without a constant.

The least squares regression method is seldom appropriate for estimating the parameters (coefficients) of an ARMA model. Rather, a maximum

Table 6.4 Parameters of a moving average (2) model of Washington, D.C. hotel/motel room demand differenced series

Model/parameter	Estimated value	t-statistic	t-statistic significance level
Constant included			
Constant	−0.849	−0.708	0.481
$q(1)$	0.595	4.35	0.000
$q(2)$	0.167	1.19	0.236
No constant			
$q(1)$	0.590	4.33	0.000
$q(2)$	0.165	1.19	0.238

likelihood estimation is used in most computer programs. The process is iterative. The program selects starting values for the parameters and tries different values until if finds the combination that minimizes the sum of the squared errors. Occasionally, the parameter estimates in a program may not converge after 50 iterations or so. This is a signal to try different starting values for the parameters.

Table 6.4 shows the results of this process for the second order moving average model of our twice-differenced series.

The constant turned out to be not significantly different from zero (note the *t*-statistic is significant only at the 0.48 level), so we drop it and focus on the moving average model without a constant. The order 2 moving average model has one significant parameter, $q(1)$, or the first error term. The second error term is significantly different from zero only at the 0.238 level of confidence. This does not appear to be a good model for forecasting the differenced series of hotel/motel room demand.

Since it is the second moving average term that is not significantly different from zero, we are tempted to drop it and estimate a one-period moving average model, or MA(1). Such a model does have a significant parameter when estimated. However, by its nature, this model cannot forecast our differenced series more than one month ahead since it is based on the error of one such forecast. This is not satisfactory practice.

Instead, we investigate whether one of the alternative ARMA models may prove more successful in achieving significant coefficients. Indeed, the ARMA(1, 2) and ARMA(2, 2) models produce parameters all significantly different from zero at the 0.05 level of significance or lower. We decide to drop the MA(2) model and submit these alternatives to the next phase: diagnostic checking.

Diagnostic checking phase

We have identified two ARMA models that appear to be valid for forecasting hotel/motel room demand in Washington, D.C. In this phase, we examine these models to see if they provide sound estimates of parameters that fit the time series well. Four tests are available for checking the validity of the model (Vandaele 1983, p. 123):

1. stationarity analysis
2. residual analyses
3. fitting extra parameters
4. omitting parameters

We will focus here on one of the most important diagnostic checks: residual analyses.

If a model accurately represents the ARMA process governing our time series, the errors of the model should have a mean of zero, a constant covariance, and be uncorrelated with each other over time. We can examine the first two assumptions by viewing plots of the errors of our ARMA(1, 2) and (2, 2) models in Figures 6.14 and 6.15.

Each model indicates errors with a mean of zero, but a variance that increases over time. This is evident in the growth of the size of the fluctuations somewhat over the time series in both figures. The magnitude of this increase is troublesome, but not fatal for either model. This, coupled

Source: author

Figure 6.14   Errors from the ARMA(1, 2) model of the differenced series of hotel/motel room demand, monthly, 1988–94

Figure 6.15 Errors from the ARMA(2, 2) model of the differenced series of hotel/motel room demand, monthly, 1988–94.

Figure 6.16 Autocorrelations of errors for ARMA(1, 2) hotel/motel room demand model

with the lack of alternative models, encourages us to move onto the next test.

An important assumption of the ARMA model is that the errors are not correlated with one another. We can investigate this assumption by reviewing the autocorrelations of the errors. If there are a number of significant autocorrelations, then the model has not been specified properly, and an alternative should be tried.

Figures 6.16 and 6.17 present the autocorrelations of the errors for the ARMA(1, 2) and ARMA(2, 2) models. The horizontal dashed lines indicate the thresholds at the 0.05 level of significance (1.96 standard errors): any autocorrelations greater than this threshold are significant at this level. In

Figure 6.17 Autocorrelations of errors for ARMA(2, 2) hotel/motel room demand model

both models, only one correlation is greater than the 0.05 level of significance: the span of 12 periods.

In summary, we selected two alternative models to the one suggested by the identification phase, because the MA(2) failed to produce significant parameters. We then submitted the alternative ARMA(1, 2) and ARMA(2, 2) models to diagnostic checking. This revealed that the error terms show variances that grow somewhat over time. The terms show significant autocorrelations only at the span of 12 months. We would expect that at the 0.05 level of significance that one out of 20 autocorrelations would appear to be significant when it is not.

We would prefer models that have constant variances and no autocorrelation of the error terms. But given the lack of viable alternative ARMA models, the ARMA(1, 2) and ARMA(2, 2) models are employed to forecast our hotel/model room demand time series to see how well they perform over the past.

Forecasting phase

The final phase of the Box–Jenkins approach is to use the best model or models that pass diagnostic checking to forecast future values of the time series. We begin by forecasting the next period from the model, and then successive periods as far out as we wish. At some point, we will be using forecast values rather than known past values for the A_{t-n}. When we run out of past values of the error term, we assume it to equal zero for all future values. The further ahead we forecast with the model, the greater the chances of substantial forecast error, however.

Once we have obtained our forecasts, we need to transform them back into the terms of our original series. If we transformed the original series into logarithms, we need to produce the anti-logarithms of the forecasts. If we differenced the series to achieve stationarity or remove seasonality, we achieve a forecast series of these differences. The forecast differences should then be added to the original series.

In our case, the ARMA(1, 2) produces a MAPE of 2.8 per cent, while the ARMA(2, 2) achieves 2.7 per cent. This difference is not significant, and, observing the principle of parsimony, the simpler model is chosen (ARMA(1, 2)) as the best for forecasting hotel/motel room demand in the Washington, D.C. area.

Figure 6.18 shows the actual hotel/motel room demand series for the Washington, D.C. area, along with the series forecast by the ARMA(1, 2) model of the differenced series. As the MAPE indicates, the forecast model follows the actual series quite closely, certainly more closely than the seasonal naive model with its 4.0 per cent MAPE.

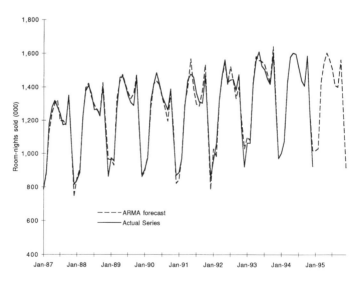

Source: Smith Travel Research and author

Figure 6.18   Actual and ARMA(2, 2) forecasts of hotel/motel room demand in Washington, D.C., monthly, 1987–95

Applications

Turner, Kulendran and Pergat (1995) compared the accuracy of ARIMA models to an exponential smoothing method for forecasting quarterly visitor arrivals in New Zealand from five countries and five multi-national regions. They concluded that where the series showed a regular trend and highly variable seasonality, then the exponential smoothing method performed better. But when trend and seasonality were not marked, then the ARIMA model produced the more accurate forecasts. However, the MAPEs for their best origin models ranged from 6 per cent to 38 per cent. This suggests that testing other methods would prove fruitful.

Witt, Witt and Wilson (1994) found a Box–Jenkins ARIMA model outperformed five other methods in forecasting quarterly visitor flows from the United Kingdom to four countries. However, it was not much more accurate than the naive, no-change model. They also found that the international terrorist activity occasioned by the U.S. bombing of Libya in 1986 depressed U.K. travel to Greece and Spain.

Di Benedetto and Bojanic (1993) used the Box–Jenkins approach to model visits to Cypress Gardens, Florida, to test the tourism area life cycle hypothesis. This hypothesis states that tourism areas go through an evolution over time, described by an S-shaped pattern. Their visitor volume rises rapidly after opening, then continues to grow for a time but at slower rates. Finally, visitor volume reaches a peak (stagnation) and will decline if efforts are not made to rejuvenate demand, such as targeting new markets or adding new attractions. Their best ARIMA model of 139 quarters of visitor volume produced accurate forecasts over periods not characterized by rejuvenation efforts. It was not quite as good as a regression model tested against it.

Conclusion

The Box–Jenkins approach is a powerful if complex approach to building a forecasting model for time series (Figure 6.19 summarizes the process). Examination of certain correlations of a series suggests the best model to forecast it. This is then diagnosed for validity and, if it passes the tests, is used for forecasting.

While the ARMA variations are nearly endless, in most cases a first or second order model will produce reliable forecast values. Going beyond this does not appear to provide significant advances in reliability or validity.

1. Check for stationarity in the mean and variance of the historical time series, and resolve any non-stationarity by transforming the original series.
2. Check for seasonality and resolve by seasonal differencing.
3. Compute the autocorrelations and the partial autocorrelations in the transformed series.
4. Examine these to rank the most likely forms of the forecasting model.
5. Compute the coefficients of this model and inspect its parameters for significance; if one or more are not significant, choose the next model suggested.
6. Use the model that produces significant parameters to forecast your transformed series.
7. Examine the residuals for stationarity of mean and variance and for autocorrelations; if any problems are found, try the next best model in step 4.
8. Once you have found a satisfactory model, use it to forecast the transformed series.
9. Transform the forecast series back into the terms of the original time series and compute its MAPE for acceptability.

Figure 6.19   Steps in applying the Box–Jenkins approach

The Box–Jenkins approach is not suited for the computer spreadsheet. Rather, the forecaster should make use of one of the statistical packages currently available for the personal computer. These programs usually have the additional advantage of identifying parsimonious models, which usually are the best. Some forecasting packages determine the best model 'behind the scenes' and only present it to you at the end. The forecaster then accepts this model on blind faith. Others present results at each step and allow the forecaster to choose the next procedure. These 'manual' packages allow the forecaster to exercise informed judgement and avoid outrageous errors.

For further information

Jarrett, Jeffrey (1991), *Business Forecasting Methods*, Basil Blackwell Ltd, 2nd edition, Chapter 9.

Makridakis, Spyros, Wheelwright, Steven C. and McGee, Victor E. (1983), *Forecasting: Methods and Applications*, 2nd edition, John Wiley & Sons, Chapters 8 and 9.

Moore, Thomas W. (1989), *Handbook of Business Forecasting*, Harper & Row, pp. 87–94

Shim, Jae K., Siegel, Joel G. and Liew, C. J. (1994), *Strategic Business Forecasting*, Probus Publishing Company, Chapter 8.

Vandaele, Walter (1983), *Applied Time Series and Box-Jenkins Models*, Academic Press, Chapters 2 to 6.

Notes

[1] Published by StatSoft™, Inc., 1994.

[2] Another test for non-stationarity of the mean is to compute the means of the series $A_t - A_{t-1}$. If this is significantly different from zero by a T-test, then there is a trend in the series, and the mean is not stationary (Vandaele 1983, p. 25).

[3] In this context, the F-test determines whether the variances of two samples are statistically equal, or, alternatively, their difference is not due to chance. Formally, the F-statistic is the ratio of the variances of the two samples. If this ratio exceeds a certain threshold value, then the differences are not due to chance. The threshold value is derived from the distribution of the F-statistic, and depends on the sizes of the samples.

7 Causal methods – regression analysis

We now move into the realm of causation, where we are interested in how one or more variables affect the one we are trying to forecast. Instead of trying to model a relationship between the current and past values of a time series, we now look for the best model that explains *why* our variable changes as it does over time.

> causal methods . . . develop projections based on the mathematical relationship between the series being examined and variables which influence that series (Moore 1989, p. 109).

There are two major approaches to causal modelling popular in tourism forecasting. One is the **linear regression method**, where our forecast variable is dependent on, or explained by, one or more independent variables. We attempt to quantify this relationship in a single equation through statistical analysis.

The other approach is to develop a set of regression equations linked together by certain variables that are both dependent and independent variables. These are often called **structural models**.[1] This approach to tourism demand forecasting is discussed in Chapter 8.

This chapter explores the advantages and limitations of the **linear regression model** and its logic. The simplest application in forecasting is presented, followed by more complex models. Then we discuss the procedures for developing a linear regression model of tourism demand, with special attention to variables that can help explain tourism demand, and how to evaluate the model's validity. Finally, applications of this method in tourism forecasting are briefly presented, followed by resources for learning more about linear regression analysis in forecasting tourism demand.

Linear regression analysis

The general form of the **linear regression model** is:

$$Y = a + b_1 X_1 + b_2 X_2 + \cdots + b_n X_n + e \qquad (7.1)$$

where

Y = the dependent, or forecast, variable (e.g. tourism demand)
a = the intercept constant
b = slope coefficients
X = independent, or explanatory, variables
n = number of explanatory variables
e = residual

The objective in forecasting is to derive sound estimates of the coefficients or parameters (a, b_1, b_2, etc.) so that we can estimate the forecast variable based on the values of the explanatory variables.

Advantages of regression analysis

The linear regression method has a number of advantages over extrapolative methods:

- **It explicitly addresses causal relationships that are evident in the real world.** These include the effects of prices, income changes, marketing programmes and competitors' actions on tourism demand.
- **It aids assessment of alternative business plans.** Managers can simulate the effects of various marketing plans or government policies (e.g. taxes, expenditures, regulation, subsidies) on tourism demand.
- **It provides several statistical measures of accuracy.** Regression models provide a great deal of information that can be used to assess their validity and improve them.
- **Regression models accommodate a wide range of relationships.** These include linear and non-linear associations, as well as lagged effects of explanatory variables over several periods.

Limitations of regression analysis

There are disadvantages of using the linear regression method for general applications:

- **The time and money costs of operating regression models can be large.** Except for the simplest models, regression analysis requires special computer programs to handle the data. Moreover, the time needed to gather, analyse and prepare the data for regression modelling is substantial. Finally, identifying a valid and statistically significant model can be quite time consuming.

- **Developing the correct relationships requires substantial skill.** Theory gives some guidance, but many important relationships must be 'teased' out of the data. The more you work with regression analysis, the better you become at discovering important connections among data series.
- **Often explanatory variables must be forecast in order to obtain forecasts of the variable of interest.** This adds additional time and money costs. Moreover, forecasting the explanatory variables increases the chances of forecasting error.
- **It assumes the explanatory variables are not affected by the dependent variable.** In many cases this assumption causes no problem. However, there may be occasions where there is a feedback of the dependent variable, say tourism expenditures abroad, on one of the explanatory variables, such as exchange rates. Another potential case is where rising visitor volumes push up prices at a destination, which is often a variable used to 'explain' visitor volume

Despite these limitations, regression analysis remains the most widely used approach in tourism forecasting.

There are two domains where one can profitably conduct regression analysis: cross-sectional analysis and time series analysis. In cross-sectional analysis, we analyse relationships among variables across space with time usually held constant. For example, we could regress the number of visitors to twenty countries in 1994 against expenditures on visitor promotional programmes, price structures, exchange rates and visitor capacities of these countries. This could be helpful in suggesting the factors that affect visitor flows among countries during a year.

In time series regression analysis, it is time that varies, not space. We look for patterns among variables over time, to determine how to quantitatively relate variables that help explain movements in our dependent variable.

We are limiting our discussion here to the use of regression analysis across time, with space held constant. We are interested in the shape of the future for a given destination, or other tourism product or market.

The logic of regression analysis

Consider Figure 7.1, which presents the annual series on hotel/motel room demand in the Washington, D.C. metropolitan area. One forecasting approach is to summarize these data in a straight line that we can then extend out into the future, in this case 1995. There are at least three different extrapolations that might provide this summary.

The **mean line** in Figure 7.1 is the mean of the time series over the 1987–94 period. While it is a summary of these data, it is not a very accurate

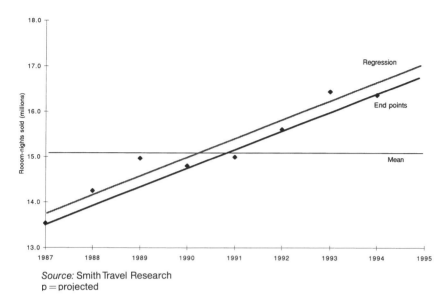

Source: Smith Travel Research
p = projected

Figure 7.1   Simple models of Washington, D.C. hotel/motel room demand, annually, 1987–95

forecasting model for 1995, because it does not capture the rising trend of the data. The **end-point line** simply connects the 1987 value to the 1994 value and extends this straight line to 1995. It, too, summarizes the data and has the advantage of actually incorporating two values from the series. However, it can be highly volatile over time, varying in slope with the last value in the series.

The **regression line** is a linear time trend regression of the room-demand values on the years they relate to. It has the advantage of providing the best 'fit' of the data. That is, it is designed to minimize the sum of the distances between the regression line and each actual value, called the **residuals**. It actually minimizes the sum of the squared vertical departures (i.e. residuals) of the data from the regression line; as a result, the technique is called 'least squares regression', or sometimes 'ordinary least squares regression' (OLS).

Simple regression: linear time trend

We begin with simple or univariate regression, where there is only one explanatory variable. One of the easiest and most popular forecasting methods is to regress a time series such as a measure of tourism demand on the periods to which it relates. In other words, it uses changes in time, such as the year or month, to 'explain' variations in the series to be forecast. In its simplest form, the **linear time trend** regression indicates the number of units the dependent variable (e.g. room-nights sold) changes for each one unit change in time (e.g. a month). If this is successful over the past values, that is, the regression equation is statistically significant and valid over our time series, then we can have confidence that it can simulate future values as well. A discussion of time trend regression will illustrate the major features of simple least squares regression models, that is, regression models that have only one equation and one explanatory variable affecting the variable of interest to us.

The form of the **simple regression model** is:

$$Y_t = a + bX_t + e_t \qquad (7.2)$$

where
- Y = the dependent or forecast variable, such as tourism demand
- t = some period of time
- a = intercept constant estimated by least squares regression
- b = slope coefficient estimated by least squares regression
- X = explanatory (independent) variable
- e = residual

In the regression line in Figure 7.1, the number of hotel/motel room-nights sold annually in the Washington, D.C. metropolitan area is the dependent variable, and the year is the explanatory variable. The intercept constant (also called the 'constant term') a is the value of the dependent variable when the explanatory variable equals zero.[2] Since it is customary to chart the dependent variable Y on the vertical axis, or Y-axis, and the explanatory variable X on the horizontal axis, or X-axis, the intercept constant marks where the regression line crosses the Y-axis when the X-axis value is zero.

The slope coefficient b indicates at what rate the regression line rises as the explanatory value increases. Formally, it is the ratio of the increase in Y to the increase in X. The intercept constant and the slope coefficient make up the **parameters** of the regression equation. Most of the effort in applying regression analysis is devoted to estimating these parameters, because they represent our best estimate of what the true values are of these character-istics over the population of all time periods.

A comment about sample and population in the context of time series is appropriate here. Our **sample** is the actual time series of data we have. In this case, our sample is hotel/motel room demand for the years 1987 to 1994. We can think of this as drawn from the **population** of all years, from the distant past to the distant future.

As a practical matter, we are seldom interested in 'forecasting' months prior to our time series (sometimes called 'backcasting') as an end in itself. But we are inherently interested in months, quarters or years to come, at least over some reasonable future. Consequently, in building forecasting models by linear regression, we are trying to infer something about the **population** of all periods from our recorded past into our future from our **sample** of only some past periods in our time series.

Finally, the residual term reminds us that we are producing estimates of the dependent variable and that these will not necessarily equal the actual values for every period. Least squares regression is designed to make the sum of the squared residuals as small as possible.

There are a number of forms of the equation for computing the intercept, *a*, and the slope coefficient, *b*. One of the easiest to compute is:

$$b = \frac{n \sum XY - (\sum X)(\sum Y)}{n \sum X^2 - (\sum X)^2} \tag{7.3}$$

$$a = \bar{Y} - b\bar{X}$$

where

b = slope coefficient
n = number of observations or data points
X = explanatory (independent) variable
Y = dependent (forecast) variable
a = intercept constant
$\bar{Y}$ = mean of the dependent variable series
$\bar{X}$ = mean of the explanatory variable series

We will deal here only with least squares regression models that are **linear in their coefficients**. That is, they take the form of equation (7.1). These need not be linear in their data, however. By transforming, or redefining, the original data series, we can employ least squares regression to produce non-linear trend lines, as we will see later.

Continuing with our example, we are attempting here to develop a regression model of annual hotel/motel room demand in Washington, D.C., that is:

$$H_t = a + bT_t + e_t \tag{7.4}$$

where

H = room-nights sold annually
t = a unit of time
a = intercept constant
b = slope coefficient
T = a year
e = residual

Table 7.1 presents the Washington, D.C. hotel/motel room demand data and the computation of the time trend regression equation for this annual series.

The resulting forecast equation is thus:

Table 7.1   Computation of hotel/motel room demand regression coefficients

1. Period (t)	2. Time (T)	3. Room-nights sold in millions (H)	4. T * H	5. T²
1	1987	13.53	26 889	3 948 169
2	1988	14.24	28 316	3 952 144
3	1989	14.96	29 763	3 956 121
4	1990	14.79	29 439	3 960 100
5	1991	14.99	29 843	3 964 081
6	1992	15.60	31 080	3 968 064
7	1993	16.44	32 758	3 972 049
8	1994	16.36	32 629	3 976 036
Sum	15 924	120.9	240 688	31 696 764
Mean	1990.5	15.11		

$$b = \frac{n\sum(TH) - (\sum T)(\sum H)}{n\sum T^2 - (\sum T)^2}$$

$$b = \frac{(8 * 240\ 688) - (15\ 924 * 120.9)}{(8 * 31\ 696\ 764) - (15\ 924 * 15\ 924)} = 0.3920$$

$$a = \bar{H} - b * \bar{T}$$

$$a = 15.11 - (0.3920 * 1990.5) = -765.2$$

$$H_t = -765.2 + 0.3920 T_t \tag{7.5}$$

To obtain a forecast for any future year n years from now $(t + n)$, simply substitute the year into equation (7.5). For example, the forecast for 1995 is:

$$H_{1995} = -765.2 + 0.3920 * 1995 = 16.92 \tag{7.6}$$

Non-linear time trends

The regression methods used in tourism forecasting are virtually all linear in their coefficients, because these can be estimated through the powerful and well-understood technique of least squares regression. However, this does not mean we are stuck with modelling only straight line time trends. We can attempt to fit non-linear time trends to our data through models that are non-linear in their data. That is, linear regression models that incorporate transformed or redefined data.

Figure 7.2 shows four non-linear time trend models that are linear in their coefficients. The equations for these curves indicate the logarithmic, parabolic and sine transformations that underlie these curves. They can handle a variety of time trend patterns.

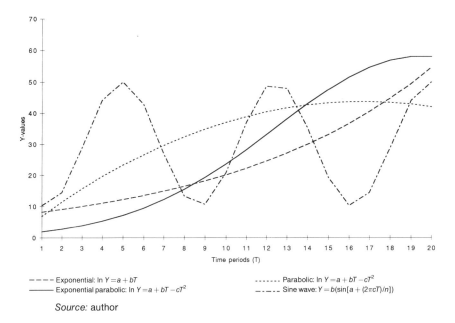

Figure 7.2   Examples of non-linear time trends linear in their coefficients

Before we move on to the multivariate regression method, we need to understand an important point. The simple regression method has limited application beyond the time trend. Tourism demand in its many aspects (airline traffic, hotel room demand, attraction attendance, etc.) is affected by more than one major variable. Consequently, when we try to model demand for a tourism product using one explanatory variable, we will necessarily misspecify the model and ensure the estimated relationship is statistically unreliable and invalid.

Misspecification, or specification error, occurs when the following assumption of linear regression analysis is violated:

the conditional expectation of the dependent variable is an unchanging linear function of known independent variables (Kennedy 1992, p. 91).

Thus there are three sources of misspecification:

- when the set of independent variables omits relevant explanatory variables or includes irrelevant ones
- when the actual relationships are non-linear in the parameters
- when the parameters do not remain constant.

Tourism demand is generated by a complex of factors relating to the traveller, the destination, characteristics of the trip, and other elements. A number of these are presented below in Figure 7.4. Since the simple regression model includes only one independent variable to explain the future course of tourism demand, it is misspecified by definition. No amount of transformation of variables or change in model structure can redress this failure.

The linear time trend model is helpful in demonstrating the long-term trend of our forecast variable. This helps us to develop the appropriate causal model that incorporates the right independent variables. This model may be useful in suggesting the general magnitude of our forecast variable in the long-term future. However, aside from these explanatory uses, simple regression models should be avoided by the forecaster who wants an accurate, valid explanatory model of the future of tourism demand.

One other clarifying point. If you are working with monthly or quarterly data, then there is no inherent numerical value to represent each observation as there is when you use annual data. Consequently, you should number each observation consecutively from the first data point (number one) to the last data point. This time series of observation identifiers then serves as your explanatory variable in the simple time trend regression.

Multiple regression

As noted above, a regression model is misspecified when one or more relevant explanatory variables are excluded from the equation. The way we deal with this misspecification is to include other variables that significantly affect the one of interest to us. This is done by expanding the simple linear regression model into a multiple (or 'multivariate') regression model by including two or more explanatory variables in our regression equation. Please note that while simple regression analysis can be accomplished in a computer spreadsheet as shown in Table 7.1, multiple regression requires statistical programs to deal with the complex calculations. Some computer spreadsheet programs include regression analysis modules that can perform multivariate regression analysis. There are also statistical programs that do so as well, such as Statistica^{TM}.

The general form of the multiple regression equation was presented as equation (7.1); it is presented here specifically as a forecasting model:

$$Y_t = a + b_1 X_{1,t} + b_2 X_{2,t} + \cdots + b_n X_{n,t} + e_t \tag{7.7}$$

where

Y = dependent (forecast) variable
a = intercept constant
b = slope coefficients
X = explanatory (independent) variables
t = a time period
n = number of explanatory variables
e = residual

If there are two explanatory variables, then the equation describes a plane in three-dimensional space, with the slope coefficients indicating its tilt. If more than two explanatory variables are present, we are in 'hyperspace' of more than three dimensions. It is difficult to imagine this and impossible to display on a two-dimensional page.

We employ the same least squares regression technique discussed with regard to simple regression analysis to minimize the sum of the squared residuals in multiple regression. That is, ordinary least squares minimizes the difference between the actual data in hyperspace and the hyperplane designated by our regression coefficients across all combinations of the values of the explanatory variables.

Figure 7.3 outlines the steps in developing and using a regression forecasting model.

Since multivariate regression forecast modelling is a complex activity and difficult to do well, we will walk through these steps using the annual Washington, D.C. hotel/motel room demand series as our example.

1. Draft your theory

To most successfully model hotel/motel room demand in Washington, D.C., we would need to break down the aggregate series into type of property (e.g. by average room rate, size, or location) or type of guest (e.g. business or leisure, group or individual, origin area), seeking to find homogeneous segments which react similarly to certain factors, such as price, season, economic cycle, etc. Such disaggregation helps us focus on the variables that are actually affecting the segment's demand, to more accurately estimate their relationships with the dependent variable.

We do not here have the information to break down this demand series below the aggregate level, however. This necessarily limits the explanatory variable time series available to us and the forecasting success of our model. However, the purpose of using this series is to illustrate the steps in applying regression analysis to forecasting tourism demand.

Figure 7.4 lists a number of variables that should be considered for inclusion in a tourism demand forecasting model. In reviewing these, our emphasis in forecasting time series by regression analysis should be on

1. **Draft your theory** of factors that affect the variable you wish to forecast, identifying the forecast (dependent) variable and important explanatory variables.
2. **Obtain time series** of the dependent and explanatory variables you have identified.
3. Examine the correlations among these explanatory variables to **identify any multicollinearity**, and remove this from your model.
4. **Specify expected relationships** of your explanatory variables to the dependent variable in mathematical form indicated by your theory (1):
   a. signs of the slope coefficients
   b. presence of lagged variables
   c. presence of dummy variables
   d. functional form, e.g. linear or non-linear.
5. **Identify initial models** as to form of the equation, explanatory variables included, and estimated parameters.
6. **Evaluate the model's validity** in light of your expectations in (4) and revise the model to deal with any aberrations.
7. **Assess the model's significance** and revise the model to rectify any problems.
8. **Use the model to forecast** future values when you are satisfied that it is theoretically correct and valid.

Figure 7.3   The regression model estimation process

variables that have changed significantly over the period of our historical series (here, 1987–94, inclusive). If a variable has not changed or changed only negligibly, it will not usually add much explanatory power to our forecasting model.

Push factors, sometimes called 'emissive' factors, are those characteristics of a population in an origin market that encourage travel away from home. For example, all else being equal, a larger **population** will generate more trips than a smaller one. This is sometimes accounted for by placing the number of trips or travel expenditures on a per capita basis from the generating country in the regression model.

GDP and income trends acknowledge that a growing economy generates more sales, jobs and personal income than a stagnant one, and can be expected to originate more business and leisure travel than a sluggish one. Indeed, measures of overall personal income appear to be the most popular explanatory variables in tourism demand regression models. Often a

1. Push factors (of origin)
   a. population size
   b. GDP and income trends
   c. income distribution
   d. education distribution
   e. age distribution
   f. leisure time
   g. family structure
   h. momentum
2. Pull factors (of destination)
   a. friends/relatives
   b. climate/weather
   c. commercial ties
   d. social/cultural ties
   e. destination marketing programmes
   f. distribution channels
   g. destination attractiveness
   h. special events
   i. complementary destinations
   j. habit
3. Resistance factors
   a. prices
      i. product price(s)
      ii. prices of substitutes
      iii. prices of complements
      iv. prices of necessities
      v. exchange rates
      vi. taxes and fees
   b. competitors' actions
   c. supply capacities
   d. distance
   e. travel time
   f. origin exchange controls
   g. border control, customs and other frontier formalities
   h. war/terrorism/crime/civil unrest
   i. natural and man-made disasters
   j. physical barriers

Figure 7.4 Potential explanatory variables in a regression model to forecast tourism demand measure of personal *disposable* income is used, by removing income-related taxes from gross personal income.

Certain **income**, **age** and **educational** groups travel more than others. If these groups are growing in an origin market, this can accelerate travel away from home. It is thought that **leisure time**, measured by number of days of paid vacation available or days in a year less work days, is positively correlated with vacation travel, although it may be inversely correlated with business travel. Certain **family structures** (e.g. husband/wife/no children) may travel more than others, such as those with school-aged children. If these are growing relative to the overall population of an area, additional travel may be generated.

Momentum refers to the effects of habit, friends' or relatives' recommendations, institutional relationships and other factors that may impel a future period's demand. This is often represented by including the value of the dependent variable lagged one or two periods as an explanatory variable. Some forecasters include time (e.g. year, quarter, month) as an explanatory variable along with others. You should avoid this as it obscures interpretation of the other explanatory variables, since time will often capture some of the effects of these on the dependent variable. However, a time trend alone can be a useful explanatory variable for certain tourism demand series, as discussed below.

Pull factors are those which attract visitors to a certain destination. Visiting **friends and relatives** is a major motivation for leisure visits, and cities with major ethnic populations may especially benefit from this travel. **Commercial ties** include the presence of head offices of major corporations at a destination, or having a concentration of financial or manufacturing firms. **Social/cultural** ties can include special ethnic neighbourhoods or institutions, such as cultural centres, religious sites, museums and monuments. Religious similarities between two countries may also be a strong influence on travel between them. Other such factors include similarity of language and the presence in one country of a large population of natives of the other.

It would seem that **destination marketing programmes**, as measured by national tourism office (NTO) expenditures, should be a useful explanatory variable for forecasting visitation to a country. However, results have been mixed (for a discussion, see Crouch 1994b, p. 15). The fact that NTO budgets are frequently dwarfed by promotional spending by airlines, cruise lines, resorts and city destination marketing agencies, and that data seldom exist on these expenditures by target market, makes teasing out the relationships quite problematic. There is some evidence, however, that the effectiveness of destination advertising appears to decrease as the distance away from the target market is increased. Moreover, this spending may affect demand with a sizeable lag, as markets, particularly distant ones, respond slowly to the promotional programmes.

Distribution channels include travel agents, tour operators, meeting and convention planners, travel clubs and other media which can help a traveller become aware of a destination, gather information about it, and make reservations for transportation, lodging and other tourism services. It is common for an emerging destination to depend upon tour operators and their packages for a substantial proportion of its leisure visitors.

Destination attractiveness includes all other factors of a permanent nature that attract visitors, such as architecture, participant and spectator sport complexes, arts and entertainment centres, topography, natural and scenic attractions, zoos and gardens. This can be increased for a city, for example, that revitalizes downtown areas and adds additional parks and other amenities. **Special events** pull visitors for short periods at certain times of the year and include festivals and fairs, conventions and trade shows, major sporting events, and concerts. Note that the special event need not occur in the destination country in order to boost travel to it. For example, Turner, Kulendran and Pergat (1995) maintain that the 1988 Expo and Bicentary events in Australia boosted U.S. visitor arrivals in New Zealand that year.

A destination may enjoy a **complementary** relationship with another, nearby one, such as Australia and New Zealand do. This effect may well operate to the extent that one destination is included with another in package tours, and to the attractiveness of both and the ease of movement between the two.

Habit in this context is similar to momentum among the push factors. Travellers may follow the pattern of visiting the same destination on their holiday trips. This is often incorporated in the causal model by a lagged value of the forecast variable.

Resistance factors comprise those variables that constrain travel between an origin and a destination. Most of these in Figure 7.4 are self-explanatory, although the price factors need some explanation.

Price is a resistance variable because most potential travellers have limited incomes, especially in relation to their day-to-day and long-term needs. The higher prices are, the fewer items this income can finance. This has been the second most popular explanatory variable in tourism demand regression models over the past three decades (Crouch 1994a, p. 48). However, tourism forecasters do not agree on the appropriate measure of price, and there are a number of choices.

Product price refers to the cost to the consumer of the item for which demand is being estimated. If a destination is the product for which demand is being modelled, then this is a complex of prices for lodging, food, entertainment and recreation, and local transportation. There is evidence that a country's consumer price index is a 'reasonable proxy for the cost of tourism', but that exchange rates are not (Witt and Witt 1992, p. 46).

Research suggests the effort of constructing a special visitors' price index is not adequately compensated in terms of improved forecasting accuracy.

Prices of substitutes represent what it costs to purchase competing alternatives to the product under study. For example, substitutes for air fares include bus fares, train fares, and automobile operating expenses. Substitutes for Jamaica include the Bahamas, Aruba, Barbados, and other destinations in the Caribbean as well as south Florida. When the price of a substitute goes up relative to your destination, then your visitor demand should rise as well. A common method of incorporating substitute process in tourism forecasting models is to include the ratio of the consumer price index in the destination country to the index in the origin country. However, this assumes that the only competitor destination for the foreign one is in the visitors' own country.

If you are trying to estimate demand for a product, such as auto rentals, for which there is another product that normally is purchased jointly, such as air transportation, then the cost of that product is a **complement price** that may affect your demand. For example, when air fares are cut, this generates more air travel and a larger demand for rental cars. Indeed, transport costs are the most important complement prices because virtually all tourism requires some transportation purchase, even if it is only gasoline. There is evidence that the 50 per cent cut in published airline fares available for U.S. domestic travel in the summer of 1992 substantially increased demand for hotel/motel rooms in many major cities during that period.

Changes in the cost of consumer **necessities** can affect travel demand. For example, rapid inflation in heating oil, gasoline, and other fuel oils during the energy crises of 1973–74 and 1979–80 dissuaded some Americans from travelling during and immediately after those periods because their household budgets were so constricted by higher energy costs. So, when the price of necessities rises, the demand for tourism may well fall.

Forecasters have found that currency **exchange rates** affect travel between countries. However, they have sometimes found it difficult to separate these effects from changes in national price levels. Some believe that potential visitors are well informed on exchange rates but relatively uninformed on price levels in destination countries. Tourism demand may be more sensitive to exchange rates in the short run than to price level changes, but research has indicated that the exchange rate is not a good representative of tourism costs. In general, as the cost of your country's currency rises in terms of the currency of an origin market, then tourism demand from that origin is expected to fall, all else being equal.

Escalating **taxes and fees** can dissuade travel as well. Here taxes include all that reduce consumer income or constrain business resources, such as income taxes, sales taxes, property taxes, value added taxes, and special business assessments. Arrival and departure taxes, including airport 'passenger facility charges', and other user fees are also an increasingly popular way for governments to attempt to increase revenues at the expense of visitors, who do not vote for elected officials of the destination. Fees include special licence charges for visitor-related activities (e.g. hunting, fishing, diving), admission fees levied by parks, museums, and similar facilities, and fines levied on visitors when they transgress traffic or foreign exchange laws. In the extreme, this latter category includes bribes forced from tourists by corrupt officials.

Effective marketing programmes and other **competitors' actions** can reduce travel to a given destination, as can inadequate transport, lodging, and entertainment/recreation **supply capacities** to or in that destination. Some countries still impose **exchange controls** on the amount of the national currency residents can take out of their country when they travel abroad. This is a deterrent to outbound travel.

Natural disasters (earthquakes, hurricanes, etc.) are well-known deterrents to visitation, but **man-made** ones are a major problem in some areas as well. The latter includes fires, plagues, illness caused by improper food handling and sanitation, and failing electrical systems.

Finally, **physical barriers** include those that prevent certain groups of potential travellers from visiting a destination. This includes access barriers to the handicapped, and asthma-sufferers' aversion to high altitudes and damp places. This category may also include topographical barriers to travel between places, such as mountains or deserts.

Given the plethora of potential explanatory variables in tourism demand regression models, it would be good if there was some guidance on which to employ. Witt and Witt (1992) built log-linear models for 24 country pairs and tested the following explanatory variables (p. 28):

1. personal disposable income
2. cost of living
3. exchange rate
4. cost of travel by air
5. cost of travel by surface
6. 1973 and 1979 oil crises
7. United Kingdom currency restrictions.

Unfortunately, they concluded

> The set of explanatory variables which appears to influence the demand for international tourism varies considerably from one origin-destination pair to another, and according to transport mode, where the data are disaggregated (Witt and Witt 1992, p. 61).

This supports the assumption that each tourism demand time series has a personality of its own, and there is no standard way to model it for forecasting.

Forecasting Washington, D.C. tourism demand

For our model of Washington, D.C. hotel/motel room demand, the origin area is primarily the United States and secondarily the rest of the world. We can incorporate a measure of U.S. economic trends, income and population size because the annual data are readily available. Information on other push factors cannot be obtained so easily.

The preferable alternative is to develop a regression equation for each origin market. However, we do not have access to the monthly distribution of room-nights sold by origin.

Turning to the pull factors, the only one that changes over time and can thus be related to changes in the dependent variable in a regression equation is the budget for the Washington Area Convention and Visitors Association, which is spent on attracting convention and other visitors to the region. The most significant recurring special event is the presidential inauguration festivities once every four years. This can be included in the model through one or more **dummy variables**.

Dummy variables

Normally, we view a time series we are attempting to forecast as being continuous and operating under the same conditions throughout the period. Every observation is affected by the explanatory variables in the same way during the period under study. However, there are situations when we should consider relaxing this constraint.

In Washington, D.C., the presidential inauguration occurs in January of each year after a presidential election. This super-annual event boosts hotel/motel occupancy towards saturation for a week or so during a month when occupancy rates are usually near their lowest. Thus, years of presidential inaugurations can be considered as falling under a different set of conditions than other years.

We can attempt to capture the effect of these different conditions on our dependent variable by including a 'dummy' explanatory variable. Such a dummy variable is dichotomous; that is, unlike other explanatory variables, this one can only take one of two values: zero or one. In this case, if the year is an inaugural one, then our dummy takes on the value of one. For other years, it takes on the value of zero.

Dummy variables are used extensively in forecast modelling by regression. They can distinguish between two or more continuous periods, such as the years of the Second World War, and the postwar period, or the years a country was under a communist government versus a period under democracy. They can distinguish periods of disaster, such as terrorist attacks or hurricanes, from normal periods. They have been used in tourism demand forecasting models to represent travel restrictions, world fairs and other special events, and oil crises.

Dummy variables can also be used to handle seasonality in a regression. Here, each of eleven months is assigned its own dummy variable. The special effects of the twelfth month are captured by the equation with all of the dummy variables equal to zero. Finally, they are sometimes used to account for measurement discontinuities, such as the use of different data sources in a time series, or changes in definitions.

This is an important principle of dummy variable analysis. The number of dummies included in an equation should always be one less than the number of different periods you are trying to distinguish. (For a lucid discussion of the use of dummy variables in other ways, see Rao and Miller 1971, pp. 88–93.)

Resistance factors

Turning back to Figure 7.4, we can include the price of a hotel/motel room in Washington, D.C. as a resistance factor. Among complementary prices, airline fares should certainly have some effect. Optimally, we need a composite fare representing air ticket prices to and from Washington, D.C. from its main origin markets. We do not have such a series, but the U.S. Bureau of Labor Statistics gathers data on representative airline fares throughout the country and prepares an index of these as a component of the Consumer Price Index. We will use this to represent fares to and from Washington, D.C.

The foreign country supplying the most visitors to Washington in a year is Canada. Therefore, the exchange rate between the U.S. and Canada may be a good measure of changing resistance on the price side for Canadian visitors.

A review of the other possible resistance factors in Figure 7.4 does not reveal any others that have changed markedly over the 1987–94 period for which we have relevant and accurate data.

2. Obtain relevant time series

At this point, we need to collect the data we plan to use to represent our dependent and independent variables. As discussed in Chapter 2, we should check to satisfy ourselves that each data series appears reasonable. Then we ensure the data are entered properly in whatever electronic medium we plan to conduct our analysis.

3. Identify any multicollinearity

This correlation among explanatory variables is called **multicollinearity**. If two explanatory variables are highly correlated, then the least squares regression procedure has difficulty in assigning coefficients to each. The result is that the two slope coefficients will show high standard errors and thus are highly unstable. Forecasters have noted that this can reach the point where different computer programs using the same data and functional form will produce different estimates of the slope coefficients. Moreover, to the extent that one coefficient is estimated as being too high, the other will be underestimated. Crouch calls multicollinearity 'the most common methodological problem encountered' in the 85 tourism demand forecasting models he reviewed (1994, p. 43).

Two standards have been suggested to identify highly correlated explanatory variables. One is to compute the correlations among all potential explanatory variables and identify those with correlations above a certain threshold, such as 0.8. However, this may cause the forecaster to incorrectly identify variables as being unfit for inclusion in the regression model when they have important explanatory powers in reality. An alternative rule is to see if the simple correlation between the two variables is larger than the correlation of either or both with the dependent variable. If so, then you have a multicollinearity problem. If this does not hold, than you can assume you do not have this problem.

The simple solution to multicollinearity is to exclude one of the two correlated explanatory variables. This is clearly warranted if you believe the two variables are measuring the same activity. But if these variables are measuring different factors affecting tourism demand, then you are not warranted in excluding one. Instead, you should seek to transform the variables to remove the multicollinearity.

Table 7.2 shows the correlations among a number of U.S. examples of variables often considered for inclusion in a tourism demand forecasting model. Those with correlations coefficients of greater than 0.8 are highlighted in **bold**. Many of these time series have grown continually over the last fifteen years and thus show high correlations. In some cases, we could reasonably exclude one or more variables which appear to be measuring the same element.

A '1' appears in each diagonal cell because each variable is perfectly correlated with itself. The top triangle is empty because the correlations are already given in the bottom triangle: the correlation between GDP and real disposable personal income is the same as the correlation between real disposable personal income and GDP.

Note that real GDP, real disposable personal income, and personal consumption expenditures are highly correlated. If we want to incorporate a measure of consumer buying power in our equation, we could exclude

Table 7.2 Intercorrelations among potential explanatory variables in a tourism demand forecasting model, U.S. annual, 1980–94

	1. Real gross domestic product	2. Real disposable personal income	3. Real personal consumption	4. Population	5. Non-agricultural employment	6. Domestic airline ASM*	7. Consumer price index	8. Travel price index	9. Domestic airline yields	10. Canadian dollar/$U.S.
1. Real gross domestic product	1									
2. Real disposable personal income	0.995	1								
3. Real personal consumption	0.995	0.996	1							
4. Population	0.982	0.988	0.984	1						
5. Non-agricultural employment	0.994	0.984	0.984	0.966	1					
6. U.S. domestic airline ASM*	0.978	0.973	0.979	0.946	0.983	1				
7. Consumer price index	0.972	0.981	0.976	0.997	0.957	0.937	1			
8. Travel price index	0.965	0.974	0.966	0.995	0.952	0.925	0.998	1		
9. Domestic airline yield**	0.529	0.539	0.518	0.585	0.518	0.464	0.632	0.635	1	
10. Canadian dollar/$U.S.	0.117	0.159	0.148	0.112	0.046	0.098	0.086	0.062	-0.162	1

* ASM is available seat-miles, a measure of airline supply of passenger travel
** Airline yield is average revenue per passenger-mile of paying passengers

Source: U.S. Department of Commerce, U.S. Department of Labor, Air Transport Association of America, U.S. Travel Data Center, Federal Reserve Board

GDP and personal consumption expenditures in favour of including only disposable personal income as an explanatory variable.

However, population, non-agricultural employment, consumer prices, travel prices and airline capacity (available seat-kilometres) are also highly correlated with disposable personal income. This is probably because they are all following a secular trend upward rather than because they are directly related to consumer buying power. Indeed, this correlation does not extend to these series' first differences for the most part, confirming a lack of relationship among these series. We are not justified in excluding them just because they are following an upward trend: each may be measuring different forces that could affect hotel/motel room demand.

Table 7.3 shows the correlations of the first differences of the same variables as in Table 7.2. Note that only two sets of series show correlations of 0.8 or higher: non-agricultural employment and GDP, and the Consumer Price Index (CPI) and the Travel Price Index (TPI). We can decide against including both employment and GDP in our regression model, since we use disposable personal income to represent some force that is represented by GDP: overall economic activity and income.

By the same reasoning, we might wish to include both overall consumer prices (CPI) and travel prices (TPI) even though they are highly correlated over the long run: the CPI measures the costs of all items Americans purchase while the TPI measures the costs of travel, which may compete with the other consumer items. Indeed, there have been times in the past when these two series have diverged, such as during petroleum crises and prolonged droughts.

If you have reason to believe that both variables are important in explaining your dependent variable, then, instead of eliminating one, you can transform your explanatory variables to remove the multicollinearity. The most common transformation is to take the first differences of one of the variables and include this in the equation, along with the original values of the other variable. Another choice is to transform the series into logarithms and include this redefined series as an explanatory variable.

Table 7.4 shows correlations between each explanatory variable considered for estimating hotel/motel room demand in Washington, D.C. and between each explanatory variable and all other such variables. Correlations of 0.8 or greater are marked in **bold**.

In Table 7.4, for example, we find the correlation of real disposable personal income and room-nights sold in the second column, row 4: 0.964. This indicates real disposable personal income is the prime candidate for an explanatory variable in our model.

It is clear that average room rates, airline fares, and real disposable personal income are highly correlated with our dependent variable, hotel/motel room-nights sold (note correlation coefficients in **bold** in column 2). This will help us identify the initial equation. However, average room rate is

Table 7.3 Intercorrelations among the first differences of potential explanatory variables in a tourism demand forecasting model, U.S. annual, 1980–94

	1. Real gross domestic product	2. Real disposable personal income	3. Real personal consumption	4. Population	5. Non-agricultural employment	6. Domestic airline ASM*	7. Consumer price index	8. Travel price index	9. Domestic airline yields	10. Canadian dollar/ $U.S.
1. Real gross domestic product	1									
2. Real disposable personal income	0.775	1								
3. Real personal consumption	0.684	0.412	1							
4. Population	−0.144	−0.154	−0.193	1						
5. Non-agricultural employment	**0.895**	0.671	0.473	−0.270	1					
6. U.S. domestic airline ASM*	0.393	0.169	0.383	−0.342	0.507	1				
7. Consumer price index	−0.468	−0.345	−0.697	0.120	−0.309	−0.356	1			
8. Travel price index	−0.360	−0.296	−0.761	0.217	−0.140	−0.210	**0.856**	1		
9. Domestic airline yield**	0.122	0.003	−0.274	−0.043	0.148	−0.068	0.727	0.569	1	
10. Canadian dollar/$U.S.	0.128	0.337	0.147	0.270	−0.001	0.007	−0.186	−0.187	−0.187	1

* ASM is available seat-miles, a measure of airline supply of passenger travel
** Airline yield is average revenue per passenger-mile of paying passengers
Source: U.S. Department of Commerce, U.S. Department of Labor, Air Transport Association of America, U.S. Travel Data Center, Federal Reserve Board

Table 7.4 Intercorrelations among potential explanatory variables in a hotel/motel room demand regression model for Washington, D.C., annual, 1987–94

1. Variable	2. Room nights sold	3. Average room rate	4. Airline fare price index	5. Real disposable personal income	6. Canadian dollar cost of $U.S.	7. Promotional budget
2. Average room rate	**0.962**	1				
3. Airline fare price index	**0.931**	**0.916**	1			
4. Real disposable income	**0.964**	**0.958**	**0.957**	1		
5. Canadian dollar cost of $U.S.	0.225	0.0798	0.331	0.283	1	
6. Promotional budget	0.755	0.753	**0.806**	0.769	−0.146	1
7. Presidential inauguration	0.362	0.265	0.130	0.118	−0.0204	−0.008

Sources: Smith Travel Research, U.S. Department of Commerce, U.S. Department of Labor, Air Transport Association of America, Washington Metropolitan Area Convention and Visitors Association

highly correlated with domestic airline fares and real disposable personal income. These high correlations suggest multicollinearity will be a problem in estimating the equation's parameters correctly.

It is clear from our theory, however, that the three correlated explanatory variables are measuring different factors that can influence room demand, so to simply exclude one or two of them from our equation would reduce the explanatory power and probably the accuracy of our model. Rather, we need to transform the explanatory variables so they no longer correlate highly with each other.

Transforming them into logarithms retained high correlations among several. However, taking the first differences of each reduced all inter-correlations to below 0.8, as indicated in Table 7.5. Consequently, the multivariate regression model for forecasting hotel/motel room demand in Washington, D.C. is stated in terms of annual differences.

4. Specify expected relationships

Based upon our theory of how hotel/motel room demand is determined in an area, we can outline how we expect our model to look once it is complete. This procedure helps us to assess the validity of our model, that is, that it is indeed incorporating relationships that actually hold in the real world.

Table 7.5 Intercorrelations among potential explanatory variables in a hotel/motel room demand regression model for Washington, D.C., annual differences, 1987–94

1. Variable	2. Average room rate	3. Airline fare price index	4. Real disposable personal income	5. Canadian dollar cost of $U.S.	6. Promotional budget
2. Average room rate	1				
3. Airline fare price index	0.069	1			
4. Real disposable income	0.440	−0.457	1		
5. Canadian dollar cost of $U.S.	−0.292	0.334	0.187	1	
6. Promotional budget	−0.562	0.006	−0.765	−0.520	1
7. Presidential inauguration	0.432	0.530	0.323	−0.118	−0.163

Sources: Smith Travel Research, U.S. Department of Commerce, U.S. Department of Labor, Air Transport Association of America, Washington Metropolitan Area Convention and Visitors Association

Table 7.6 lists the explanatory variables we have selected for our forecasting model, and what we expect their relationship will be to hotel/motel room demand.

Economic theory posits that demand is inversely related to price, so we expect the coefficient of average room rate (expressed in rate of change) to be negative.[3] Airline fares are considered to be the price of a complementary product, so we expect that as they rise, travel is retarded and hotel/motel demand slows: a negative relationship as well. Finally, the Canadian dollar cost of purchasing U.S. dollars is a price to potential Canadian visitors of travelling in the U.S., so as this price rises, it is also expected to have a negative impact on hotel/motel demand.

Table 7.6 Theoretical characteristics of potential explanatory variables in a regression model of hotel/motel room demand

1. Explanatory variable	2. Coefficient sign	3. Dummy variable?	4. Lagged variable
1. Average room rate	negative	no	no
2. Domestic airline fares	negative	no	no
3. Real disposable personal income	positive	no	possibly
4. Canadian dollar cost of £U.S.	negative	no	possibly
5. Presidential inauguration	positive	yes	no

Rising real disposable income should stimulate travel away from home, so this is expected to show a positive relationship to hotel/motel demand. Similarly, the quadrennial presidential inauguration boosts room demand in the years in which it occurs.

Looking at the third column in Table 7.6, only one of these variables, the presence of the inauguration, is represented by a dummy variable. In the years of this event (1989 and 1993 in our time series), it will be represented by a dummy with a value of one. For other years, the value is set at zero.

Finally, we need to consider whether the impact of any of our explanatory variables is a lagged one. In other words, is the value one or two years earlier expected to be more highly correlated with current room demand than the current value. It appears that current hotel/motel rates, airline fares, and the presence of an inauguration will affect room demand in the current period, rather than a year or two later.

On the other hand, last year's personal income may affect this year's decision to travel. And since foreign visitors often book tour packages to the U.S. as much as a year in advance, a previous year's exchange rate may affect this year's visitation. So lagged values of these should be considered in building our model. We do not have enough advance information, however, to specify that these variables must be lagged in our model. We can test both current and lagged effects during the model-building process.

One final phase of this step is to specify the mathematical, or functional, form of these relationships. The simplest form is to assume the levels of the explanatory variables are associated with the levels of the dependent variables. Another simple form is to relate changes in the dependent variable from period to period to the explanatory variables. Under this form, the series are all transformed into new series of the first differences, with one fewer data point than the original series. This is the form of the variables we will use, to avoid the multicollinearity problem identified earlier.

A popular functional form in tourism forecasting is the log-linear equation, where the logarithm of the dependent variable is regressed on the logarithms of the explanatory variables. This is an elasticity model, where the relationship of the logarithmic terms indicates that percentage changes in the explanatory variables produce a certain percentage change in the dependent variable. There is evidence that this is the preferred form for forecasting tourism flows among places because it usually yields significant coefficients with expected signs. Crouch found it was by far the most popular form for models forecasting tourism demand among countries (1994a, p. 42). One deficiency of such models is that they assume the demand elasticity is constant which 'can produce absurd results when explanatory variables extend well beyond their original range' (Ibid.).

Other forms that could be used in a tourism demand regression forecasting model correspond to those depicted in Figure 7.2. These all produce non-linear relationships yet the regression equations remain linear in their parameters, a basic requirement for valid least squares regression analysis.

Once we have thoughtfully outlined how we expect our explanatory variables to affect hotel/motel room demand, the next step is to identify an initial model.

5. Identify initial model

At this stage, we take the expected form of our equation and enter various combinations of explanatory variables into it to find combinations of variables that produce the best fits of the dependent variables' historical data series. One of the most popular methods of arriving at an initial model is called **stepwise regression**. This procedure for identifying a regression model tries different combinations of explanatory variables to identify one or more combinations that fit the data well and produce slope coefficients significantly different from zero.

Several procedures have been suggested for stepwise regression. The one detailed in Figure 7.5, sometimes called 'forward stepwise regression', is based on the recommendations of Makridakis, Wheelwright and McGee (1983, pp. 279–281).

The objective is to derive two or three equations that produce high $\bar{R}^2$ or F-statistics and significant parameters. Then, these models should be tested against your theoretical expectations of the parameters, and those that do not pass this test can be discarded. Finally, you will examine a number of tests of the validity of your models to select the best one.

The stepwise regression process is quite tedious in a spreadsheet even with a efficient regression application, and it is better to use a statistical program with this capacity. In a number of such programs, the computer actually tests all combinations of explanatory variables and indicates the most successful. However, it is wise to examine the results of each step yourself rather than to accept the program's choice of explanatory variables, because some programs ignore the significance of the coefficients and focus exclusively on achieving the highest $\bar{R}^2$. You may end up with several irrelevant explanatory variables in your model, a clear case of misspecification.

In our collection of explanatory variables for hotel/motel room demand, the one with the highest correlation with annual changes in room demand is the dummy variable for the presidential inauguration years (Table 7.7). Consequently, the stepwise regression procedure began with this explanatory variable and added and subtracted additional variables in order to maximize the F-statistic. Several equations were identified that produced good fits with the room demand time series, and these are detailed in the next section.

Note that a **lagged** series of real disposable personal income (RDPI) changes was included as a potential explanatory variable (Table 7.7). This is

1. Examine the simple correlations of the explanatory variables with the dependent variable.
2. Regress the dependent variable on the explanatory variable with the highest correlation and record the $\bar{R}^2$ or F-statistic (both are measures of the goodness of fit and are discussed below) and the t-statistic for the slope coefficient (a measure of the significance of the slope coefficient, also discussed below).
3. Add the potential explanatory variable with the next best correlation with the dependent variable and run the regression again. If the $\bar{R}^2$ increases and the slope coefficient for both explanatory variables is significant at some specified confidence interval (e.g. 90 or 95 per cent), record the t-statistics and the $\bar{R}^2$ and move to the next step. If $\bar{R}^2$ declines, drop this explanatory variable. If one or more of the slope coefficients become insignificant, reject the variable(s) with the insignificant coefficient and move to the next step.
4. Add the potential variable with the next highest correlation with the dependent variable. If the $\bar{R}^2$ increases and all t-statistics remain significant, move on to step 5. If the $\bar{R}^2$ decreases or the t-statistic of the new variable is not significant, delete the latest variable and move on to the next step. If the $\bar{R}^2$ increases, but the t-statistic for one of the earlier variables becomes insignificant, drop this variable and run a regression again. If the new regression produces a higher $\bar{R}^2$ than the original and t-statistics of all slope coefficients are significant, move on to the next step.
5. Continue the step 4 process until no additional variable increases the $\bar{R}^2$ or produces a significant slope coefficient. This is an initial model.

Figure 7.5   Stepwise regression estimation process

because several equations in the stepwise process included RDPI but with a negative coefficient, indicating that as consumer income rose, room demand in Washington, D.C. declined, and vice versa. This did not appear reasonable, so the lagged variable was incorporated to test the hypothesis that income affected room demand with a one-year lag. The promotional budget series was lagged as well, for the same reasons.

Table 7.7 reveals some surprises, given our theoretical expectations of the signs of the explanatory variable coefficients in Table 7.6. Annual changes in average room rate are positively correlated with room-night sales increments, suggesting raising rates is the way to increase occupancy. If this were true, then we would expect occupancies to be nearly 100 per cent for each year, since hoteliers would have no reason to restrain rates. On the contrary,

Table 7.7 Correlations of potential explanatory variables with Washington, D.C. hotel/motel room demand, annual differences, 1987–94

Variable	Correlation
Average room rate	0.594
Airline fare price index	−0.066
Real disposable personal income (RDPI)	0.013
Canadian dollar cost of $U.S.	−0.105
Promotional budget	−0.318
Presidential inauguration	0.616
Lagged RDPI	0.215
Lagged promotional budget	−0.0197

the monthly data indicate that room rates appear to 'chase' demand: hoteliers try to increase demand during months with traditionally low occupancies and lower rates than high occupancy months. The same may be true for the annual series as well.

The Washington, D.C. promotional budget is also negatively correlated with room demand. Again, this contradicts theory, and suggests that the budget may be chasing demand as well. This is supported by the fact that even lagged changes in the series are negatively correlated with room demand increments.

6. Evaluate the model's validity

At this step in our regression modelling, we should now have a small number of equations, say two or three differing in the explanatory variables included. We can order these by their measures of goodness of fit and coefficient significance, such as below for our hotel/motel demand problem:

$$\Delta RNS = 1.86 - 28.5 \times \Delta LRDPI - 2.31 \times \Delta\$CAN - 0.137 \times \Delta RR$$

$$\qquad \text{(21.8)} \quad \text{(−22.8)} \qquad\qquad \text{(−11.9)} \qquad\qquad \text{(−10.2)}$$

$$-0.263 \times \Delta LPB + 2.53 \times PID \quad (7.8)$$

$$\text{(−10.0)} \qquad\qquad \text{(27.3)}$$

$$\bar{R}^2 = 0.996 \qquad F = 288 \ (p = 0.044)$$

$$\Delta RNS = 1.12 - 21.5 \times \Delta LRDPI + 0.188 \times \Delta PB + 2.05 \times PID \qquad (7.9)$$

$$\text{(7.27)} \quad \text{(−5.81)} \qquad\qquad \text{(2.26)} \qquad\qquad \text{(7.09)}$$

$$\bar{R}^2 = 0.906 \qquad F = 20.4 \ (p = 0.017)$$

$$\Delta RNS = 0.973 - 16.3 * \Delta LRDPI + 1.64 * PID \tag{7.10}$$

$$\quad\text{(4.91)}\quad\quad\text{(3.96)}\quad\quad\quad\quad\quad\text{(5.12)}$$

$$\bar{R}^2 = 0.811 \quad\quad F = 13.8 \, (p = 0.016)$$

where

ΔRNS = annual change in hotel/motel room-nights sold (millions)

$\Delta LRDPI$ = annual change in real disposable personal income lagged one year ($\$10^9$)

$\Delta\$CAN$ = annual change in Canadian dollar cost of U.S. dollar ($C)

ΔRR = annual change in annual room rate ($)

ΔLPB = annual change in promotional budget, lagged one year $millions)

PID = dummy variable for presidential inauguration years

ΔPB = annual change in promotional budget ($millions)

The figure shown in parentheses below each coefficient is the *t*-statistic for that coefficient. All are significant at the 0.10 level, and those in **bold** are significant at the 0.05 level.

We now examine each to see how it compares to our set of expected relationships listed in Table 7.6. Our objective is to select the best valid equation, that is, the one with best fit that conforms to our theory of the correct relationships between the dependent variable and the explanatory variables, and that passes the tests for a significant regression model.

7. Assess the model's significance

Once we have developed our most valid causal model, we must then examine it for significance. That is, we try to determine whether the estimated relationships embodied in our regression model truly depict associations among the variables, or are an artifact of the estimation process. If a model's relationships accurately reflect the data describing the present world, then we can be much more confident they can be used to describe the future. If the quantified relationships instead reflect features of the way we have organized and processed the data, then we cannot expect them to be good descriptions of how the world works now and how it will in the future.

To determine whether we have indeed achieved a valid least squares regression model for forecasting tourism demand, there are five basic questions we should ask about it:

1. Does it accurately simulate the historical data?
2. Is our test for simulation accuracy valid?
3. Have we included any irrelevant explanatory variables?
4. Have we excluded any important explanatory variables?
5. How stable is the model?

Each of these questions will be discussed in turn, with appropriate tests presented and remedies suggested.

A. Accurate simulation of the historical series

We can have much more confidence that our model can predict the future course of a data series if it successfully simulates its past course. We employed a test for the extrapolative models discussed in Chapter 4 based on the average percentage error, the MAPE.

For regression analysis, we have a useful analogue in the coefficient of determination adjusted for degrees of freedom, or $\bar{R}^2$. This statistic indicates the per cent of the variation of the dependent variable around its mean that is explained by our explanatory variables. As such, it varies between zero and one, with zero indicating the explanatory variables have no power to explain the variation in the dependent variable, and one indicating they explain all of this variation. Formally, $\bar{R}^2$ is computed by the following formula:

$$\bar{R}^2 = 1 - \left[\left(1 - \frac{\sum (\hat{Y}_t - \bar{Y})^2}{\sum (Y_t - \bar{Y})} \right) \left(\frac{n-1}{n-k-1} \right) \right] \qquad (7.11)$$

where

$\bar{R}^2$ = coefficient of determination adjusted for degrees of freedom
$\hat{Y}$ = dependent variable as estimated by the regression equation
t = a time period
$\bar{Y}$ = the mean of the dependent variable data series
Y = actual dependent variables in the data series
n = number of observations in the dependent variable data series
k = number of parameters (explanatory variables plus one)

Note that this statistic is an altered version of the simple coefficient of determination, or R^2. As you add explanatory variables to a regression equation, the R^2 naturally rises, since each added variable usually can explain some of the variance in the dependent variable. $\bar{R}^2$ adjusts for the number of explanatory variables, so that we can truly determine whether a model with five explanatory variables is more significant than one with only two.

We should, of course, prefer models with high values of $\bar{R}^2$, but there is no standard as to what 'high' means. The $\bar{R}^2$ value can depend very much on what we are trying to forecast. For a tourism demand series affected by many factors, such as the number of Mexican visitors to the United States, an $\bar{R}^2$ of 0.7 might be considered high. Models forecasting first differences of a tourism demand series are also considered reliable if they achieve with $\bar{R}^2$

of 0.7 or more, because first differences tend to be more volatile than their underlying time series.

However, for a series showing stable trends over time, such as hotel/motel room demand in the Washington, D.C. metropolitan area, an $\bar{R}^2$ of 0.7 may well be considered too low. There is no definitive guide to the significance of this statistic. Fortunately, we have a related statistic that is accompanied by a guide to its significance: the F-statistic.

In our use of it in regression analysis, the F-statistic is the ratio of an equation's explained variance in the dependent variable to its unexplained variance. The equation is:

$$F = \frac{\sum (\hat{Y} - \bar{Y})^2 / k}{\sum (Y - \hat{Y})^2 / (n - k - 1)} \tag{7.12}$$

where

F = F-statistic
$\hat{Y}$ = dependent variable estimated by the regression equation
$\bar{Y}$ = the mean of the data series
Y = actual dependent variables in the data series
n = number of observations in the dependent variable data series
k = number of parameters (explanatory variables plus one)

In essence, the F-statistic can tell us whether movements in the explanatory variables do indeed 'explain' changes in the dependent variable, or, alternatively, that the apparent correlation is just random. You can look up the value of your F-statistic in tables found in most statistical textbooks and determine whether it is significant or not according to some level of confidence (usually set at 0.1 or 0.05). As a rule of thumb, if you have two explanatory variables or more, and the number of observations less the number of explanatory variables equals six or more, then an F-statistic of 5 or more indicates your regression model is significant at the 0.05 level. Since the $\bar{R}^2$ and the F-statistic are linearly related, this indicates your coefficient of determination is 'high enough' as well. In short, your forecast equation provides a good fit with the historical data series.

As suggested by the equations, computation of $\bar{R}^2$ and the F-statistic can be tedious on a spreadsheet. Fortunately, statistical packages for personal computers that conduct regression analysis print out these two statistics as a matter of course. In the case of the F-statistic, its level of significance is indicated as well.

Note that $\bar{R}^2$ is not available for time series analysis models, so you need to compute MAPEs when comparing these to regression models. Indeed, it is always wise to compare the MAPEs of alternative regression models among themselves, for a high $\bar{R}^2$ is no guarantee of a low MAPE.

There is a tendency among forecasters to focus on the $\bar{R}^2$ value to indicate the most accurate forecasting model. However, this is to confuse explanatory power of a regression model with its ability to correctly forecast future values. Witt and Witt (1992) have clearly documented the two are not the same in tourism demand forecasting. They found in a comparison of a number of regression models for international travel flows among countries that in less than one-fifth of the cases did the regression model with the highest $\bar{R}^2$ produce the most accurate forecast of future levels of tourism demand. Other forecasters agree that a 'high $\bar{R}^2$ alone is not a convincing reason for accepting a forecasting model' (e.g. Calantone, di Benedetto and Bojanic 1987, p. 37).

B. *Validity of the test for simulation accuracy*

One of the critical assumptions of least squares regression analysis is that the residuals, or errors of fit, are random, that is, independent of one another. The alternative is that they show a pattern. This pattern indicates that the model is not taking account of all the important information on relationships to the dependent variable. In particular, this signals that at least one important explanatory variable has been left out of the equation, that is, that the model is misspecified. (The ramifications of this are discussed below.)

In addition, this pattern, called 'serial correlation' or 'autocorrelation of the residuals', will bias the estimates of our equation's goodness of fit: $\bar{R}^2$ and the F-statistic. The most common case in time series data is positive serial correlation, where residuals in one time period are positively correlated with residuals in the next time period. If this is present in a regression model, then the goodness of fit measures as estimated appear higher than they actually are, giving an overly optimistic picture of the success of the regression.

The most popular way to identify serial correlation of the residuals is the Durbin–Watson (DW) statistic:

$$DW = \frac{\sum (e_t - e_{t-1})^2}{\sum e_t^2} \tag{7.13}$$

where

DW = the Durbin–Watson statistic
e = residual
t = a time period

The numerator computes the squared differences between successive residuals for each time period in the data series and adds them up. Then the sum of the squared residuals are added up in the denominator and divided into the numerator. If the residuals show a slow-moving course, that is, are close to one another, the DW statistic will be small. If there is a distinct, fast-moving pattern, then the successive residual differences will be large and the

DW statistic will be large. These are the two cases of serial correlation that will bias our measures of a regression model's goodness of fit to the historical data.

The DW statistic ranges from zero to four. If the DW statistic is 2.0, the residuals are completely independent and there is no serial correlation. Most statistical textbooks contain tables of the critical values of this statistic to suggest whether there is serial correlation, there is no serial correlation, or we are in an indeterminate region where we do not know whether serial correlation is present or not. These regions vary substantially by number of observations and number of explanatory variables in the equation. As a rule of thumb, if the DW statistic falls between 1.5 and 2.5, we can be reasonably sure that no serial correlation exists among the residuals in most cases.

If your Durbin–Watson statistic falls outside of this region, there is a good chance you have serial correlation of your residuals. The best remedy is to look for missing explanatory variables and include them in your model. Another remedy is to transform some of your explanatory variables by differencing or taking their logarithms. There are methods that directly correct serial correlation in the residuals, but these ignore the problem of omitted variables: even though you may remove the serial correlation, you will still have a misspecified model.

Heteroscedasticity

A second assumption of the linear regression model is that the residuals all have the same variance. If this is assumption is violated, we are said to have **heteroscedasticity**, the name given to the condition where the residuals do not maintain constant variance across the entire time series.

This condition is frequently found over long time series showing a marked trend, such as many tourism demand series. In some long tourism demand series, such as U.S. air passenger travel in Figure 6.2 in Chapter 6, the order of magnitude changes over the course of the series. In the complete series, the value for 1994 is 49 times the value for 1950. In some series of this kind, as the variable becomes larger in magnitude, its variance tends to become larger too. This is heteroscedasticity. (The opposite, and preferred condition, where the variance of the residual terms does not change over the series, is called **homoscedasticity**.)

When heteroscedasticity occurs, the major practical implication is that the variance of the estimated parameters is biased and our t-test of their significance may give false signals of significance. That is, we may accept an explanatory variable as being significantly related to our dependent variable when we should not. Moreover, heteroscedasticity also biases the F-test, and we may accept an overall equation as our best model when we should not.

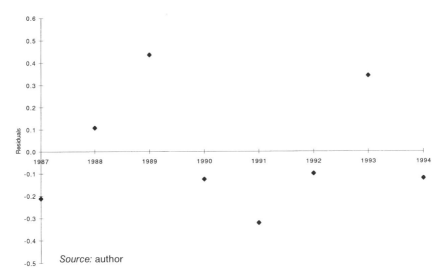

Figure 7.6   Residuals from the time trend regression of hotel/motel room demand in Washington, D.C., annually, 1987–94

One way to identify heteroscedasticity is to chart the residuals and examine them to see if their variance changes over time. Figure 7.6 charts the residual terms from the linear time trend shown in Figure 7.1. It appears that they get larger in the latter half of the series than they were in the first half, the sign of heteroscedasticity. However, it is not clear that this is the case.

Johnston (1972, p. 219) suggests a five-step test for the presence of heteroscedasticity in a regression equation:

1. Order the observations by size
2. Omit a certain number of observations in the centre of the series (Johnston suggests omitting 8 for a 30-point time series and 16 for a 60-point series. You can interpolate for series of different lengths.)
3. Fit separate linear time tend regressions to the remaining observations in the first part of the remaining time series and the second part.
4. Compute the sum of the squared residuals, and divide the larger sum by the smaller.
5. Apply the F-test to this ratio; the degrees of freedom are one-half the number of observations in the first part of the series less four, and one-half the number of observations in the second part of the series less four. If the resulting ratio is smaller than the F-statistic for these degrees of freedom, then the variances are equal and we have homoscedasticity and thus no problem.

In the Figure 7.6 example, the ratio is 9.3 without excluding any values since the series is so short. The degrees of freedom are $(13 - 4)/2$ and $(13 - 4)/2$, or 4,4. The F-statistic for these degrees of freedom at the 0.05 level of significance is 6.4. Since the F-statistic for our ratio exceeds this, then we accept the hypothesis that the variances of the two parts of our time series are not equal. In short, we have identified heteroscedasticity in this series.

If you find heteroscedasticity in your time series, try to remove it by transforming the dependent variable into first differences, logarithms or square roots as discussed in Chapter 6. Then use the transformation that removes it as in your forecast variable.

C. Irrelevant explanatory variables

Relying on theory or intuition, the forecaster may include a number of explanatory variables that are not statistically related to the dependent variable. This violates the principle of parsimony and may contribute to higher forecast errors in the future. Fortunately, there is a simple test for the significance of the relationship between an explanatory variable and its dependent: the t-test.

The t-statistic is computed as follows:

$$\text{ts} = \frac{b_i}{se_{b_i}} \tag{7.14}$$

where

  ts = the t-statistic
  b = slope coefficient
  i = one of the explanatory variables
  se = standard error (in this case, of the slope coefficient)

The standard error of the slope coefficient is computed as follows:

$$se_{b_i} = \frac{\sum (Y_t - \check{Y})^2/(n - k)}{\sum (X_{i,t} - \bar{X})^2} \tag{7.15}$$

where

  se = standard error
  b = a slope coefficient
  i = one of the explanatory variables
  Y = dependent variable
  $\check{Y}$ = estimate of the dependent variable
  n = number of observations
  k = number of parameters (i.e. explanatory variables plus one)
  X = an explanatory variable
  $\bar{X}$ = mean of the explanatory variable data series

Since the t-statistic is obtained from the least squares regression, it has a statistical distribution. Based on the degrees of freedom (number of data points less the number of explanatory variables plus one) and the degree of confidence you seek, you can look up the critical value in tables in most statistical textbooks. Assuming a 95 per cent confidence interval[4] and six or more degrees of freedom, a t-statistic of 2.0 or more indicates the coefficient is significantly different from zero, and thus its explanatory variables should be retained in the forecasting model.

Note that since the coefficient can be negative, the t-statistic can be negative, too. Consequently, look for a t-statistic with an **absolute** value of greater than 2.0.

If a coefficient fails to pass this test, you should exclude the related explanatory variable from your equation. Its coefficient has a value only due to sampling, and this value is as likely to be zero as to be any other number. In other words, there is no evidence that this explanatory variable explains any of the variation in the dependent variable, and should be omitted from the model as irrelevant.

D. Omitted explanatory variables

A forecasting model is designed to be a simplified representation of a complex reality. By its very nature, the model cannot include all factors that affect tourism demand in reality. However, we should take pains to ensure the most important explanatory variables are included.

If we exclude an important explanatory variable, we obtain biased estimates of the slope coefficients for the variables we do include. This means they are not accurate representations of past relationships between the explanatory variable and the dependent variable. We can assume they will fail to be so in the future as well.

One way to guard against omitting relevant variables is to carefully develop a theory of what affects tourism demand and how. This will suggest variables that can explain the course of your dependent variable over time. Variables that offer the potential for explaining tourism demand are listed in Figure 7.4, above.

One way to explore whether relevant explanatory variables have been left out of the equation is to examine the residuals of your model. If these show a non-random pattern (i.e. serial correlation), this indicates one or more important variables related to your dependent variable have been left out. A popular test for such patterns is the Durbin–Watson statistic explained in B, above.

E. Stability of the forecasting model

Throughout this discussion of causal forecast modelling, we have been focusing on estimating the intercept constant and slope coefficients through least squares regression. Once we have assured ourselves (and our clients or supervisors) that we have accurately estimated these according to statistical tests of significance and validity, we need to have confidence that they are stable. That is, that we do not stretch reason too far in assuming these coefficients will apply in the future we are forecasting.

While we can never be certain that what pertains now will operate in the future, we can test our model for stability, that is, that the coefficients have remained fairly constant over our historical time series. We can drop out the most recent year's worth of data, rerun the regression and see whether this substantially changes our coefficients.

Substantial changes include those where the sign changes or where the value changes significantly. This last can be determined by applying a t-test to see if the difference between our original coefficients and those from the revised model differ significantly at the 5 per cent level of significance.

If the slope coefficients do vary significantly when the last year's worth of data are removed, then we do not have a stable model. You need to develop a new model with a different set of explanatory variables that does show stability, as well as meeting our other criteria for a sound forecasting model.

One of our preferred regression models (7.8) for forecasting hotel/motel room demand could not be tested for stability because it had too many explanatory variables for the number of data points available in a six-year test period. However, below is a comparison of the parameters of equations (7.9) and (7.10) as estimated from the seven-year time series and the six-year series.

1988-94

$$\Delta RNS = 1.12 - 21.5 * \Delta LRDPI + 0.188 * \Delta PB + 2.05 * PID \qquad (7.9)$$
$$\text{(7.27)} \quad \text{(−5.81)} \qquad \qquad \text{(2.26)} \qquad \qquad \text{(7.09)}$$

$$\bar{R}^2 = 0.906 \qquad F = 20.4 \, (p = 0.017)$$

1988-93

$$\Delta RNS = 1.20 - 25.0 * \Delta LRDPI + 0.265 * \Delta PB + 2.34 * PID \qquad (7.11)$$
$$\text{(6.23)} \quad \text{(−4.28)} \qquad \qquad \text{(2.02)} \qquad \qquad \text{(4.88)}$$

$$\bar{R}^2 = 0.880 \qquad F = 13.2 \, (p = 0.071)$$

1988-94

$$\Delta RNS = 0.973 - 16.3 * \Delta LRDPI + 1.64 * PID \qquad (7.10)$$
$$\text{(4.91)} \quad \text{(3.96)} \qquad \qquad \text{(5.12)}$$

$$\bar{R}^2 = 0.811 \qquad F = 13.8 \, (p = 0.016)$$

1988-93

$$\Delta\text{RNS} = 0.956 - 15.2 * \Delta\text{LRDPI} + 1.53 * \text{PID} \qquad (7.12)$$

$$\quad\;\; \textbf{(4.48)} \quad\;\; \textbf{(–3.25)} \qquad\qquad\; \textbf{(4.08)}$$

$$\bar{R}^2 = 0.757 \qquad F = 8.77 \,(p = 0.055)$$

where

ΔRNS = annual change in hotel/motel room-nights sold (millions)
ΔLRDPI = annual change in real disposable personal income lagged one year ($\$10^9$)
ΔPB = annual change in promotional budget ($millions)
PID = dummy variable for presidential inauguration years

Both equations (7.9) and (7.10) are remarkably stable. Their parameters hardly change as a result of one less period. Moreover, their t-statistics remain significant at the 0.05 level (those in **bold**), except for one in equation (7.9) that remains significant at the 0.10 level. While the measures of overall goodness of fit ($\bar{R}^2$ and the F-statistic) decline somewhat, this can be expected when a period is removed from the end of a short time series.

Table 7.8 summarizes the various validity tests applied to our three acceptable forecast equations for hotel/motel room demand in the Washington, D.C. area. The results of the earlier examination of the signs of the coefficients are included, as well, in the last row. Those characteristics in **bold** are the best for a given test.

Model (7.10) shows the most superior characteristics (i.e. six are in bold). Model (7.9) is a close second, and posts a lower MAPE. Equation (7.8)

Table 7.8 Comparisons of three hotel/motel demand forecasting models on tests of validity

Characteristic	Model (7.8)	Model (7.9)	Model (7.10)
$\bar{R}^2$	**0.996**	0.906	0.811
F-statistic (significance level)	288 (0.04)	20.4 (**0.02**)	13.8 (**0.02**)
MAPE	**0.1%**	0.5%	0.8%
Durbin–Watson statistic	1.45*	**2.18**	1.44*
Heteroscedasticity	NA	NA	NA
Parameters' significance			
Intercept constant	0.03	**0.01**	**0.01**
Coefficients not significant at 0.05	3	1	**0**
Coefficients not significant at 0.10	**0**	1	**0**
Stability	NA	**good**	**good**
Coefficients with questionable signs	2	**1**	**1**

* The Durbin–Watson test for serial correlation is inconclusive here
NA = not applicable (time series is too short to exhibit this)

holds third place in these tests, and is the most complex with five explanatory variables. However, its MAPE is by far the lowest.

Personal judgement is required to distinguish among these three choices for our forecasting model. This author prefers model (7.9) since it is a close second place and produces a lower MAPE than (7.10). Model (7.8) claims the lowest MAPE and highest $\bar{R}^2$, but could not be tested for stability due to the number of explanatory variables and the short period available.

8. Use the model to forecast

Once we have settled on our best regression model for forecasting tourism demand, we should employ it to develop forecasts of our future. At its most basic, this involves substituting values for the explanatory variables that will produce the forecast for the period we are interested in.

If lagged explanatory variables appear in the regression model, then we can often use the actual values for these since they are known. More often, however, we must resort to forecast values for our explanatory variables to forecast our dependent variable. This requirement necessarily increases our forecast errors. The less reliable the forecast explanatory variables available to us, the less reliable will be our forecast of the dependent variable.

In many cases, you can obtain forecasts of important economic variables for reputable forecasting firms. Sometimes, you will need to contact tourism industry sources for predictions of tourism-related variables. In any case, try to evaluate the quality of these forecasts just as carefully as you evaluate your own forecasting model. The tests for such evaluation have been discussed above, and are summarized in the next section.

Since the three 1995 explanatory variables in equation (7.9) are a lagged value (change in real disposable personal income), a policy variable known with precision (change in the promotional budget), and one known with certainty (presence of a presidential inauguration), it is easy to substitute to obtain a forecast for 1995 (RNS_{1995}). The 1995 values of the explanatory variables are shown in **bold** in equation (7.13):

$$\Delta RNS_{1995} = 1.124 - 21.5 * \mathbf{0.132} + 0.188 * \mathbf{0.220} + 2.05 * \mathbf{0} \qquad (7.13)$$

$$\Delta RNS_{1995} = 1.124 - 2.838 + 0.0414 = -1.673 \qquad (7.14)$$

$$RNS_{1995} = \Delta RNS_{1995} + RNS_{1994} = -1.673 + 16.363 \text{ million}$$
$$= 14.7 \text{ million} \qquad (7.15)$$

The best regression model indicates a drop of nearly 1.7 million room-nights sold in 1995, far greater than in any year of the time series. This does not appear reasonable. The alternative model represented by equation (7.9) indicates a drop of 1.2 million room-nights, also greater than any year in the time series.

In this situation, regression analysis has failed to produce reasonable forecasts for a future year. We are best advised to search for alternative regression models using other explanatory data, or employ a time series model that produces reasonable forecasts.

In our example, we forecast the change in hotel/motel room demand in the next year. This was to eliminate multicollinearity among explanatory variables. More often, your regression model will be designed to produce forecasts of the level of demand in the next year or two. This raises a problem. Unless your regression equation fits your time series perfectly, or by chance the last value in your historic time series is correctly forecast by your model, your forecast will be inconsistent with your actual time series. As a result, the change from your last historic value to your first forecast value will be exaggerated. Appendix 3 discusses this problem and solutions for it.

Applications

Witt and Witt (1992) examined the relationship between validity and forecasting accuracy in 35 regression models of tourism flows between country origins and destinations. Their validity criteria comprised:

- coefficient of determination adjusted for degrees of freedom ($\bar{R}^2$)
- coefficient of determination (R^2)
- Durbin–Watson statistic
- relative number of significant coefficients at the 0.5 per cent level.

Their conclusion is not encouraging:

> The assessment of the likely forecasting ability of econometric models of tourism demand on the basis of common criteria such as goodness of fit, statistical significance of the coefficients, and the like may well be misleading. Conditions such as high goodness of fit and large proportion of statistically significant coefficients do not appear to be sufficient to ensure a high level of forecasting accuracy (p. 66).

In other words, these four criteria do not ensure an accurate model for forecasting tourism flows among countries.

This conclusion may be due to

1. employing the wrong validity criteria for regression models (for example, they did not deal with possible multicollinearity, heteroscedasticity or stability in their time series)
2. idiosyncrasies in the time series used (however, there is no evidence presented that data irregularities characterized the series used)

3. the failure of validity criteria to indicate the most accurate regression model.

Of these three, the third reason is the most disturbing. If we accept this conclusion, then we are left without an *a priori* method of determining the best regression forecasting model. Moreover, the ultimate implication is that regression methods are useless for building accurate tourism forecasting models because their tests of validity do not ensure accurate forecasts.

This author's conclusion is that the tests of regression model validity are necessary but not sufficient conditions for selecting the most accurate model for forecasting the future. They should all be applied, including the test for stability. The model or models that best satisfy these criteria are then those most likely to produce accurate forecasts. (The forecasts may even be averaged as Witt and Witt suggest (p. 66).) This is the best insurance against accepting an inaccurate model, but will not guarantee accuracy.

These two authors have also investigated the explanatory variables that influence international tourism through the use of regression analysis (Witt and Witt 1994). They found that the set of such variables varies from one origin-destination pair to another, and that their relative influence does as well. This confirms the potential for error in assuming that one regression model can suffice for several pairs of destinations.

Smeral (1988) has suggested a 'two-stage decision process, separable for each country', as a forecasting model of international tourism. In the first stage, the total amount of real expenditures on individual consumer products by the residents of a country are each forecast, including domestic tourism and international tourism specifically. In the second stage, the country of destination and expenditures in that country are determined by the size of the foreign tourism promotion budget for the country and the dollar prices of tourism goods and services in all countries. He provides the theoretical foundation in Smeral (1994), along with forecasts of average rates of tourism demand growth for 18 countries.

Using three forms of the regression model estimated for travel among nine west European countries, he investigated the effects of different income growth rates and price changes. He found that the distribution of travel expenditures differed significantly depending on the model used and the rate of income growth or price change. He also found that reductions in tourism prices in one country can increase tourism demand for that country as well as others. Smeral noted his models failed to take into account variables other than price and income, such as age structure, leisure time, tastes and supply constraints.

Smeral, Witt and Witt (1992) extended this model to project the impact of post-1992 European Union integration and political changes in eastern Europe on national tourism imports and exports to 2000. They estimated a tourism import equation and a tourism export equation for each of 18 countries by ordinary least squares regression, employing annual data for 1975 through 1988. Explanatory variables for tourism imports (associated with outbound tourism) in terms of $U.S. adjusted for inflation included GDP of the generating country, the ratio of tourism import prices to consumer prices in the generating country and a dummy variable representing trend influences. On the export side (associated with inbound tourism), the explanatory variables were total tourism imports (representing the 'foreign travel budget'), the ratio of country consumer prices to other countries' prices, and a dummy trend variable. They also added dummy variables for the petroleum crises of 1974 and 1979, and well as national recessions.

They achieved high R^2 for most equations. The income coefficient was significant at the 0.5 per cent level and had the correct sign in all cases. The relative price coefficients were significant at the 0.5 per cent level with the correct signs for most equations. One result is that the European Union travel deficit with the rest of the world is expected to increase at a greater rate than before integration. Another report on this study concluded that Canada is likely to enjoy an increase in its tourism balance with the European Union as a result of integration (Smeral and Witt 1992).

Two of the authors modified the original model by incorporating more recent data, including the demise of the Iron Curtain and German reunification, and allowing for different export demand structures for each country, that is, shares of visitors by origin country (Smeral and Witt 1995). Tourism flows to and from 18 major industrialized countries were estimated annually to 2005, employing two different scenarios for countries' GDP growth.

di Benedetto and Bojanic (1993) investigated the tourism area life cycle hypothesis at Cypress Gardens, Florida, over 139 quarters through regression analysis. This hypothesis states that demand for a tourism area goes through six stages over time, marking out an S-shaped curve. They used a 'step-logarithmic' form of the regression equation, which incorporated a trend variable from the series' beginning and another trend variable when Walt Disney World opened in 1971, boosting visitor volume to the entire area. They employed dummy variables to handle seasonality, the addition of new attractions on site, and eternal events, such as the world oil crises of 1973–74 and 1979.

These authors employed nearly all of the tests of a valid, reliable regression forecasting model and concluded theirs did follow the life cycle curve traced out by the actual series. They tested it against a Box–Jenkins ARIMA model and found they performed equally as well as when measured by MAPE.

Crouch, Schultz and Valerio (1992) developed a regression model of annual inbound visitors, 1970 to 1989, from five origin countries specifically to investigate the power of the marketing expenditures of the Australian

Tourist Commission (ATC) to increase arrivals. Explanatory variables included personal income in the origin country, consumer prices in Australia relative to those in the origin country, the cost of travel to Australia, ATC marketing expenditures, a trend term to allow for changing 'tastes', and dummy variables for special events and disturbances, both positive and negative. They reported $\bar{R}^2$, the Durbin–Watson statistic, significance of the coefficients, the sign of the coefficients, and a measure of multicollinearity of the explanatory variables.

They concluded marketing expenditures were significantly related to inbound tourism, and produced benefit-cost ratios of between 9 and 220: that is, the ratio of increased international visitor receipts to the increase in marketing expenditures was 9 for the U.S. and 220 for New Zealand. They also found that marketing expenditures appear to work with a lag of up to one year.

Jørgensen and Solvoll (1996) developed log-linear regression equations to forecast Norwegians residents' demand for inclusive tour charters in each of three seasons of the year over the 1969–93 period. Their explanatory variables comprised real disposable personal income, consumer expectations of future prosperity (measured by the national government's forecast of changes in personal consumption), indexes of tour prices, and an index of the summer weather. The last was included to account for the fact that nearly 40 per cent of annual tours are taken in the June–August period and appear to be related to the previous summer's weather conditions: the cooler and wetter the summer was, the more Norwegians tend to buy inclusive tours during the subsequent summer.

Their reported R^2s were relatively low, but each of their three equations were significant by the F-test. They had difficulty with serial correlation, however. They found that tour demand in the winter is least sensitive to income in the winter and most sensitive in the summer. Prices had the most adverse effects in the winter and least in the summer. They found that the poorer the summer weather in a year, the higher the demand for tours during the following 12 months. Finally, contrary to intuition, they found that their measure of consumer expectations was inversely related to tour demand: the more optimistic consumers became, the fewer tours they bought.

Darnell, Johnson and Thomas (1990) used a log-linear regression equation to model quarterly visitor volume to the North of England Open Air Museum at Beamish. Their explanatory variables included visitor volume lagged one period, admission price, real disposable personal income, the retail price index, and dummy variables for new attractions, Easter Sunday falling in the first quarter or second quarter, and exceptionally good weather. They reported nearly all tests of regression model accuracy and validity, except the MAPE. They found admission prices and income to be the most significant explanatory variables.

Brady and Widdows (1988) developed regression models of U.S. travel to three European countries during the summer months in order to quantify the effects of the Chernobyl nuclear disaster, the *Achille Lauro* attack, and terrorism directed against the U.S. as a result of raids on Libya on this tourism in the summer of 1986. They used air fares, disposable personal income, exchange rates, dummy variables for months, and hotel/motel room rates in the U.S. as explanatory variables. They concluded this travel declined from one-quarter to two-thirds during the summer of 1986, with Greece taking the greatest hit.

Choy (1984) used a linear time trend method to develop models of visitor arrivals in the Asian/Pacific region, and Hong Kong from individual origin areas. He found it to be considerably more accurate than the naive model as measured by MAPE over the 1974–82 period. He also found that low MAPEs did not necessarily accompany high $\bar{R}^2$ or vice versa, and that models for several of the origin area series produced unacceptably high MAPEs. Choy (1985) extended the usefulness of this model by relating it to demand for hotel room-nights in Hong Kong.

Witt and Martin (1987) report on a study of the impact of destination advertising on international arrivals in Greece from eight generating countries over the 1972–82 period. Per capita personal income in the origin countries, cost of travel between the origin and Greece, the ratio of the consumer price index in Greece to the origin country's index, Greece's promotional expenditures in the origin country and a dummy variable for the threat of war with Turkey in 1974 were included as explanatory variables. While they achieved high $\bar{R}^2$ values for most of the origin country models, in only five of eight equations did they obtain a significant coefficient for advertising expenditure. They note that determining the effect of such advertising on arrivals is complicated by the fact that the impact may be spread over several years and may vary by media purchased.

The Austrian Institute for Economic Research carried out a lengthy econometric investigation of tourism demand for Austria by Austrians (domestic tourism), and other countries' residents (inbound tourism), and by Austrians for other country destinations (outbound tourism) over the 1961–77 period (Schulmeister 1979). The Institute was particularly interested in developing models to forecast the long-term demand for tourism, short-term demand as affected by the general business cycle, and before and after the 1973–74 worldwide petroleum crisis to determine if changes in the structure of tourism demand had taken place.

This study found that Austrian residents' rising demand for tourism, both domestic and international, over the long run was mainly due to increases in income, which short-term fluctuations were primarily influenced by changes in school vacations (duration and timing), weather conditions, and fluctuations in private consumption (p. 26) This last variable showed an inverse relationship to overall tourism demand, explained by the reasoning that rapid domestic price inflation accelerated consumption expenditures for necessities and tourism demand suffered as a result.

The petroleum crisis depressed Austrian outbound tourism through high rates of inflation, and demand was shifted to domestic destinations. However, there was no evidence that the structure of tourism demand changed as a result of the crisis: the list of explanatory variables remained the same and their coefficients changed little (pp. 65–66). However, the Institute found that during political and economic crises, 'sudden fluctuations in the expectations of private households have a very strong short-term effect on the demand for tourism' (p. 76). Fluctuations in indexes of 'consumer sentiment' (i.e. personal evaluations of current or future general economic conditions) may be important explanatory variables in regression models during such crisis periods.

Chan (1994) fitted a linear trend and a sine wave to monthly seasonally adjusted tourist arrivals in Singapore over a 12-year period, and found a complete cycle lasted 170 months. This model achieved a MAPE of 2.6 per cent, far lower than those produced by naive 1, naive 2, simple linear regression or ARIMA models.

Conclusion

This chapter presents the linear regression model, a powerful and popular model for estimating the quantitative relationship between tourism demand and one or more variables associated with that demand. It is important to recognize the limitations of this very popular method. Above all is the limitation that regression analysis does not prove that a cause and effect relationship exists between a dependent variable and its explanatory variables. Rather, it indicates variations in the former are associated with certain variations in the latter variables. Cause and effect can only be proved by experimentally manipulating changes in an explanatory variable and measuring the resulting changes in the dependent variable. As one group has observed, 'regression analysis results should therefore be treated as *prima facie* evidence of a cause–effect relationship and not as conclusive proof' (Crouch, Schultz and Valerio 1992, p. 206).

Since tourism demand is generally the product of a complex set of factors, simple linear regression models employing one explanatory variable are rarely successful and never valid for simulating the time series. Rather, the forecaster needs to consider carefully a range of variables that stimulates tourists to travel away from home, that attracts visitors, and that acts as barriers to tourism flows between origins and destinations.

Table 7.9   Characteristics of a sound forecasting model and their indicators

Characteristic	*Test indicators*
Is the model valid?	Expected signs of coefficients, lagged variables, dummy variables
Are explanatory variables uncorrelated with one another?	Examine intercorrelations for multicollinearity
Does the model accurately simulate its time series?	$\bar{R}^2$, F-statistic, MAPE
Are the $\bar{R}^2$ and F-statistic tests valid?	Durbin–Watson statistic; test for heteroscedasticity
Are any irrelevant variables included?	t-test
Are any relevant explanatory variables omitted?	Durbin–Watson statistic
Is the model stable?	Remove several of the last points in the time series, estimate the parameters again, and check for significant changes in parameters

As the discussion of building a multiple regression model of hotel/motel room demand in the Washington, D.C. area showed, it is sometimes difficult to derive a valid, significant, accurate forecasting model by this technique. Even a model that passes the myriad tests with flying colours can fail to make reasonable forecasts. Considerable experience with such models will aid you in knowing when you have a model that 'works' or not.

In some cases, you may need to review a model someone else has developed and its products. If so, you should look for the characteristics of sound regression models presented above to aid your assessment. These are summarized in Table 7.9.

In a thorough comparative study of various international tourism forecasting methods, Witt and Witt (1992) found that regression models (which they call 'econometrics') were less accurate than the naive method of assuming the next period's value equals the last period's in forecasting the level of tourism demand. They were, however, the most accurate among seven methods examined in forecasting changes in the direction of a series, i.e. whether next year's value would be higher or lower than this year's.

It appears the considerable time and expense required to build a valid regression model for forecasting tourism demand may not be justified on the basis of its accuracy in forecasting next year's values. However, such a model is indispensable if we want to understand what factors affect tourism demand and how. Indeed, Witt and Witt conclude

the main use of econometric [i.e. regression] models to a practitioner is with respect to the identification of the size of the effects that changes in the explanatory variables are likely to have upon tourism demand, and not as a direct forecasting tool (1992, p. 166).

In short, we may not expect a great deal of accuracy in forecasting levels from such models, but we should demand they perform well in predicting whether next year's value will be greater or less than this year's.

For further information

Calantone, Roger J., di Benedetto, C. Anthony and Bojanic, David (1987), 'A comprehensive review of the tourism forecasting literature', *Journal of Travel Research*, Vol. XXVI, No. 2, pp. 28–39.

Clifton, Peter, Nguyen, Hai and Nutt, Susan (1992), *Market Research: Using Forecasting in Business*, Butterworth-Heinemann, pp. 127–151.

Cunningham, Stephen (1991), *Data Analysis in Hotel & Catering Management*, Butterworth-Heinemann, Chapter 12.

Johnston, J. (1972), *Econometric Methods*, 2nd edition, McGraw-Hill Book Company, Chapters 2, 3, 5, 6 and 8.

Kennedy, Peter (1992), *A Guide to Econometrics*, 3rd edition, The MIT Press, xii + 410 pp.

Levenbach, Hans and Cleary, James P. (1981), *The Beginning Forecaster: The Forecasting Process through Data Analysis*, Lifetime Learning Publications, Chapters 12 to 17 and 20.

Makridakis, Spyros, Wheelwright, Steven C. and McGee, Victor E. (1983), *Forecasting: Methods and Applications*, 2nd edition, John Wiley & Sons, Chapters 5 and 6.

Moore, Thomas (1989), *Handbook of Business Forecasting*, Harper & Row, Chapters 5 to 7.

Pindyck, Robert S. and Rubinfeld, Daniel L. (1981), *Econometric Models and Economic Forecasts*, McGraw-Hill Book Company, Chapters 1 to 10.

Rao, Potluri and Miller, Roger LeRoy (1971), *Applied Econometrics*, Wadsworth Publishing Co., Chapters 1 to 3.

Saunders, John A., Sharp, John A. and Witt, Stephen F. (1987), *Practical Business Forecasting*, Gower Publishing Company, Chapters 5 and 6.

Schulmeister, Stephan (1979), *Tourism and the Business Cycle*, Austrian Institute for Economic Research, 141 pp.

Shim, Jae K., Siegel, Joel G. and Liew, C. J. (1994), *Strategic Business Forecasting*, Probus Publishing Company, Chapters 4 and 5.

Smeral, Egon (1994), 'Economic models', in *Tourism Marketing and Management Handbook*, second edition (Stephen F. Witt and Luiz Moutinho, eds), Prentice Hall, pp. 497–503.

Smith, Stephen L. J. (1989), *Tourism Analysis, A Handbook*, Longman Scientific & Technical, Chapter 5.

Witt, Stephen F. (1994), 'Econometric demand forecasting', in *Tourism Marketing and Management Handbook*, second edition (Stephen F. Witt and Luiz Moutinho, eds), Prentice Hall, pp. 516–520.

Witt, Stephen F. and Witt, Christine A. (1992), *Modeling and Forecasting Demand in Tourism*, Academic Press Ltd, vii + 195 pp.

Witt, Christine A. and Witt, Stephen F. (1994), 'Demand elasticities', in *Tourism Marketing and Management Handbook*, second edition (Stephen F. Witt and Luiz Moutinho, eds), Prentice Hall, pp. 521–529.

Witt, Stephen F. and Witt, Christine A. (1995), 'Forecasting tourism demand: A review of empirical research', *International Journal of Forecasting*, pp. 447–475.

Notes

[1] 'Econometric model' is also used by some to include both one equation models as well as multiple equation models (see Witt and Witt 1992, pp. 13–15). To avoid confusion, the term 'structural model', will be used herein to describe systems of regression equations that are linked together and attempt to represent salient causal relationships at work.

[2] Some statisticians object to this interpretation of the constant term in a regression equation. They argue that it represents the mean effect on the dependent variable of all of the excluded variables (Rao and Miller 1971, p. 6).

[3] Crouch (1992) maintains that demand for a tourism product may not always be inversely related to its price, nor does demand for a destination always rise with increasing incomes in its origin markets. However, there is no reason to assume that the normal economic relationships of price and income to demand do not hold here.

[4] This appears to be the most popular confidence internal in tourism demand forecasting models. It means that over a large number of samples, 95 per cent of them would contain the population mean within the confidence interval. This statement is the same as postulating a '5 per cent level of significance'. These statements are used interchangeably in this book (Pindyck and Rubinfeld 1981, pp. 36–37).

8 Causal methods – structural models

Recall the discussion in Chapter 7 that economic theory suggested that the following model might explain most of the variance in hotel/motel room-nights sold in Washington, D.C.:

$$\text{HRS} = a + b_1\text{RDPI} - b_2\text{ARR} - b_3\text{AF} - b_4\text{CAN} + b_5\text{PB} + b_6\text{PI} \quad (8.1)$$

where
$\quad$ HRS = hotel/motel room-nights sold
$\quad$ RDPI = real disposable personal income
$\quad$ ARR = average hotel/motel room rate
$\quad$ AF = airline fares
$\quad$ CAN = Canadian dollar cost of the U.S. dollar
$\quad$ PB = promotional budget for Washington, D.C.
$\quad$ PI = a presidential inauguration year

A multivariate regression was run to estimate the parameters (the intercept, a, and the slope coefficients, b_n). The parameters, then, quantify the relationship between the explanatory variable and the dependent variable. The nature of regression analysis assumes the relationship is all one way, that is, from the explanatory variables to the dependent variable. Moreover, it assumes minimum relationships among the explanatory variables. If we found high correlations among potential explanatory variables, we either transformed them or dropped them from consideration to guard against the deleterious effects of multicollinearity.

In short, the single multivariate regression equation assumes the only causality operating in the world is from each explanatory variable to the forecast variable. A little reflection suggests this may well do violence to reality.

For example, there may be a feedback mechanism operating from hotel/motel room-nights sold to average room rate. If demand for rooms is pushing against capacity thus raising the occupancy rate, this may well encourage hoteliers to raise room rates more rapidly than when occupancy rates are low, so that we might envision:

$$\text{ARR} = a_2 + c \times \text{HRS} \quad (8.2)$$

Moreover, the budget available for promoting Washington, D.C. is partially financed by hotels and motels in the area. A year's budget may be based on some proportion of the past year's hotel sales, so we could well have:

$$\text{PB}_t = a_3 + d\text{HRS}_{t-1} \tag{8.3}$$

There may also be relationships at work among the explanatory variables. Some have found the demand for air travel from U.S. carriers (AD) is closely related to the growth in the U.S. economy, as measured, say, by real disposable personal income (RDPI). And as air travel demand pushes against airline capacity, air fares (AF) rise more rapidly. This suggests:

$$\text{AD} = a_4 + e\text{RDPI} \tag{8.4}$$
$$\text{AF} = a_5 + f\text{AD} \tag{8.5}$$

Finally, years of presidential inaugurations (PI) may be associated with higher hotel/motel room rates, as follows:

$$\text{HRS} = a_6 + g\text{PI} \tag{8.6}$$
$$\text{ARR} = a^2 + h\text{HRS} \tag{8.2}$$

These feedback and cross-dependencies cannot be captured in a single equation multivariate regression model. Rather, economic forecasters have developed systems of interdependent equations to more faithfully represent the important relationships in the real world, and these are called **structural models** because they attempt to replicate the important structures of the economy and other elements of the real world.

In reviewing equations (8.1) to (8.6), it is clear that the terms 'dependent variable' and 'explanatory variable' have lost their distinctions. In some equations (8.1 and 8.6) hotel room-nights sold are the dependent variable, but in others (8.2 and 8.3) they are explanatory variables. Instead, forecasters make use of the terms **endogenous variable** and **exogenous variable** in a structural model.

Endogenous variables are all those determined within the structure. That is, they appear at least once on the left-hand side of an equation in a structural model, such as hotel room-night sales in equation (8.6) and average room rate in equation (8.2). Exogenous variables are determined outside the structure, by forces that do not appear within the structure. In this model, these include presidential inaugural years and the exchange rate between the Canadian dollar and the U.S. dollar. These never appear on the left-hand side of an equation as affected by another variable in the model.

How many endogenous variables and exogenous variables to include is up to the structural model builder. You will base this decision and that concerning the number of equations to include on theory and the availability of valid data.

Most structural models are composed of **simultaneous equation systems**. The distinctive characteristic of these systems is that all of the relationships involved are needed for determining the value of at least one of the endogenous variables. Correctly solving these systems to estimate valid parameters is at the heart of structural model estimation.

A tourism demand structural model

The following is an example of a structural model for forecasting hotel/ motel room sales.

$$\text{HRS}_t = a_1 + b_1\text{GDP}_t + b_2\text{ARR}_t + b_3\text{AF}_t + e_{1,t} \tag{8.8}$$

$$\text{GDP}_t = a_2 + c_1 C_t + c_2 I_t + c_3 G_t + e_{2,t} \tag{8.9}$$

$$C_t = a_3 + d_1\text{GDP}_{t-1} + e_{3,t} \tag{8.10}$$

$$\text{AF}_t = a_4 + f\frac{\text{RPM}_{t-1}}{\text{ASM}_{t-1}} + e_{4,t} \tag{8.11}$$

$$\text{RPM}_t = a_5 + g\text{GDP}_t + e_{5,t} \tag{8.12}$$

$$\text{ARR}_t = a_6 + h\frac{\text{TC}_{t-1}}{\text{HRS}_{t-1}} + e_{6,t} \tag{8.13}$$

where

$\quad$ HRS = hotel/motel room-nights sold
$\quad$ GDP = gross domestic product
$\quad$ ARR = average hotel room rate
$\quad\;$ AF = average airline fare
$\quad\;\;$ C = personal consumption expenditures
$\quad\;\;$ I = capital investment
$\quad\;\;$ G = net government purchases of goods and services
$\quad$ RPM = airline revenue passenger-miles
$\quad$ ASM = airline available seat-miles
$\quad$ TC = total hotel operating costs
$\quad\;\;$ e = residual
$\quad\;\;$ t = some time period

There are three types of equations that can appear in such models. First are those that describe the **behaviour** of consumers and other actors: equations (8.8), (8.10) and (8.12). Second are equations that describe **technical relationships,** such as production functions and price functions: equations (8.11) and (8.13). Third are **identity** equations, which are true by definition: equation (8.9) defines gross domestic product. It is not necessary to include

all of these three types in a structural model, but you shou.
might productively be included in each category.

Advantages and disadvantages

Structural models offer a number of advantages over single-equation
models:

- They more fully represent the interdependencies of variables in the real
  world.
- They allow detailed simulations, that is, forecasting the results of changes
  in certain exogenous variables for policy analysis.
- The process of building a structural model improves understanding of
  how the portion of the world we are interested in works.

There are, of course, limitations of structural models that the forecaster
should understand:

- They are far more complex and costly to build than single regression
  equation models.
- They require a great deal of input data.
- Multicollinearity is an even more serious problem than in multiple
  regression models.
- Omission of an important explanatory variable will result in great forecast
  error (called the 'specification problem').
- The ordinary least squares estimation procedures lead to biased and
  inconsistent estimates of parameters in these models and cannot be used.
- Random errors can become magnified by the structural relationships.
- There are no standard set of rules for building these models.
- They must be continually monitored and adjusted.

Since ordinary least squares regression produces biased estimates of
parameters in structural models, it is not used for such estimation. Rather,
one or a combination of the following methods are employed:

- two stage least squares, the most popular method
- indirect least squares
- full information maximum likelihood
- limited information maximum likelihood.

Discussion of these is beyond the practical orientation of this book, but the
interested reader is directed to the sources at the end of this chapter for
further information.

Given the challenges of constructing, operating and maintaining such models, it is not surprising that there now appear to be no such models for forecasting tourism demand. Rather, there are sets of independent equations for forecasting tourism demand from an origin for a number of different destinations, or for projecting visitor flows among countries. These employ a large number of multivariate regression equations, where the explanatory variables for each equation are drawn from a large set of possible variables.

The inherent complexity of developing structural models ensures they are not likely to appeal to any but large business organizations, government, and the occasional university. There are several consulting firms that have specialized in building large structural models of national economies. These can be queried should a manager seek to have a structural model of tourism demand developed.

The estimation process

Figure 8.1 outlines the steps in building and using a structural model.

There are two special problems associated with structural equation models that must be resolved in order to achieve valid models and reduce forecast error. The **specification problem** arises when one or more important variables are omitted from the model. This produces biased parameters in single equation regression models as well, but the error is magnified in a structural model because a number of equations are affected.

There is a requirement in structural models that there be one and only one equation for each endogenous variable included. If an endogenous variable does not have an equation explaining it, then it should be treated as exogenous. If there are more endogenous equations than endogenous variables, a result is errors of estimation and reduced significance of the parameters estimated.

The **identification problem** is a mathematical question associated with simultaneous equation systems. It is concerned with the possibility of obtaining meaningful estimates of the model's parameters, so it is an issue of validity.

One way to view this problem is to consider the forecasting of hotel room demand. The actual values we have in our time series reflect actual demand behaviour. However, they also reflect the realities of supply: the number of rooms purchased on a given day is the intersection of the demand curve and the supply curve. Unfortunately, we do not know which is dominating the outcomes we observe: hotel/motel room-nights sold. To resolve this, we must transform the structural equations so that no single equation can be mimicked by a linear combination all of the equations. For example, we

1. Detail your theory of what variables are important to explaining the course of your tourism demand variable and how they are related.
2. Designate the exogenous and endogenous variables.
3. Specify the expected relationships in mathematical form, including
   a. parameter signs
   b. parameter approximate magnitudes
   c. functional form, e.g. linear, log-linear
   d. leads and lags
4. Choose the estimation procedures, e.g. indirect least squares, two-stage least squares, etc.
5. Assemble relevant data.
6. Estimate the coefficients, which show the relationships between individual explanatory variables and the forecast variable.
7. Conduct statistical tests of the model to evaluate validity.
8. If satisfactory, use the model to forecast future values.
9. Monitor the residuals and make appropriate changes to improve the model's accuracy.

Figure 8.1 Structural model estimation process

might add a measure of consumer income to the demand equation but exclude it from the supply equation.

Applications

Jenkins and Frechtling (1991) experimented with an existing large-scale global structural model (the Fair World Model) to indicate how terrorist attacks against tourism targets, such as occurred in 1985–86, and rapid increases in the cost of petroleum would affect the travel of West German residents to ten major destination countries. The Fair World Model indicated the linkages between the consumer, government, business and financial sectors of West Germany and the ten other countries. These and the airline distances, along with dummy variables for the petroleum price inflation in 1973–74 and 1979–80, were correlated with the outbound tourism that West Germany generated to these countries. The estimation method was unusual in that it allowed elasticities to vary over time rather than remain constant as is assumed in most tourism demand regression models.

The authors generated baseline forecasts for West German travel to each of the ten countries, assuming no terrorist attacks and petroleum remaining at \$20 per barrel in 1989 prices. The 1985–86 terrorism was found to produce no measurable impact on German travel to Australia, Austria, France, Italy and Japan. With the price of oil doubling, and the presence of terrorism, West German travel was projected to drop by one-third to the UK and three-quarters to the U.S. Travel to Canada, Greece and Iceland dropped by percentages between these extremes.

Conclusion

Structural equation models have the advantage of explicitly reflecting the interdependencies among variables that exist in the real world. However, they are costly to build and difficult to build well. There appear to be no such models for estimating tourism demand today, and the above discussion suggests why. They require a great deal of resources in terms of time, money, expertise and input data.

However, this discussion should help you to evaluate structural models proposed by others.

For further information

Almon, Clopper (1989), *The Craft of Economic Modeling*, 2nd edition, Ginn Press, iv + 307 pp.

Granger, C. W. J. (1989), *Forecasting in Business and Economics*, 2nd edition, Academic Press, Chapter 5.

Holden, K., Peel, D. A. and Thompson, J. L. (1990), *Economic Forecasting: An Introduction*, Cambridge University Press, Chapter 5.

Jarrett, Jeffrey (1991), *Business Forecasting Methods*, second edition, Basil Blackwell Ltd, Chapter 6.

Kennedy, Peter (1992), *A Guide to Econometrics*, 3rd edition, The MIT Press, Cambridge, MA, Chapter 10.

Kmenta, Jan (1971), *Elements of Econometrics*, The Macmillan Company, Chapter 13.

Makridakis, Spyros, Wheelwright, Steven C. and McGee, Victor E. (1983), *Forecasting: Methods and Applications*, 2nd edition, John Wiley & Sons, Chapter 7.

Moore, Thomas W. (1989), *Handbook of Business Forecasting*, Harper & Row, pp. 222–231.

Pindyck, Robert S. and Rubinfeld, Daniel (1981), *Econometric Models & Forecasts*, 2nd edition, McGraw-Hill Book Company, Chapter 11.

Rao, Potluri and Miller, Roger LeRoy (1971), *Applied Econometrics*, Wadsworth Publishing Co., Chapter 8.

9 Qualitative forecasting methods

Chapters 4 through 8 have presented various quantitative techniques for forecasting tourism demand. These seek to state the relationship of the forecast value to its earlier values or to explanatory variables in numerical terms. We now turn to qualitative forecasting methods, also called 'judgemental methods' or 'subjective forecasting'.

Qualitative forecasting methods rely on the experience and the judgement of individuals assumed to be experts in the field under study. The expert, or 'judge', is the processor of information rather than the computer. Moreover, the qualitative forecaster is usually not trying to estimate a value for a given variable but to suggest the boundaries within which the future value will lie.

Specifically, we will look at four qualitative forecasting techniques in the context of tourism demand in this chapter:

1. jury of executive opinion
2. subjective probability assessment
3. Delphi method
4. consumer intentions survey.

All of the qualitative forecasting methods discussed here follow a simple four-step process, as shown in Figure 9.1. The methods differ in how the judges are selected, what information is provided along with the questions, the degree of interaction among judges, and how the judges' reports are processed to obtain the final forecasts. The first three methods follow the Biblical admonition that 'plans fail for lack of counsel, but with many advisers they succeed' (Proverbs 15:22, New International Version).

---

1. Select the judges
2. Pose the questions to the judges
3. Ask for answers
4. Obtain forecasts

Figure 9.1　Steps common to qualitative forecasting models

Occasions for qualitative methods

Qualitative forecasting methods are normally applied under one or more of the following conditions:

There are insufficient historical data. In some cases, we do not have enough past data for use in a quantitative model to produce valid forecasts. This is especially true in the case of a new product, such as a supersonic aircraft, a new luxury resort in a country that has none, or a new reservations technology for consumer use.

The time series available is not reliable or valid. We may have a long time series of data that is suspect as to quality and relevance to what we wish to measure. Measuring same-day visitors, or day-trippers, is difficult for a number of countries and the series they publish may not be accurate. Some countries, such as Austria, have no counts of total overnight visitors. The only available counts are of arrivals in registered accommodations. This may not be a sound measure of total visitor volume for modelling the future.

The macroenvironment is changing rapidly. The macroenvironment comprises external factors that are beyond the control of the tourism marketer but which affect demand. These include the economies of major source markets, exchange rates, political changes, weather, labour unrest, the spread of digital technologies, to name a few. It is difficult, for example, to imagine accurate quantitative model forecasts of visitor volume to Czechoslovakia, Yugoslavia and Russia for the post-1989 period, or tourism generated from these countries. Similarly, quantitative models would prove ineffective in forecasting travel to and from Hong Kong after it reverts to the People's Republic of China, and from a united Germany after reunification.

Major disturbances are expected. Whereas macroenvironmental changes may be slow to develop and last for years, disturbances are essentially unanticipated, short-term major changes in factors affecting tourism. These include wars, terrorism, political upheavals, and floods and other natural disasters. This condition appears to characterize tourism to and from most Middle Eastern countries at the current time, and several north African ones.

Long-term forecasts are desired. Reliable forecasts for periods three to five years or more in the future are difficult to generate from quantitative models. This is primarily due to the greater number of factors that may then affect visitor flows and to their greater variability in the long run. Yet sometimes tourism managers, planners and others need to understand the possible shapes of a distant future which qualitative techniques can provide.

Questions often asked about the long-term future of tourism demand include:

- what events may occur in the next ten years that could critically affect our product or markets?
- by what year will a new technology be widely used?
- what will our visitor volume be in ten years?

Advantages and disadvantages

Advantages of qualitative techniques are that they are usually inexpensive, they do not require a high level of statistical skill, and they often comprise the only methods of dealing with certain forecasting problems.

However, errors can arise due to the lack of expertise or bias of chosen judges, the human tendency to confuse desires for the future with forecasts of it, and judges' predisposition to be anchored in the present and underestimate future changes. Moreover, there is less restraint on the forecaster from asserting his or her own views in a qualitative forecast than a quantitative one.

Jury of executive opinion

One of the simplest and most widely used forecasting approaches is the jury of executive opinion. In its most basic form, the method comprises corporate executives or government officials meeting together and reaching consensus estimates of key variables in the future. The output is specific values or a range of values expected at specific points in the future.

An advantage of this technique is its simplicity. Very little skill or training is required to participate, and only knowledge about the variables to be forecast is required. It does not require much historical data, although describing the recent past may be helpful in establishing a common foundation for the discussion. The method serves to pool the experience and judgement of those most familiar with the variables to be forecast. Finally, it is eminently feasible without long historical series.

The disadvantages are several. Perhaps the most damaging is that often the most forceful or most senior executives' opinions carry the most weight in this group discussion. Yet these may not have the best ability to describe

1. Select the judges: people familiar with the variables you are forecasting, their recent history, and what affects them.
2. Pose the questions to the judges in a group setting where discussion is encouraged.
3. Ask for answers: record the various forecasts of point estimates from the group where all can see them.
4. Obtain forecasts: discuss the various forecasts until a consensus on point forecasts of the variables is reached.

Figure 9.2   The jury of executive opinion process

the most likely future. Related to this is the fact that this method disperses responsibility for developing accurate forecasts, with the result that the judges may not devote serious effort to the task. When a group is responsible, no one person can be held accountable for forecasting errors.

Another disadvantage is that the jury of executive opinion requires costly executive time. This cost may be hidden, but careful accounting may well show that other forecasting methods are cheaper and more accurate. Finally, this method does not necessarily produce detailed forecasts that are consistent with one another. For example, using this group consensus method to forecast arrivals in a hotel generated by various market segments (e.g. meetings and conventions, individual business travellers, group leisure travel and individual leisure travellers) may produce expected arrival volumes for certain months that are larger than the hotel's capacity.

Figure 9.2 summarizes the four-step process for the jury of executive opinion.

Research outside the tourism area has suggested that better forecasts are derived from structured meetings involving a facilitator who works for the group rather than a leader for whom the group works (Armstrong 1985, p. 121). The facilitator:

● prepares for the meeting by decomposing the problem into smaller topics
● encourages participation by all members of the group
● avoids expressing judgement and helps the group to do so as well
● avoids introducing his/her own ideas to the group.

Despite its limitations, the jury of executive opinion will remain a popular method for forecasting tourism demand for individual facilities, attractions and destinations due to its celerity and simplicity.

Applications of the jury of executive opinion

Moutinho and Witt (1995) chose the jury of executive opinion over the Delphi method to rank the importance and impact of 25 possible future developments in science and technology affecting tourism, the probability of the occurrence of each, and the most likely year of occurrence up to 2030. They felt it was important to permit discussion among the 25 experts to facilitate the exchange of ideas and allow for clarification of reasoning before the forecasts were made due 'to the rather innovative/radical nature' of these developments. They found among other things that mean probability of occurrence was inversely correlated with the mean year of expected occurrence.

Subjective probability assessment

The jury of executive opinion forecasting method usually produces point estimates of future variables as the most likely forecast, with perhaps a range on either side of possible values as well. In the subjective probability assessment method, the members of a group are each asked to suggest a probability distribution for the forecast variable. This is often easier for a judge to deal with than trying to specify a single future value.

To begin, we select the judges. These may be corporate executives, government officials, outside experts or some combination of these. In posing the questions, it is useful to include background information that helps to bring all judges up to the same level of knowledge.

The questions themselves should be straightforward and cover basic variables. You should avoid asking about aggregate variables that combine various levels of uncertainty. For example, instead of asking hotel executives to forecast total room-nights that will be sold in an area, you could break this down by market segment, e.g. meetings and conventions, individual business travellers, group leisure, etc. This takes advantage of the fact that some of the sub-variables may be known with more certainty than others.

The next step is to ask for answers. This should be done to elicit probability distributions from the judges. Figure 9.3 is an example of how to pose the questions and ask for responses.

You, as forecast manager, then process the returned reporting forms. If the number of judges reporting is 20 or more, you can show the distribution of the expected values reported by the judges. The expected value for an individual judge is simply the sum of the products of the values with their probabilities. For example, assume a judge using the reporting form in Figure 9.3 reported the following probabilities:

1. Room nights sold in 2000 (millions)	2. Probability of this outcome	3. Product of value and probability (2 ×
13	0%	0
14	0%	0
15	5%	0.75
16	35%	5.6
17	40%	6.8
18	20%	3.6
Total	100%	16.8
	(Should sum to 100%)	

The numbers in the third column are simply the product of the value in the first column and the probability in the second column. When the third column values are summed, we obtain the expected value for this particular judge. We can array all of the expected values reported in a distribution and determine the expected value (mean) of the distribution and its dispersion (standard deviation). These then serve as the group's best forecast value and its range.

If the number of judges is fewer than 20, then the distribution may not be a smooth one. You can still calculate the mean, but the standard deviation may not make much sense.

Figure 9.4 summarizes the process for the subjective probability assessment method.

Delphi method

The Delphi method is designed to produce a group consensus on forecasts while avoiding some of the problems of other group forecasting methods, such as the jury of executive opinion. These problems include:

- specious persuasion
- undue influence of 'recognized experts'
- unwillingness to abandon publicly expressed views
- the 'herd' or 'bandwagon' effect where individuals are reluctant to state views at odds with a developing consensus.

The following are historical statistics on hotel/motel room demand in the Washington, D.C. metropolitan area.

	Room-nights sold (millions)
1987	13.5
1988	14.2
1989	15.0
1990	14.8
1991	15.0
1992	15.6
1993	16.4
1994	16.4

Based on your best judgement, please assign probabilities to each of the possible values of total room demand in the Washington, D.C. metropolitan area in the year 2000. The probabilities for this measure must sum to 100%. No individual probability can be less than 0% or greater than 100%.

Room nights sold in 2000 (millions)	Probability of this outcome
13	_____ %
14	_____ %
15	_____ %
16	_____ %
17	_____ %
18	_____ %
Total	_____ %
	(Should sum to 100%)

When you have completed your form, please return it to the forecast manager. Thank you for your cooperation.

Figure 9.3 Form for gathering subjective probability assessments of hotel/motel room demand in 2000

1. Select the judges: people familiar with the variables you are forecasting, their recent history, and what affects them.
2. Pose the questions to the judges either individually or in a group where discussion is discouraged.
3. Ask for answers: the judges record their probability distributions on paper or computer and transmit these to the forecast manager.
4. Obtain forecasts: the forecast manager combines the forecasts into one probability distribution for each variable and presents the mean and standard deviation for each.

Figure 9.4   The subjective probability assessment process

Specifically, the Delphi method has three distinctive characteristics which set it apart from other judgemental techniques:

1. respondent anonymity – reducing unwanted group discussion effects
2. iteration and controlled feedback – the forecaster conducting the Delphi method transmits a summary of the emerging group consensus back to the judges, who are encouraged to reassess their prior responses and provide new ones based on this feedback over several iterations or 'rounds'
3. statistical group response – the group opinion is defined by certain statistics from the final round.

Since successful application of the Delphi method requires adherence to a relatively complex process, each of the four steps in qualitative forecasting applied to this method will be discussed in detail.

1. Select the judges

You should recognize from the beginning that the quality of Delphi forecasting depends heavily on the expertise of the judges and their willingness to remain involved over a substantial period of time. Panels of Delphi judges have numbered from a dozen to as many as 900. Some researchers believe that 15 to 20 members are the minimum panel size required (Yong, Keng and Leng 1989, p. 38).

Some researchers have found that the reliability of Delphi method results is directly related to the size of the group, but this has not been confirmed for tourism forecasting. Recruiting these judges may take a substantial amount of time, to ensure they have the qualifications and the judgement required for serious forecasting, and that enough of them make a firm commitment to participate to the end of the process. Studies have indicated that the Delphi method is more accurate than the jury of executive opinion, so the extra time involved may be more than compensated for.

You should make special efforts to recruit a panel of judges representing a wide range of tourism interests and experience. For example, it would be wise to include qualified managers, business researchers, academics, government officials, consultants and even business forecasters. If you are focusing on destination demand, then the judges should represent lodging, food service, transportation (both inbound/outbound and local), attractions, and other specific elements of the tourism industry at the destination.

A significant threat to the validity of the Delphi method is attrition. It is not uncommon for one-half of the panel to drop out over the course of the project. This raises serious issues as to the validity of the results, because the drop-outs may unbalance the panel in a significant way. Moreover, attrition makes interpretation of progress toward consensus more difficult: is the developing convergence due to true consensus or just the withdrawal of maverick judges? Investing time in informing judges of the time requirements of the study and securing their commitment to remain through to the end will pay handsome dividends in terms of study validity.

You should plan carefully for your Delphi study by laying out a schedule of contacts, response stimulation, processing and reporting of the results. You should tighten it as much as possible, allowing for a maximum of four rounds. The more you can shorten the Delphi process by quick processing and contacting judges with results, the less attrition you are likely to have. (Communicating over the Internet may dramatically reduce response times.) A four-round Delphi study, from beginning to end, should take no longer than six months.

2. Pose the questions to the judges

Three elements need to be considered in forming Delphi questions:

1. the probability that some event will occur
2. the date that it will occur
3. the magnitude of the event.

Delphi questions comprise some combination of these three elements. In our consideration of the future of hotel/motel room demand in the Washington, D.C. metropolitan area, we might ask for forecasts in one of the following three questions or 'event statements':

1. what is the probability that room-nights sold will reach 20 million annually by the year 2000?
2. in what year will room-nights sold reach 20 million?
3. what will the volume of room-nights sold in the year 2000 be?

You should clearly understand the nature of the forecasting problem you are trying to solve with the Delphi technique in order to choose one of these three event statements. For example, if a hotel developer wants to know if total market size will be large enough to make a profit in a hotel that would open in 2000, you as the forecast manager will choose the third question. In contrast, if a city convention and visitors bureau is concerned whether there will be enough room capacity to serve demand when it exceeds 20 million room-nights, you would pose event statement 2. Finally, if management is interested in the certainty among qualified experts that room demand will reach a certain level in the year 2000, you should pose question one.

Sometimes, the Delphi method is used to assess the timing of a range of factors that could affect tourism demand in the future. Here, you can ask each of the judges for a list of such factors, and the results will comprise event statements in the Delphi questionnaire.

It is important to phrase the questions clearly and unambiguously. It is wise to break complicated topics down into simple questions. It is even wiser to pretest the Delphi questionnaire by sending it to a sample of a dozen or so individuals and asking for their identification of ambiguous or confusing questions. You can then use this information to revise your language to promote understanding during the actual Delphi survey.

You may want to provide background information so that the judges have a common basis to start from. This background could, for example, include the recent history of the variables you wish to forecast. Make sure you enclose a postage-paid return address envelope, and include the return address on the questionnaire in case it and its envelope become separated.

3. Ask for answers

An important part of the Delphi process is the recording of judges' forecasts and the processing of these responses for re-submission to the panel. This process comprises a number of 'rounds', normally two to four in number, where responses are received, summarized, and sent back to the judges. During rounds subsequent to the first, judges are asked to reconsider their forecasts based on the emerging group consensus.

Figure 9.5 presents two sample questionnaires for a very simple Delphi survey of demand for hotel/motel rooms in the Washington, D.C. metropolitan area. (Normally a Delphi questionnaire will ask for responses to a number of event statements, not just one.) The first questionnaire differs from the others in that it presents the recent history of the forecast variable and asks only for the judge's initial forecast. The round 2 questionnaire reminds the judge of his/her initial forecast and summarizes the entire panel response through the median and the interquartile range. It is typical of the questionnaires to be used in successive rounds, as well.

Round 1

Name of respondent:_____

Thank you for agreeing to participate in this Delphi survey of future hotel/motel room demand in the Washington, D.C. area.

The following is the recent history of hotel/motel room demand in the Washington, D.C. metropolitan area:

	Room-nights sold
Year	*(millions)*
1990	14.79
1991	14.99
1992	15.60
1993	16.44
1994	16.36

Based on your knowledge of the hotel/motel business and tourism demand in this area, please record below your forecast of the volume of room-nights that will be sold in the year 2000. Please record at least one decimal point in your forecast.

Hotel/motel room-nights that will be sold in the year 2000: _____ million

Your response will be kept confidential and will not be reported outside of the research staff.

Please complete this form and return it as soon as possible in the envelope provided to Dr D. C. Frechtling, International Institute of Tourism Studies, The George Washington University, Washington, D.C. 20052, U.S.A.

Thank you for your help.

Figure 9.5 Delphi survey of hotel/motel room demand in the Washington, D.C. metropolitan area

---

Round 2

Name of respondent:_____

Some time ago you reported your forecast of the number of hotel/motel room-nights that will be sold in the Washington, D.C. area in the year 2000, as follows. Below this is the summary of the responses by the complete Delphi panel:

<u>20.95</u> million room-nights

Median (the mid-point in the range of all values reported)
= 19.45 million room-nights

Interquartile range (comprises the middle two quarters of the values reported) = 18.10–20.00 million room-nights

Based on this information, please record your forecast hotel/motel room demand in the Washington, D.C. area in the year 2000, below.

_____ million room-nights

If your forecast falls outside of the interquartile range reported above, please indicate your reasons for this high or low forecast value, below:

_____

_____

_____

Your response will be kept confidential and will not be reported to anyone outside of the immediate research staff.

Please complete this form and return it as soon as possible in the envelope provided to Dr D. C. Frechtling, International Institute of Tourism Studies, The George Washington University, Washington, D.C. 20052, U.S.A.

Thank you for your help.

Figure 9.5 *Continued*

Summarizing consensus: median or mean?

The median is one of three statistics often used to summarize a distribution of values by indicating the 'centre' or typical value of the distribution. It is computed by listing the values in the distribution in order of size (usually from lowest value to highest) and determining the middle value that divides this list into two equal parts. If there are an odd number of values in the distribution then the median is the middle of the order listing. If there are an even number of values, then the median is the mean of the two middle values.

Managers of tourism demand Delphi studies have variously used the mean and standard deviation, or the median and interquartile range, to summarize the group consensus. The original Delphi studies used the median, and it has three advantages over the mean as the summary of the panel.

First, it is not sensitive to extreme outliers that may be reported by the panel. For example, assume the mean reported by 20 Delphi judges is 20 million room-nights sold in 2000, with a range of 18 to 22 reported. If the 21st judge reports 30 million room-nights, then this value alone increases the mean to 20.5, or by 2.5 per cent. On the other hand, such a value generally will have little impact on the median, moving it only toward the next highest value reported above the original median.

A second advantage of the median is that it deals with ordinal values – those that can be ranked from lowest to highest but do not have the properties of either interval (e.g. years) or ratio (e.g. distance) data – in a valid way. Theoretically, the mean of an ordinal data set is meaningless because the intervals are arbitrary. While most forecast data you may wish to gather in a Delphi survey may be interval or ratio data, this is not always the case. For example, often the response 'never', is permitted when asking in what year the judge thinks an event will occur. 'Never' cannot be part of computing the mean year, but it is enlisted to compute the median: it takes the position just above the highest year reported.

Finally, there is a theoretical reason for preferring the median over the mean as the representative value of the distribution of responses. The sum of the absolute deviations around the median is smaller than for any other measure of the distribution's centre. Looking at this another way, the median is always closer to the actual value than 50 per cent of the responses given, and may well be closer than more than 50 per cent. The mean, on the other hand, may be farther away from the true value than two-thirds or more of the Delphi responses.

The standard deviation or the variance is the appropriate measure of a distribution's dispersion around the mean. The analogous measure of dispersion for the median is the **interquartile range**. It is the range for the middle 50 per cent of the values reported. In other words, it is the range of

1. Order the values reported from lowest to highest.
2. Count the values and add 1 to the count.
3. Divide this sum by 4 and round to nearest whole number: this is the number of steps or reported values in a quartile.
4. Beginning with the highest value, count the number of steps found in (3) toward the lowest value: this is the lower bound of the third quartile.
5. Beginning with the smallest value, count the number of steps in (3) toward the highest: this is the upper bound of the first quartile.
6. The interquartile range is the range of values between these two bounds.

Source: After Witte (1989), p. 68

Figure 9.6   Calculating the interquartile range

reported values when the highest one-quarter and the lowest one-quarter of these values have been eliminated from the distribution. Its centre is the median and, like the median, it is not very sensitive to extreme values.

Calculating the interquartile range is conceptually simple but computationally complex. Figure 9.6 presents a simple set of steps to compute this range for any set of data.

Reporting the median and interquartile range to Delphi judges in the second and successive round questionnaires gives each a summary of the panel's reports as to the typical value and how tightly the consensus is grouped around it. If a judge reports a value outside of the interquartile range, then ask him or her to provide a written reason for being outside of the consensus. Then report this reason anonymously to the Delphi judges during the next round so that each might consider it in re-evaluating his or her next forecast.

4. Obtain the forecast

An important decision in the Delphi method is how many rounds to conduct before settling on the group's forecasts. On the initial round, there will normally be a wide range of answers. Over successive rounds the distribution of responses will narrow toward convergence, and this convergence is expected to be a more accurate estimate of the variable sought than either an individual's response or the simple median of a number of responses. The most severe rule is to continue the process until there is no significant change in the median or the interquartile range from the penultimate round to the last one; a clear signal the panel will not move further towards consensus.

A somewhat less severe rule is to continue the process until the interquartile range becomes relatively narrow around the median, say no more than 10 per cent higher or lower than the median. This suggests consensus has been achieved.

Finally, the loosest guide to the number of rounds is to cut them off after three or four. There is no theoretical foundation for this rule but it does reflect monetary and time cost considerations. There is a natural decay in response rate as the process is extended. Achieving the consensus of five remaining judges after seven rounds is certainly less meaningful than accepting the consensus of twenty judges after three rounds.

When you report your results, be sure to include both the median and the interquartile range. The latter indicates the strength of the consensus, which may vary widely among the variables you are seeking to forecast.

Delphi advantages and disadvantages

Compared to other qualitative forecasting methods where groups are brought together to develop consensus, the Delphi method has the following advantages:

- it prevents specious persuasion, dominant individuals, and the 'herd' effect from biasing the consensus result
- redundant or irrelevant 'noise' is controlled by the forecast manager
- it presents the spread of opinion as well as consensus points
- it allows judges to consider the opinions of others without emotion
- it allows judges to re-consider their own forecasts in light of information on the group consensus and reasons for outliers
- the method has proved more accurate than jury of executive opinion and traditional group meetings.

Disadvantages include the following:

- Delphi results are extremely sensitive to
     a. level of judges' expertise
     b. clarity of the events and schedules presented
- it requires a substantial period of time from start to finish, potentially resulting in significant panel attrition
- the Delphi forecaster can exercise considerable influence over the panel results through the way he/she reports reasons for outliers
- it treats events as independent of one another
- it assumes each judge bases his or her forecast of outcomes on perspectives shared with other judges.

Applications of the Delphi method

Yong, Keng and Leng (1989) recruited 67 members for a Delphi panel on future factors affecting tourism in Singapore, and 23 judges agreed to participate. The study was concluded after three rounds, with 17 judges participating in the last round. Twenty-six event statements were assessed as to (a) the likelihood of occurrence, (b) the year of probable occurrence, and (c) the important of the event to tourism in Singapore. The major factors affecting tourism demand to the country included the People's Republic of China becoming a major tourism destination, technological advances lowering travel costs to Singapore, and tourism spending becoming a non-discretionary part of household budgets in developed countries.

Liu (1988) conducted a Delphi survey in 1984–5 among 42 tourism managers in Hawaii regarding the volume of visitor arrivals in the state in 2000 and the split between international and domestic visitors, Oahu island's share and the maximum accommodation capacity on the island in 2000. Seventeen judges returned completed second-round questionnaires, and it is unclear why the process was cut off at this point. The consensus was that visitor arrivals will total nine million by 2000, with an increase in the international visitors' share of the state total but a decline in total visitation to Oahu.

Kaynak and Macaulay (1984) reported on a Delphi study conducted among public officials, educators, tourism business operators and other business people with an interest in tourism in Nova Scotia, Canada. Questions regarding changes in society's values that may affect tourism development to 2000, structural changes in the tourism industry and their impact, and events that would impact tourism training were posed to 150 judges, and, after two rounds, 44 completed questionnaires were returned.

The authors reported means and standard deviations, but it is unclear how they concluded that maximum convergence of opinion was achieved after two rounds. Consensus included relatively little change in society's values by 2000, and a significant increase in bus tours to the province and in government involvement in tourism. The event statements with the greatest likelihood of occurrence and critical impact on Nova Scotia's tourism include more specialized educational programmes for hotel and restaurant managers, increased demand for part-time training programmes, and one-half of the world's cash transactions occurring through computerized systems.

Moeller and Shafer (1994) describe a Delphi study conducted in 1973–74 among 900 experts as to the social, managerial and technological events likely to shape the future of park and recreation management to 2000 and beyond. Four rounds were conducted, and the number of judges dropped to nearly 400. The forecasters summarized the judges' consensus as an 'optimistic future'.

Uysal and Crompton (1985, pp. 8–9) discuss some early applications of the Delphi method to forecast the occurrence of events that would affect tourism demand in the distant future.

The consumer intentions survey

The three qualitative methods used so far rely on the forecasts of experts as judges and the processing of these to achieve a consensus. An alternative in the tourism demand forecasting situation is to ask the source of the demand himself: that is, survey consumers as to whether they anticipate taking a trip over some short to medium term, say six months to a year. Asking the actual purchaser may provide advantages over the expert judges.

'Intentions' are statements that consumers make about their planned behaviour or about events they can control. Consumer intentions models assume there is a quantifiable relationship between intentions and actual behaviour in the future. Intentions data are most useful if they meet the following conditions.

The event is important. The more important the event, the more likely it is that intentions will provide good forecasts. Consumers are more likely to have reliable plans to take a two-week vacation trip than a weekend trip. They are more likely to follow through on a planned visit to another country than to a nearby city. An anticipated once-a-year vacation trip is more likely to occur than one among six or seven planned in a year's time.

Closely related to this is how far in the future the event is likely to occur. A visit to another continent a year from now may be known with more certainty than a weekend trip to visit friends in the next city in a month or two.

Responses can be obtained. Potential respondents must be identified and queried, and they must provide their intentions. The objective is to gather enough information from a portion of the entire population to generalize to that population. This is a classic sample survey project, and much has been written on this (e.g. World Tourism Organization 1995; Alreck and Settle 1985). There are three major types of errors that can render the intentions invalid as indicators of future behaviour:

- **sampling errors** create problems in generalizing from the sample to the population; these are estimated through applying statistical sampling theory and can be resolved through theory as well
- **non-response errors** create problems in generalizing from the respondents to the sample; these are resolved by achieving high response rates

- **response errors** create problems in generalizing from the response to the respondent; these are resolved by encouraging respondents to answer carefully constructed, practicable questions honestly and completely.

The respondent has a plan. In accessing tourism demand intentions, this includes asking whether the respondent has made lodging or transportation reservations. An even stronger plan is purchasing non-refundable airline tickets or travel packages which carry cancellation penalties. Intentions accompanied by such actions are more likely to be acted upon than those unaccompanied by any action.

The respondent can fulfil the plan. This is a major obstacle to accurate intentions on business-related trips. Management may mandate or terminate trips outside of the respondent's control. This is also problematic with family vacation travel as well. Little is known about the decision-making dynamics of these trips, and obtaining intentions from one adult may not accurately reflect the family's final behaviour.

The respondent reports correctly. In some cases, vacation trips are conspicuous consumption and the respondent may be trying to impress the interviewer or others with plans that may never be fulfilled. A guard against this is to qualify respondents as to the number of vacation trips they have taken over a previous period. Those who have not taken any such trips are less likely to follow through on plans to take a major one.

New information is unlikely to change the plan. This is another reason why it is so difficult to obtain reliable intentions of business trips. The announcement of an important meeting or problems with a customer or client that arise after the intentions have been stated will make them inaccurate. Ultimately, some information will affect many business and leisure travel plans: e.g. outbreak of war, transportation labour disruptions, petroleum shortages, airline fare wars.

Figure 9.7 outlines the consumer intentions survey process.

Applications of the consumer intentions survey to tourism

For several decades, the Conference Board in New York city has included a question about intentions to take a vacation trip in the next six months in its monthly Survey of Consumer Confidence and Buying Plans. This survey is conducted by mail among 5000 U.S. households drawn from a panel maintained by National Family Opinion, Inc., (NFO) of Columbus, Ohio, U.S.A. Each month, NFO draws a new sample of 5000 U.S. households from its database of householders who have agreed to participate in such surveys. Typically, about 3500 return completed questionnaires covering

---

1. Select the judges: define your population of consumers, design a plan for sampling a portion of them who are representative of the whole, select the sample.

2. Pose the questions to the judges in carefully worded questionnaires administered by mail, telephone, or in person.

3. Ask for answers: stimulate response through follow-up contacts and/ or incentives; receive the responses and process them.

4. Obtain forecasts: generalize from the sample responses as to the percentages of the population that will demand tourism services or absolute numbers of these; condition these with past experience on the relationship between intentions and actual behaviour.

Figure 9.7   The consumer intentions survey process

consumer appraisal of current business conditions, expected conditions, and plans to buy certain durable goods in the next six months.

Every other month beginning in 1978, the NFO panels have received questions on vacations intended in the next six months. Responses are tabulated in the following categories as a percentage of the adult U.S. population intending to take one or more vacation trips:

- destination
  - U.S.
  - foreign country
- means of travel
  - automobile
  - airplane
  - other

The Conference Board intentions survey achieves a response rate of about 70 per cent, and the respondent results are generalized to cover non-respondents as well. Research on non-response to tourism surveys has indicated that non-respondents tend heavily to be non-travellers. This suggests the percentages of the population intending to take a vacation derived from this survey may be biased upward to a significant extent.

Another problem with the Conference Board survey occurs in trying to apply step 4 of the process in Table 9.1. Since the vacation intentions sample is drawn from the NFO database of householders who have agreed to participate in such surveys, it is not a probability sample of the U.S. adult population.

Table 9.1 Relationship of Travelometer$_{sm}$ vacation intention interviews to season of intended travel

Month of interview	Season of intended travel	Months in season
January	Spring	March, April, May
April	Summer	June, July, August
July	Fall	September, October, November
October	Winter	December, January, February

Both of these drawbacks affect estimates of the absolute numbers of potential vacationers. However, they may not affect *changes* in these numbers. That is, this survey may be a good guide to trends or turning points in future vacation travel activity. This is discussed below.

The U.S. Travel Data Center of Washington, D.C. has conducted a monthly survey of U.S. tourism activity since 1979. Early each month, a new probability sample of 1500 households is selected and interviewed by telephone about their travel activities over the previous month.

Beginning in early 1992, the Travel Industry Association of America has employed this survey to develop the Travelometer$_{sm}$, a set of seasonal forecasts of travel activity away from home. In four months of the year, respondents who had taken at least one trip to a place 100 miles or more away from home are queried about their intentions to travel during the approaching season, according to the schedule in Table 9.1.

The pleasure travel results are reported for major demographic categories, purpose of trip, duration, expected participation in selected activities (e.g. visit a city, take a cruise), type of destination and planned spending. Business travel intentions are tabulated by demographic characteristics.

The Travelometer$_{sm}$ has the advantage over the Conference Board's survey of being based on the intentions expressed by a probability sample of the U.S. population. Moreover, it covers travel during a three-month period rather than the six months of the Conference Board. A final advantage is that the Travelometer$_{sm}$ can report the numbers of 'person-trips' potential vacationers plan to take. This is more useful to industry planners and marketers than the proportion of the population planning to take one or more vacation trips, the Conference Board approach. Moreover, these intentions forecasts can be directly compared to the number of vacation person-trips respondents to the National Travel Survey actually report, to assess the accuracy of the intention estimates.

A disadvantage is that the Travelometer$_{sm}$ is conducted only four times a year to the Conference Board's six. Moreover, past Travelometer$_{sm}$ reports do not report vacation person-trips intended consistently. In the 15 Travelometer$_{sm}$ reports beginning with summer 1992, vacation person-trips have been projected only five times.

Evaluation of tourism consumer intentions surveys

If the intentions forecasts were reported, we could evaluate the accuracy of the Travelometer$_{sm}$ by computing the MAPE from the National Travel Survey (NTS) estimates of actual vacation person-trips. For the five periods for which such estimates are available, the MAPE is 2.4 per cent. The seasonal naive model produces a MAPE of 2.2 per cent for the same group of periods. Consequently, it is not clear that the Travelometer$_{sm}$ provides any useful information about future vacation travel in terms of error magnitude accuracy. Given the lack of an unbroken time series of person-trip forecasts, it is not possible to evaluate the Travelometer$_{sm}$ on the directional change accuracy and trend change accuracy criteria discussed in Chapter 2.

On the other hand, with the help of the NTS monthly vacation person-trip series, the Conference Board vacation intentions series can be evaluated on all three forecasting accuracy criteria. The steps required are:

1. obtain a seasonally adjusted monthly series of NTS vacation person-trips
2. combine months into six-month blocks consistent with the Conference Board vacation intentions series; for example, the Conference Board estimate in February 1990 of the percentage of the population planning a vacation trip in the next six months should be associated with the six consecutive monthly NTS vacation person-trip estimates beginning in March 1990
3. transform the Conference Board percentage intention estimates into numbers of the population intending to take such a trip; this takes account of population growth over the time series period
4. regress the six-month NTS blocks on the Conference Board series as a regression forecast model
5. evaluate the regression model forecasts against the NTS six-month blocks on the three accuracy criteria.

This intentions regression model was significant at the 0.05 significance level according to the F-test, although the $\bar{R}^2$ is only 0.163, as is to be expected with univariate regression models of tourism demand. The coefficient of the vacation intentions variable is 1.613 and is significant at the 0.05 level. This suggests that the average number of vacation trips taken by each person with such intentions over the subsequent six months is 1.6.

The actual NTS estimates of U.S. vacation person-trips and the intentions model forecasts are shown in Figure 9.9. Table 9.2 summarizes the evaluation of this model on the three forecast measures of accuracy discussed in Chapter 2.

This vacation intentions model, based on the Conference Board's bi-monthly survey of the vacation intentions of a sample of the U.S. population, does not perform well on any of the three accuracy criteria. It

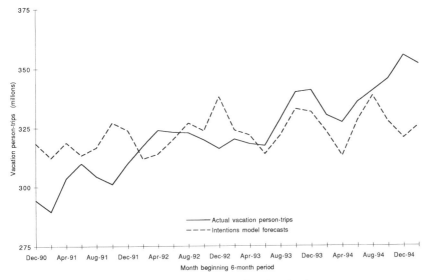

Source: U.S. Travel Data Center, The Conference Board and author

Figure 9.8   Actual and intentions model forecast U.S. vacation person-trips, six-month periods, 1990–95

Table 9.2   Comparison of forecasting accuracy measures for the vacation intentions model and the simple naive model

Measure of accuracy	*Measure*	*Intentions model*	*Simple naive model*
Error magnitude	MAPE	3.7%	1.7%
Directional change	Per cent forecast correctly	12/25 = 48%	50%*
Trend change	Per cent forecast correctly	3/8 = 38%	50%

* Since the simple naive model always forecasts no change, it will generate neither a correct nor an incorrenct forecast of direction so an alternative model must forecast directional change or trend change correctly more than 50 per cent of the time or we are better off accepting the naive model forecast of no change (see Witt and Witt 1992, pp. 125, 129) comes closest to the naive model in forecasting directional change. Overall, there is no reason to place much confidence in this particular intentions measure in forecasting future vacation travel demand on the basis of the NTS series. Perhaps other time series, validly representing actual pleasure travel activity, could be developed where the Conference Board measure would prove an accurate predictor.

In summary, surveying consumers about their future travel plans may appear to be a reasonable source of valid information about future tourism demand. However, the two efforts applied in the U.S. have not fulfilled this promise. This conclusion is based on admittedly sketchy data because that is all that has been available. Perhaps a consumer intentions survey that focuses on activities of value to tourism planners and marketers and that can be accompanied by a sound time series of actual behaviour will prove a fruitful source of tourism demand forecasts in the future.

Conclusion

Judgemental, i.e. qualitative, forecasting methods are appropriate, and often the only feasible alternative, when any one or more of the following conditions obtains:

- a valid time series of the variable being forecast is not available or is unacceptable
- a long-term (3 years or more) forecast is desired, or
- major disturbances in the future macroenvironment are likely.

In contrast to quantitative forecasting methods, qualitative methods use individual judges to organize information and present the futures. These judges may be experts on the tourism demand variable at hand, or consumers likely to generate the demand.

Armstrong (1985, pp. 147–149) provides a number of recommendations to improve the accuracy of judgmental forecasting methods. The following seem most applicable to forecasting tourism demand.

I. On selecting judges

    A. for expert opinion studies, do not use judges who have a personal stake in the situation being forecast

    B. use probability samples for consumer intentions surveys to select samples most representative of their populations

II. On posing questions

    A. word each question carefully so that all judges understand it in the same way and know how to answer it

    B. word the question in different ways in the same questionnaire when uncertainty is high, e.g. very long-range forecasting

    C. provide the minimum background information in an easy-to-understand format.

III. On obtaining the forecast

    A. consider potential judge–judge and researcher–judge interactions that could bias results, and implement ways of preventing this

    B. if group meetings must be held to obtain a forecast, structured meetings are more effective than unstructured ones, although participants prefer the latter.

IV. On assessing uncertainty

    A. ask judges to rate their own confidence in their predictions, although they tend to overestimate this

    B. groups in consensus tend to make riskier predictions than individuals.

V. Use combined forecasts of futures from different methods (e.g. subjective probability and Delphi) where uncertainty is high, using different methods

For further information

Alreck, Pamela L. and Settle, Robert B., *The Survey Research Handbook*, Richard D. Irwin Inc., xix + 429 pp.

Armstrong, J. Scott (1985), *Long-range Forecasting, from Crystal Ball to Computer*, 2nd edition, John Wiley & Sons, Chapter 6.

Calantone, Roger J., di Benedetto, C. Anthony and Bojanic, David (1987), 'A comprehensive review of the tourism forecasting literature', *Journal of Travel Research*, Vol. XXVI, No. 2 (fall), pp. 34–35.

Dalkey, Norman C. (1969), *The Delphi Method: An Experimental Study of Group Opinion*, The Rand Corporation, ix + 79 pp.

Jarrett, Jeffrey (1991), *Business Forecasting Methods*, 2nd edition, Basil Blackwell Ltd., Chapter 10.

Granger, C. W. J. (1989), *Forecasting in Business and Economics*, 2nd edition, Academic Press Inc., pp. 215–221, 153–157.

Makridakis, Spyros, Wheelwright, Steven C. and McGee, Victor E. (1983), *Forecasting: Methods and Applications*, 2nd edition, John Wiley & Sons, Chapter 13.

Moeller, George H. and Shafer, Elwood L. (1994), 'The Delphi technique: A tool for long-range travel and tourism planning', in *Travel, Tourism, and Hospitality Research, A Handbook for Managers and Researchers*, second edition, John Wiley & Sons, pp. 473–480.

Moore, Thomas W. (1989), *Handbook of Business Forecasting*, Harper & Row, Chapter 10.

Moutihno, Luiz and Witt, Stephen F. (1995), 'Forecasting the tourism environment using a consensus approach', *Journal of Travel Research*, Vol. XXXIII, pp. 46–50.

Saunders, John A., Sharp, John A. and Witt, Stephen F. (1987), *Practical Business Forecasting*, Gower Publishing Company, Chapter 10.

Shim, Jae K., Siegel, Joel G. and Liew, C. J. (1994), *Strategic Business Forecasting*, Probus Publishing Company, pp. 384–387.

Smith, Stephen L. J. (1989), *Tourism Analysis, A Handbook*, Longman Scientific & Technical, pp. 125-31.

Uysal, Muzaffer and Crompton, John L. (1985), 'An overview of approaches used to forecast tourism demand', *Journal of Travel Research*, Vol. XXIII, pp. 8–9.

10 Conclusion

Forecasting is essentially organizing information about the past in order to predict one or more futures. In this book, we are specifically interested in saying something intelligent about the future of tourism demand in order to reduce the risks of operating a tourism organization in that future.

In the previous chapters, we have discussed the reasons for undertaking tourism forecasting, how to approach such a forecasting project, how to evaluate forecasting models, and the application of thirteen different quantitative and qualitative methods of forecasting tourism demand. In this final chapter, we review the accumulated wisdom of those who have studied business forecasting, especially tourism demand forecasting. This advice may well save you time and money by indicating the most fruitful paths to follow, as well as blind alleys and false leads you need to know about in advance of your forecasting efforts.

However, first we present an essential topic for determining how well your preferred forecasting model is operating in actually predicting your measure of tourism demand as the future unfolds.

Monitoring your forecasts

Ideally, your tourism forecasting model, chosen after much blood, sweat, toil and tears in examining alternatives, testing validity, and checking accuracy, should produce forecasts over time that fluctuate narrowly around the actual time series. If this is so, then the cumulative sum of your forecast errors will tend toward zero as time goes by.

Occasionally, however, due to randomness in the forecasting error or the actual data, several positive (or several negative) errors may accumulate in a row, pushing the sum away from zero. It is helpful to have a rule for determining when this sum has strayed too far from reflecting random forecast errors, indicating that the model needs to be revised or a new model chosen.

Forecasters have developed a 'tracking signal' for this very purpose:

$$TS = \frac{\sum (A_t - F_t)}{\sum |A_t - F_t|/n} \tag{9.1}$$

where

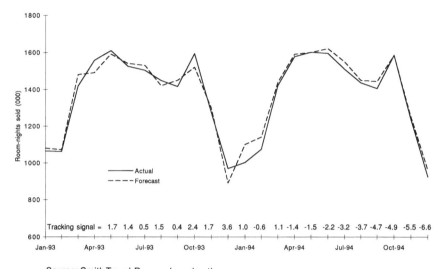

Source: Smith Travel Research and author

Figure 10.1 Tracking actual and forecast hotel/motel room demand in Washington, D.C., monthly, 1993–94

TS = tracking signal
A = actual value
F = forecast value
t = some time period
n = number of time periods

Ideally, the forecast values should fluctuate around the actual values. If so, the numerator of equation (10.1) will approximate zero. But if the forecasts tend to exceed or fall short of the actual series as time goes by, then the numerator will depart from zero. If the ratio of these cumulative errors to the cumulative mean absolute errors (the denominator of equation (10.1)) falls outside of the range of −4 to +4, this is the signal that your model is not tracking actual behaviour correctly. Forecasters prefer to use all data available, including those from backcasting, to compute this cumulative mean, not just the values from the beginning of the forecast period.

Consider Figure 10.1, where a forecaster has developed a model to forecast monthly hotel/motel room demand in the Washington, D.C. area for 1994. The forecast model values do not track the actual series perfectly through 1993, but fluctuate around them. This is consistent with a random pattern of errors, suggesting the forecast model is adequate to its task.

However, as 1994 unfolds, the errors tend toward the negative as the forecast values uniformly exceed the actual series. The tracking signals are shown at the bottom of the chart, associated with their months. Reflecting this path, they begin to decline in April 1994. By September, they have exceeded the lower bound of our tracking range of −4. At this point, we need either to re-estimate the parameters of this model or go through the model selection process again as described in Chapter 3.

Through experience and management's preference, you can adjust the tracking signal threshold. For example, if your data are very well behaved and management places a premium on accuracy, you might set the threshold at between −3.0 and +3.0. On the other hand, if you have difficulty fitting a good forecasting model to your time series, you may want to set the threshold at −5.0 to +5.0.

What we have learned about tourism demand forecasting

Serious tourism demand forecasting spans nearly three decades. Over this period, the published experiences of many forecasters give rise to a number of generalizations about forecasting this demand. The following are provided as signposts for the tourism forecaster, to help you avoid dead ends, traps and pitfalls that waste time and money.

As with any generalization, you will encounter exceptions to one or more of the following. But they are a fruitful place to start.

Note that most of them deal with quantitative forecasting. By their idiosyncratic nature, qualitative forecasting methods do not give rise to many generalizations.

Every tourism demand time series has a personality. Some grow strongly year after year while others are flat or even in decline. Some show seasonality that varies from year to year while others display a regular pattern that changes little. Some appear to follow linear paths while others follow curves or even waves over time. Some fluctuate wildly while others show mild increases and decreases. It is the forecaster's challenge to tease out these patterns from a time series for replication in a forecasting model.

No one method works best for all. Related to the previous finding, there is no one forecasting method that works best for all measures of tourism demand. Even in the limited arena of international tourism flows, no one model stands out as the most reliable. There is evidence, however, that simple extrapolative models, such as exponential smoothing, produce more accurate forecasts than complex regression models.

No one method is best in minimizing all three types of forecasting error. For a given tourism demand series, it is quite unlikely you will find a single model that will be the most accurate predictor of magnitude, direction and trend. Rather, it appears that regression models are somewhat more accurate on forecasting direction and trend while extrapolative models work better on reducing forecast error. But this is not a firm finding across time series.

Parsimony rules in tourism demand forecasting. A number of tourism forecasters have noted that complex forecasting models are seldom more accurate in predicting the future than simple ones. (This appears to be true in most business forecasting situations: Makridakis 1990, p. 65.) This is especially true of the short to medium term (up to three years). The seasonal patterns and momentum found in most tourism demand series can be expected to continue, unless large shocks (energy crises, wars, economic recessions, etc.) occur. The latter are unlikely in the short to medium term.

Visitor volume is easier to forecast than expenditures. Methods of measuring international and domestic tourism are more accurate in counting people than their expenditures. The latter are usually developed through visitor surveys, records of financial institutions, tourism industry records, or some combination of these. This idiosyncratic approach prevents generation of valid and consistent data series for visitor expenditures, and forecasting models applied to them fall prey to these measurement irregularities.

International tourism demand series tend to be more valid than domestic ones. Validity is the art of measuring precisely what you intend to measure. International visitor counts tend to be more valid than domestic visitor estimates, because the former cross international borders. Even though border formalities are declining throughout the world in the name of facilitating visitor flows, the physical international boundaries remain and at a minimum serve as points to count visitors. There are normally no such boundaries within most of the world's nations where domestic travellers can be observed and surveyed.

Domestic tourism demand is easier to forecast than international. While international tourism demand series more accurately reflect visitor flows among countries, they are more difficult to forecast accurately. This is because in addition to all of the factors that influence domestic travel away from home, international travel is also affected by exchange rates, changing government policies toward international tourism, bilateral treaties covering air transportation and other activities affecting tourism, and political upheavals such as war, insurrections, and terrorism.

Whenever possible, disaggregate your demand series. An aggregate tourism demand series may include several components with homogeneous behaviour. The most evident are leisure travel and travel for business purposes. Different motives mean different trends in extrapolative models, and different explanatory variables in causal ones. However, avoid disaggregating too finely, because very small series may be volatile due to their measurement processes rather than the behaviour they attempt to represent.

Consumer price indexes appear to be good proxies for the cost of travelling within a country. A good deal of experimentation with consumer price indexes versus indexes specifically designed to track the prices that visitors pay has indicated that the former is just as good as the latter in forecasting visitor flows. Since the former are available for nearly all countries, the rule of parsimony requires they be used in demand models. However, the costs of transport among countries should be considered separately from in-country prices.

Exchange rates do not represent travel costs well. Exchange rates have been found to indicate poorly trends in international transport costs or in-country visitor-related prices. However, they are quite visible to the traveller and should be considered carefully for inclusion in causal models.

Relationships can change dramatically in causal models in the long-run. The coefficients that indicate the relationship of each explanatory variable to a measure of tourism demand should not be considered fixed in the long run. Major shocks, such as petroleum shortages, wars, terrorism and natural disasters can change their values. But minor shocks operate on them as well. These include changes in political structures, increased capacity in infrastructure and superstructure, dramatic marketing programmes, and reduced restraints on international trade, to name a few. In tourism, the long run appears to be about three years or more, arguing for the application of qualitative forecasting models to signal the shapes of these futures.

Use qualitative models to forecast events that can be verified. Like all other approaches, qualitative forecasting methods should be continually evaluated as to their accuracy in suggesting the shapes of the future. If the events they predict are too vague to be observed, such as 'visitor flows from Canada will increase substantially', such assessment is prevented. A good rule in phrasing an event statement is to clearly define the future situation that would correspond to the event's non-occurrence.

Seasonality is an ally in tourism model building. Tourism demand in many areas is extremely sensitive to the passing of months, seasons and quarters, and this sensitivity appears to be quite regular. By first describing seasonal patterns accurately, you remove a good bit of the volatility of sub-annual series. This enables you to concentrate on simulating the non-seasonal series, a less daunting challenge.

Look for convergent validity. You can be much more confident in your forecasts if you have two or more models converging on a prediction than if you have only one. Compare the results of several models, looking for corroboration among them and with informed judgement. Combining quantitative and qualitative forecasting methods is an especially effective way of achieving convergent validity.

Doing sound forecasting

Each of the 13 tourism demand forecasting methods discussed in this book are accompanied by a set of rules for applying them. These serve several essential purposes:

- they distinguish one method from another
- they embody important theories, reasoning and common sense
- they have proved superior to alternative rules in producing sound forecasts in practice
- they allow the valid comparisons of results across various studies that help build a body of knowledge about a phenomenon such as tourism demand.

When a researcher ignores or intentionally violates the rules of a forecasting method, he or she cannot:

- claim to have applied the method
- claim to have incorporated the theories inherent in that method in his or her forecasting model
- avoid the implicit declaration that his or her judgement supersedes the accumulated experience of other forecasters
- confirm or deny the conclusions of other forecasters who have rightly applied the method.

In short, the rules of a method are its discipline applied to data about the past of a phenomenon. In the absence of such discipline, sloppy forecasts and ignorance reign.

Using forecasts wisely

Reviewing the process applied in a given forecasting method, that is, the sequential steps followed, is the best technique for evaluating forecasts prepared by others. Test a forecast study, in its assumptions, method and results, by examining its underlying rationality embodied in its process. In order to do this fruitfully you need to:

- determine the nature of the time series or other past information used
- understand the assumptions on which the model is based
- review the process applied
- test the results for statistical significance and/or reasonableness.

This frequently means that you must request information additional to what is usually published on a forecasting study. For some reason, forecasters seldom detail all of the process they employed when writing up the results. But without this, you cannot validly assess the validity of a forecasting model or the accuracy of its future forecasts.

A final word

It is wise never to underestimate the role that judgement plays in successful tourism demand forecasting. Initially, you use judgement to select the demand series to forecast and the range of methods to apply in doing so. If using a causal model, you choose carefully which explanatory variables to include and the valid measures of these. Moreover, you must decide on the form or structure of your causal model, using sound judgement. Then, you must assess the quality of alternative models to choose the most effective one for your purposes. Finally, monitoring your model over time requires judgement as to when to estimate new parameters or test a new set of models.

When applying a qualitative forecasting technique, judgement plays a more critical role. You must carefully choose the judges and select from among alternative ways of phrasing the questions or event statements. Finally, you employ judgement in deciding when a consensus is reached and its shape.

The point is, tourism demand forecasting is as much an art as it is a science. As you become familiar with the series you are forecasting, or are reviewing from someone else's forecasts, you gain insights into what makes it tick. This knowledge is invaluable to you and the managers who use your forecasts. Never rely strictly on a mechanical process to produce tourism forecasts. For, like the activity itself, tourism demand forecasting is a diverse, dynamic, changeable process that rewards the quick and observant but leaves the careless and inattentive behind.

For further information

Choy, Dexter J. L. (1984b), 'Forecasting tourism revisited', *Tourism Management*, Vol. 5, No. 3 (September), pp. 171–176.

Crouch, Geoffrey I. (1994a), 'The study of international tourism demand: A survey of practice', *Journal of Travel Research*, Vol. xxii, No. 4 (spring), pp. 41–57.

Faulkner, Bill and Valerio, Peter (1995),), 'An integrative approach to tourism demand forecasting', *Tourism Management*, Vol. 16, No. 1 (February), pp. 29–37.

Gardner, Everette S., Jr. (1992), 'How to monitor your forecasts', *Lotus*, April, pp. 54–57.

Shim, Jae K., Siegel, Joel G. and Liew, C. J. (1994), *Strategic Business Forecasting*, Probus Publishing Company, pp. 152–153.

van Doorn, Jozef W. M. (1984), 'Can futures research contribute to tourism policies', *Tourism Management*, Vol. 3, No. 3 (September), pp. 24–39.

Witt, Stephen F. and Witt, Christine A. (1992), *Modeling and Forecasting Demand in Tourism*, Academic Press Ltd, vii + 195 pp.

Appendix 1

Hotel/motel room demand in the Washington, D.C., metropolitan area, 1987–94

Month-year	Room-nights sold	Month-year	Room-nights sold	Month-year	Room-nights sold
Jan-87	786 152	Jan-89	974 188	Jan-91	885 370
Feb-87	887 466	Feb-89	955 943	Feb-91	971 191
Mar-87	1 179 318	Mar-89	1 269 982	Mar-91	1 282 507
Apr-87	1 279 396	Apr-89	1 455 327	Apr-91	1 440 099
May-87	1 317 952	May-89	1 463 003	May-91	1 475 659
Jun-87	1 277 096	Jun-89	1 411 940	Jun-91	1 456 850
Jul-87	1 239 127	Jul-89	1 348 487	Jul-91	1 362 356
Aug-87	1 170 964	Aug-89	1 307 840	Aug-91	1 309 305
Sep-87	1 177 436	Sep-89	1 289 197	Sep-91	1 302 742
Oct-87	1 349 938	Oct-89	1 458 479	Oct-91	1 466 332
Nov-87	1 054 226	Nov-89	1 159 213	Nov-91	1 181 893
Dec-87	813 315	Dec-89	869 957	Dec-91	854 615
Jan-88	839 670	Jan-90	903 905	Jan-92	959 456
Feb-88	886 806	Feb-90	974 746	Feb-92	1 059 044
Mar-88	1 220 361	Mar-90	1 317 009	Mar-92	1 321 280
Apr-88	1 376 184	Apr-90	1 414 099	Apr-92	1 468 333
May-88	1 408 277	May-90	1 484 942	May-92	1 561 624
Jun-88	1 361 691	Jun-90	1 421 063	Jun-92	1 425 970
Jul-88	1 262 819	Jul-90	1 342 884	Jul-92	1 442 066
Aug-88	1 267 118	Aug-90	1 301 696	Aug-92	1 444 047
Sep-88	1 225 871	Sep-90	1 261 578	Sep-92	1 380 209
Oct-88	1 405 643	Oct-90	1 388 512	Oct-92	1 473 327
Nov-88	1 125 935	Nov-90	1 113 859	Nov-92	1 146 961
Dec-88	863 217	Dec-90	869 067	Dec-92	920 010

Month-year	Room-nights sold	Month-year	Room-nights sold	Month-year	Room-nights sold
Jan-93	1 063 319	Jan-94	1 001 666		
Feb-93	1 061 060	Feb-94	1 073 196		
Mar-93	1 417 406	Mar-94	1 421 423		
Apr-93	1 556 240	Apr-94	1 577 321		
May-93	1 608 882	May-94	1 600 991		
Jun-93	1 524 063	Jun-94	1 594 481		
Jul-93	1 503 225	Jul-94	1 510 052		
Aug-93	1 448 443	Aug-94	1 436 164		
Sep-93	1 416 191	Sep-94	1 404 978		
Oct-93	1 593 538	Oct-94	1 585 409		
Nov-93	1 274 462	Nov-94	1 234 848		
Dec-93	969 445	Dec-94	923 115		

Source: Smith Travel Research, 105 Music Village Blvd, Hendersonville, TN 37075 U.S.A. Telephone 615-824-8664. Used with permission.

Appendix 2

Dealing with super-annual events

Seasonality refers to recurring patterns of demand within a year, a common feature of tourism demand series. Sometimes, however, an event occurs periodically over a period of years that affects tourism demand related to a destination. For example, the U.S. presidential inauguration occurs in Washington, D.C. in January of the year following every year evenly divisible by 4. This boosts the demand for hotel and motel rooms in and around the city to capacity levels for a week to ten days.

You may have to deal with a similar periodic super-annual event in forecasting demand to a destination. It poses two problems for the forecaster:

1. it inflates somewhat the value of the seasonal factor for the month in which it occurs and deflates somewhat the values for the other months
2. your forecasting model will underestimate this month's value in any future year in which the event takes place.

Figure A.2.1 helps us deal with the bias in number 1 for the hotel/motel room demand series for Washington, D.C. The solid line makes it clear that the inaugural festivities in 1989 and 1993 boosted January room-nights considerably above the more typical January. How do we keep this recurring bulge from affecting the seasonal factors for the more typical Januarys?

One option is to determine the long-term trend of January room demand and use the resulting trend values for 1989 and 1993 in computing the seasonal factors. A popular representation of this trend is the linear time trend regression model, discussed in the context of regression analysis in Chapter 7. This causal model employs the years as the explanatory variable and room demand as the dependent or forecast variable to develop a straight line that has the virtue of minimizing a measure of the distances from it to the actual values.

The linear time trend for the eight years for which we have annual hotel/ motel room demand data is shown as the line with the long dashes in Figure

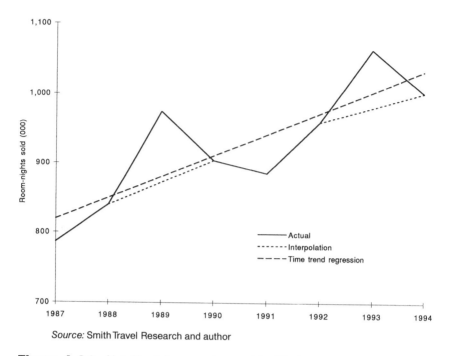

Figure A.2.1   Hotel/motel room demand in Washington, D.C. in January, 1987–94

A.2.1. It clearly shows that the Januarys of 1989 and 1993 lie significantly above the trend for all Januarys. We could compute the additional boost that presidential inaugurations give to January room demand as the distance from the trend line to the actual value for the two years.

This boost will be understated because of the logic of the time trend model. It minimizes the squared differences between it and the actual time series. As a result, it responds to the high values in 1989 and 1994 by moving upward closer to these values. In so doing, it underestimates the bonus associated with the inaugural Januarys and still biases the seasonal factor for the month upward.

A better solution to separate out the impact of the inaugural festivities on certain Januarys is to estimate what their values would be in their absence by interpolation. The interpolated value for January 1989 hotel/motel room demand is the average of the actual values for the years immediately prior and subsequent to it, 1988 and 1990. The interpolated value for January 1993 is similarly computed. Both of these are represented by the short dashed lines in Figure A.2.1.

These estimates have the virtue of being unaffected by the size of the inaugural boost and being anchored by two actual values. Both of the

Table A.2.1   Comparison of actual and interpolated values for January room demand in Washington, D.C. affected by presidential inaugurations (thousands of room-nights sold)

	January 1989	*January 1993*
Actual value	974	1063
Interpolated value	872	981
Actual value compared to interpolated value		
Absolute difference	102	83
Percentage difference	12%	8.4%

interpolations follow an upward trend as the time trend regression model does, but are positioned somewhat lower.

The interpolated values shown in Table A.2.1 are substituted for their actual values in computing the seasonal adjustment factors for the Washington, D.C. hotel/motel room demand time series. These cause the seasonal factors for January to be reduced somewhat, and the factors for the other months each to increase a little. Figure A.2.2 compares the two sets of seasonal factors.

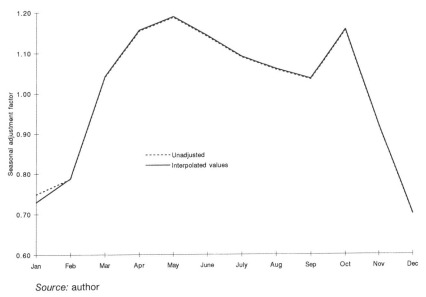

Source: author

Figure A.2.2   Comparison of unadjusted and adjusted seasonal factors for Washington, D.C. room demand

The differences between the two series are negligible except for January. However, the seasonal factors resulting from the interpolated values should improve the decomposition forecasting model for the non-inaugural Januarys. The forecasts for inaugural Januarys (1997, 2001, etc.) will need to be adjusted for the boost to room demand that the festivities give (problem 2 noted above). This can be done by applying either a percentage increase from Table A.2.1 or an absolute increase. We might average the values in Table A.2.1 or pick a value within their ranges.

In summary, this discussion suggests how to deal with special events that affect tourism demand and recur over periods of years in forecasting that demand. The above method deals with biased seasonal adjustment factors and inaccurate monthly or quarterly forecasts resulting from such events. It can be applied whether the event occurs in a regular pattern, or varies by number of years when it occurs. It is designed to improve forecasts of tourism demand for the periods affected.

Appendix 3

Splicing a forecast to a time series

Consider Figure A.3.1, which utilizes the linear time trend model shown in Figure 7.1 to produce forecasts of annual demand for hotel/motel room-nights in the Washington, D.C. area for 1995, 1996 and 1997. (This is not the best model for forecasting annual room demand but is used here simply for explanatory purposes.) This model comprises the equation:

$$RD_t = -764.4 + 0.3916 \cdot Y_t \qquad \text{(A.3.1)}$$

where

    RD = hotel/motel room-nights sold (millions)
    t = some time period
    Y = a year

Entering the years 1994 through 1997 in this equation produces the forecasts shown in Table A.3.1.

If the forecast for 1995 is simply spliced onto the actual time series, the change from 1994 to 1995 appears as 2.9 per cent or more than 500 000 room-nights, yet the forecast model reckons this at 2.4 per cent, or fewer than 300 000 room-nights. This is because the model produces a value for 1994 that is 0.5 per cent (89 000) higher than the actual value.

There are two methods commonly used to splice the first forecast value onto the last actual value in such situations. The 'per cent change' method takes the annual per cent changes from the forecast model and applies these to the actual time series. In our example, the 2.4 per cent increase for the time trend forecast series from 1994 to 1995 shown in the fourth column of Table A.3.1. is added to the actual value for 1994 to obtain 16.75 million room-nights as the forecast for 1995. For the next year, the per cent change in the time trend forecast model is 2.3 per cent (again from column 4), and this is added to our 16.75 million forecast for 1995 to obtain a 1996 forecast of 17.13 million room-nights.

While this is a simple approach with some intuitive appeal, it has a major drawback. As evident in Figure A.3.1, this forecast never reaches the values forecast by our time trend model. Rather, it is always about 0.5 per cent

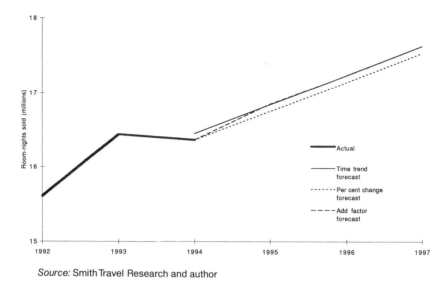

Source: Smith Travel Research and author

Figure A.3.1 Alternative forecasts of hotel/motel room demand for Washington, D.C., annually, 1995–97

Table A.3.1 Hotel/motel room demand in the Washington, D.C. area, actual and forecast, annually, 1994–97

1. Year	2. Actual value (millions)	3. Time trend forecast value (millions)	4. Forecast change from previous year (per cent)
1994	16.36	16.45	2.4
1995	NA	16.84	2.4
1996	NA	17.23	2.3
1997	NA	17.63	2.3

NA = not available

below the forecast line. For another forecasting model, this difference could be considerably greater. By adopting this method, we abandon the values our preferred model predicts for the future.

There is a second technique that both links the last actual value to our model's forecast values and reaches our model's forecast series. Called the 'addfactor method', it is based on the Durbin–Watson statistic, which we observed earlier in Chapter 7, and indicates the degree of autocorrelation among the residuals in our regression equation.

To begin the addfactor method of adjusting our forecast values, we compute a factor represented by the Greek letter rho, or ρ:

$$\rho = 1 - \frac{DW}{2} \qquad (A.3.2)$$

where

ρ = rho factor
DW = Durbin–Watson statistic

The next step is to compute the addfactor that will be applied to our first forecast value after the last actual data point:

$$AF_{f+1} = \rho \cdot (A_f - F_f) \qquad (A.3.3)$$

where

AF = addfactor
ρ = rho factor
A = actual value
F = forecast value
f = time period of the last actual value

This addfactor is added to the first forecast value after the last actual data point $(f + 1)$ to obtain the revised forecast:

$$RF_{f+1} = F_{f+1} + AF_{f+1} \qquad (A.3.4)$$

where

RF = revised forecast value
F = forecast value
AF = addfactor
f = time period of the last actual value

The revised forecast for the second period after the last actual data point $(f + 2)$ is produced by adding the product of rho times the previous period's addfactor to the forecast value for period $f + 2$:

$$RF_{f+2} = F_{f+2} + (\rho \cdot AF_{f+1}) \qquad (A.3.5)$$

where

RF = revised forecast value
F = forecast value
ρ = rho factor
AF = addfactor
f = time period of the last actual value

If the value for RF_{f+2} is not sufficiently different from zero, you have reached the forecast line and need apply no more adjustments. If RF_{f+2} is sufficiently different from zero, then apply equation (A.3.5) again for period $f + 3$. Continue this until RF_{f+2} approximates zero for the number of significant digits you are working with.

Table A.3.2 illustrates the computational process embodied in equations (A.3.2) to (A.3.5) using the linear time trend model shown in Figure A.3.1, which produces a Durbin–Watson statistic of 2.21.

Table A.3.2   Process for splicing hotel/motel room demand forecasts for the Washington, D.C. area to the actual time series

Step	Computation
1. Compute the rho factor through equation (A.3.2)	$\rho = 1 - (2.21/2) = -0.105$
2. Compute the addfactor by multiplying the rho factor by the error for the last actual value in the time series (from Table 6.A.1) through equation (A.3.3)	$AF_{f+1} = 0.105 \cdot (16.36 - 16.45)$ $= -0.00945$
3. Add the addfactor to the first forecast value after the last actual value (from Table 6.A.1) through equation (A.3.4)	$RF_{f+1} = 16.84 - 0.00945 = 16.83$
4. Compute the addfactor for the next period after the last actual value $(f + 2)$ through equation (A.3.5)	$AF_{f+1} = 0.105 \cdot -0.00945 = 0.000992$
5. If this addfactor is sufficiently different from zero, then add it to the forecast value for period $f + 2$	The addfactor 0.000992 approximates zero and will not change our forecast, so we do not complete this step or go to the next one

In this case, we have reached the forecast line during the first forecast year and future forecasts can be taken directly from our model. In other cases, you may not reach the forecast line for three or four periods.

In conclusion, as Figure A.3.1 indicates, the addfactor procedure develops transition values that smooth the path between the last actual value of the time series and the values forecast by the model. It avoids both simply jumping up to the forecast line for the first future year and trending up at the same rate as the forecast model but never reaching its values.

For further information

Moore, Thomas W. (1989), *Handbook of Business Forecasting*, Harper & Row Publishers, pp. 209–218.

Glossary

Note: terms defined in this glossary are indicated by **bold type**. 'WTO' refers to definitions established by the United Nations and the World Tourism Organization.

Accuracy – the degree of conformity of a forecast to the actual event being forecast, i.e. the correctness of a forecast; for **quantitative forecasting methods**, this is measured by the **MAPE**, among other measures.

ARIMA – the **time series forecasting method** that adds differencing a time series to the **ARMA** method.

ARMA – 'autoregressive moving average' method combines the **autoregressive model** and the **moving average model**; used in the **Box–Jenkins approach**.

Autocorrelation – refers to correlation that may occur between adjacent values of **residual** or **error** terms after the application of a **forecasting method**.

Autoregressive model – a **regression** model where the forecast variable is related to past values of itself at varying time lags.

Backcasting – the process of applying a **forecasting model** to the period covered by the **time series** on which it is based; used to establish the **accuracy** of a **forecasting model**.

Bias – refers to the amount by which an estimation method fails to produce the actual value of the statistic being estimated.

Box–Jenkins approach – a popular process for applying **ARIMA** models to time series forecasting.

Causal forecasting method – a class of **quantitative forecasting methods** that attempts to mathematically simulate cause and effect relationships among **time series**.

Coefficient – a number multiplying a variable to produce an equation's solution; in **regression analysis**, the coefficients are determined by **least squares estimation**.

Coefficient of determination – in **regression analysis** the square of the correlation between the values in the **time series** being forecast and the **forecast series**; it indicates the proportion of the **variance** in the latter explained by the former; indicated by R^2 ('*R* squared'); it should be adjusted for the number of **explanatory variables** in a **regression model**, in which case it is indicated by $\bar{R}^2$ ('*R*-bar squared').

Confidence level – see **level of confidence**.

Correlation coefficient – a standardized measure of the relationship between two **variables**, representing the amount by which they vary together in deviating from their respective **means**.

Country of residence – the country where the **visitor** has lived for most of the past 12 months, or for shorter periods if he or she intends to return within 12 months to live there. (WTO)

Data point – an individual value in a **time series**.

Data series – same as a **time series**.

Decomposition method – a **forecasting method** designed to break down the patterns in a **time series** into season, cycle, trend and random components.

Delphi method – that **qualitative forecasting method** designed to develop group consensus by following specific rules that ensure respondent anonymity, iteration and controlled feedback and statistical group response.

Dependent variable – see **forecast variable**.

Deseasonalize – the process of removing the recurrent seasonal variations in a monthly, quarterly or other sub-annual **time series**.

Destination – a place where a **visitor** stops, either overnight or for a shorter period not necessarily including a night. (WTO)

Differencing – the act of creating a new **time series** by subtracting the previous value of the original time series from the current one (called 'short differencing') or subtracting the **sub-annual time series** value one year earlier from the current value ('long differencing').

Domestic visitor – any person residing in a country who travels to a place within the country outside his/her usual environment for a period not exceeding 12 months and whose main purpose of visit is other than the exercise of an activity remunerated from within the place visited. (WTO)

Double exponential smoothing method – an exponential smoothing method that adjusts a **single exponential smoothing** model for trend in a **time series**.

Downward trend series – a **time series** that declines rather steadily in a linear fashion; its **mean** decreases over time.

Dummy variable – an artificial **variable** constructed such that it takes the value of one whenever the qualitative phenomenon it represents occurs, and zero otherwise.

Durbin–Watson statistic – allows us to test the hypothesis that there is no **autocorrelation** among the **residuals** obtained by forecasting.

Endogenous variable – a variable whose value is determined within a **structural forecasting model**.

Error – the value obtained by subtracting a **forecast value** from the actual value for the same point in time; same as **residual**.

Establishment – a single physical location at which business is conducted; distinct from a **firm**, which is a business organization or entity consisting of one or more establishments under common ownership or control.

Exogenous variable – a variable whose value is determined outside a **structural forecasting model**.

Explanatory variable – a variable that affects the **forecast variable** in a **regression** model but is not affected by it; same as **independent variable**.

Exponential smoothing method – one of several **extrapolative forecasting methods** that uses one or more smoothing constants and past **errors** to simulate a **time series**; includes **single exponential smoothing** and **double exponential smoothing**.

Extrapolate – to estimate a value of a **variable** outside a known range from values within a known range by assuming that the estimated value follows logically from the known values.

Extrapolative forecasting methods – also called 'time series methods' employ patterns in a **time series** to project or **extrapolate** future values, ignoring causal relationships.

Firm – a business organization or entity consisting of one or more **establishments** under common ownership or control.

Forecast process – the formal structure of sequential steps that produce a forecast.

Forecast series – a **time series** of future values produced by some method.

Forecast variable – the **variable** to be forecast based upon its **time series**; the dependent variable in a **regression** equation that is determined by some other factor or factors.

Forecast, tourism demand – a prediction of **tourism demand** for some time period subsequent to the most recent period for which such data are available.

Forecasting method – a systematic way of organizing information from the past to infer the occurrence of an event in the future; a forecasting method normally permits more than one **forecasting model** to be developed.

Forecasting model – one specific application of a **forecasting method**.

Forecasting –the process of organizing information about a **phenomenon**'s past in order to predict a future.

Functional form – the form of the mathematical relationship between the **forecast variable** and one or **more explanatory variables**, e.g. linear, exponential, quadratic.

GDP – **gross domestic product**.

Gross domestic product – a measure of the total flow of goods and services produced within a country's borders over a specified period of time, usually one year or quarter.

Heteroscedasticity – the condition where the **variance** of a **time series** increases or decreases over the series; opposite of **homoscedasticity**.

Historical time series – a **time series** of past values.

Homoscedasticity – the condition where the **variance** of a **time series** remains constant over the series; opposite of **heteroscedasticity**.

Inbound international tourism – the activities of non-residents of a given country travelling to and within the country as **visitors**. (WTO)

Independent variable – see **explanatory variable**.

Intercept – the constant term in a **regression** equation, often viewed as estimating the value of the **forecast variable** when all **explanatory variables** equal zero.

Interquartile range – the range of the middle 50 per cent of the values in a distribution; its centre is the **median**.

Judge – an expert chosen to provide forecasts according to the rules of a specific **qualitative forecasting method**.

Least squares estimation – a statistical estimation method that estimates the **coefficients** or **parameters** of a **regression** equation by minimizing the squared **errors** between the **forecast series** and the **time series**.

Level of confidence – the probability that a confidence level around an estimated **regression** model statistic encompasses the analogous **population parameter**.

Level of significance – the risk of rejecting the hypothesis that a **regression model** parameter, such as the coefficient of an **explanatory variable**, is significantly different from zero when it is not.

Linear time trend regression – a **regression model** where time is the only **explanatory variable**.

MAPE – see **mean absolute percentage error**.

Market segment – a subgroup of an overall **market** that comprises consumers who are similar in their response to a **tourism** product and its marketing.

Market – those people who may have an interest in purchasing a good or service and have the financial means to do so.

Mean – the value found by dividing the sum of all **observations** by the number observations.

Mean Absolute Percentage Error (MAPE) – a measure of forecasting **error** equal to $[(1/N) * \sum (|F_t - A_t|/A_t) * 100]$, where '$N$' is the number of time periods covered, 'F' is the forecast for specific time period, t, and 'A' is the actual value for the specific time period t.

Median – the point in a distribution of values, ranked from lowest to highest, that divides the distribution into two equal parts.

Microcomputer – a compact and relatively inexpensive computer consisting of a microprocessor and other components of a computer, miniaturized where possible; sometimes called a 'personal computer'.

Misspecification – the condition of a **regression model** where the **dependent variable** is not an unchanging linear function of the model's **explanatory variables**; that is, important explanatory variables are missing.

Model – a simplified representation of reality that attempts to capture the major relationships at work among certain **variables**.

Moving average model – an **extrapolative forecasting model** employing current and past **errors** to explain current values of a **time series**; not related to **moving average**.

Moving average – the **time series** produced by computing the **means** of some number of past consecutive values of a time series at each point in time; not related to **moving average model**.

Multicollinearity – in a **regression model**, the condition where two or more **explanatory variables** are highly correlated with each other.

Multiple regression model – see **regression model**.

Naive forecasting model – the simplest **forecasting model**, predicting that the next period's value will be the same as the current period's (the 'simple naive model'), or if a seasonal series, the same as the value one year earlier (the 'seasonal naive model').

Non-linear trend series – a **time series** that does not follow a straight line as it rises or falls over time, but often follows a curve or wave.

Observation – same as a **data point**, reminding us that each data point must be observed and measured, introducing the possibility of measurement **error**.

Origin country – the country where the **visitor** has lived for most of the previous 12 months or has lived for a shorter period and intends to return within 12 months. (WTO)

Outbound international tourism – the activities of **residents** of a given country travelling to and within another country. (WTO)

Outlier – an extreme **observation** in a **time series**.

Paradigm – a **model** of the world or view of how the world works.

Parameter – an **intercept** constant or slope **coefficient** in a quantitative **forecasting model**.

Parsimony – the principle that, all else being approximately equal, the simpler of two **forecasting models** is the better one.

Partial autocorrelation – a measure of **correlation** indicating the strength of the relationship between current values of a **variable** and an earlier value at a specific time lag while holding the effects of all other time lags constant.

Partial correlation – a measure of correlation between a **forecast variable** and an **explanatory variable** while holding the effects of all other explanatory variables constant.

Person-trip – a standard measure of **tourism** activity, this is recorded each time one person goes on a qualified **trip**; for instance, four persons travelling together correspond to four person-trips.

Personal income – income received by persons from employment, investments, and transfer payments in the form of wages, salaries, other forms of labour earnings, dividends, interest and rent.

Phenomenon – an occurrence, a circumstance, or a fact that is perceptible by the senses.

Population – all values, objects or people of interest to the survey researcher and from among whom the **sample** will be selected.

Precision – the exactness with which a number is specified, indicated by the number of significant digits with which it is expressed.

Probability sample – a **sample** where every element of the **population** it represents has a known, non-zero chance of being included.

Qualitative forecasting methods – also called 'judgemental methods' these employ experts or judges to organize past information about the **forecast variable** by following some rule or set of rules.

Quantitative forecasting method – a **forecasting method** that organizes past information about a **phenomenon** by specific mathematical rules.

R^2 - see **coefficient of determination**.

$\bar{R}^2$ - see **coefficient of determination**.

Receiving country – a country that receives **visitors** who are **residents** of another country. (WTO)

Regression analysis – the method of determining the statistical relationship between a **forecast variable** and one or more **explanatory variables** utilizing their **time series** and least squares estimation or other statistical method.

Regression model – an equation where the **coefficients** relating one or more **explanatory variables** to the **forecast variable** are estimated by least squares estimation or some other statistical method; if there is only one explanatory variable then it is a simple regression model; if there are two or more explanatory variables, then it is a multiple regression model.

Reliability – the extent to which repeated use of a **forecasting model** will yield the same results.

Research – the process by which we gather, organize and analyse information in a systematic manner to solve problems or confirm solutions.

Resident of a country – a person who has lived in the country for most of the past 12 months, or for a shorter period if her or she intends to return within 12 months to live there. (WTO)

Residual – in forecasting, commonly used as a synonym for **error**.

Same-day visitor – a **visitor** who does not spend the night in a collective or private accommodation in the place visited; this includes cruise passengers who debark in a country but spend their nights on board ship. (WTO)

Sample – the number and/or identification of respondents in the **population** who will be or have been included in a **sample survey**.

Sample survey – a research technique where a **population** is identified, a **sample** is selected and systematically questioned, and the results analysed and expanded to represent the **population**.

Scatter diagram – a graphical display showing two **time series** as a single point at each time period.

Seasonal factor – a value associated with a given month, quarter or other sub-annual period which represents the average ratio of that value to the value for the average period for the year; this is used to compute **seasonally adjusted time series**.

Seasonal naive model – see **naive forecasting model**.

Seasonality – movements in a **time series** within a year which recur roughly the same every year; these are usually the result of weather, social customs, holidays, or business policies.

Seasonally adjusted time series – a **time series** of monthly, quarterly or other sub-annual data from which recurring seasonal fluctuations have been removed; these series are usually produced through computing **seasonal factors**.

Serial correlation – same as **autocorrelation**.

Single exponential smoothing method – an **extrapolative forecasting method** where a single smoothing constant and **errors** are used to adjust the forecast series to the **time series**; works best with a **stationary series**.

Spreadsheet – a type of software for **microcomputers** that offers the user a matrix of rows and columns into which data can be entered and processed.

Stationary series – a **time series** that exhibits a constant **mean** and constant **variance**.

Stepped series – a **time series** that exhibits a series of increases (or decreases) followed by a horizontal or level trend indicating no change.

Structural forecasting model – a set of inter-related equations intended to simultaneously represent how **endogenous** and **exogenous variables** are related.

Sub-annual time series – a **time series** for regular periods of time less than one year, such as months, seasons or quarters.

Survey – a sampling, or partial collection, of facts, figures, or opinions taken from a **population** and used to approximate or indicate what a complete collection of information, or census, might reveal.

Time plot – a graph that displays a **time series** related to its periods at equally spaced intervals.

Time series forecasting methods – see **extrapolative forecasting methods**.

Time series – an ordered sequence of values of a **variable** observed at equally spaced time intervals.

Time trend method – a **forecasting method** that uses **regression analysis** to estimate the relationship of a deseasonalized **time series** to time, expressed in months, quarters or years.

Tourism – the activities of persons travelling to and staying in places outside their usual environment for not more than one consecutive year for leisure, business and other purposes. (WTO)

Tourism demand – a measure of **visitors**' use of a quantity of a good or service; such measures commonly found in **tourism** forecasting include **visitors** to a destination, transportation passengers and **tourism expenditures**.

Tourism expenditure – the total consumption expenditure made by a **visitor** or on behalf of a visitor for and during his/her **trip** and stay at a **destination**. (WTO)

Tourism industry – the set of **firms, establishments** and other organizations one of whose principal activities is to provide goods and/or services to tourists.

Tourist – a **visitor** who stays at least one night in a collective or private accommodation in a place visited. (WTO)

Tracking signal – an indicator of whether the **errors** occurring as the future unfolds are due to chance or indicate that the **forecasting model** no longer simulates the **time series** and should be revised or replaced.

Transformation – changing the measurement scale of one or more **variables**; used to achieve a **stationary series** and to improve the accuracy of a **regression model**.

Travel party – members of a single household travelling together on a **trip**.

Travel – the act of taking any **trip**.

Traveller – any person on a **trip** between two or more localities. (WTO)

Trip – a basic measure of **tourism** from the standpoint of the generating place or country (the origin) and covers the whole period that a person travels away from home. (WTO)

Upward trend series – a **time series** that moves upward rather steadily in a linear fashion; its **mean** increases over time.

Vacation trip – a pleasure **trip**, usually of several days or more and often requiring a leave of absence from work.

Validity – the extent to which a **variable** or a regression model actually measures what it is intended to measure.

Variable – any phenomena that can be measured; in this book, it usually refers to a **phenomenon's time series**.

Variance – a summary statistic that represents how closely the values of a **time series** cluster around its **mean**; it is the mean of the squared deviations from the mean.

Visitor party – same as **travel party**.

Visitor – any person travelling to a place other than that of his usual environment for less than 12 consecutive months and whose main purpose of travel is other than the exercise of an activity remunerated from within the place visited. (WTO)

World Tourism Organization – an affiliate of the United Nations, is an intergovernmental body devoted to the promotion and development of domestic and international **tourism** throughout the world.

WTO – abbreviation of **World Tourism Organization**.

Bibliography

Almon, Clopper (1989), *The Craft of Economic Modeling*, 2nd edition, Ginn Press, iv + 307 pp.

Alreck, Pamela L. and Settle, Robert B. (1985), *The Survey Research Handbook*, Richard D. Irwin, Inc., xix + 429 pp.

Archer, Brian (1994), 'Demand forecasting and estimation', in *Travel, Tourism and Hospitality Research, A Handbook for Managers and Researchers*, 2nd edition (J. R. Brent Ritchie and Charles R. Goeldner, eds), John Wiley & Sons, pp. 105–114.

Armstrong, J. Scott (1985), *Long-range Forecasting, From Crystal Ball to Computer*, 2nd edition, John Wiley & Sons, xxvii + 689 pp.

Brady, John and Widdows, Richard (1988), 'The impact of world events on travel to Europe during the Summer of 1986', *Journal of Travel Research*, Vol. XXVI, No. 3 (winter), pp. 8–10.

Calantone, Roger J., di Benedetto, C. Anthony and Bojanic, David (1987), 'A comprehensive review of the tourism forecasting literature', *Journal of Travel Research*, Vol. XXVI, No. 2 (fall), pp. 28–39.

Chan, Yiu-Man (1993), 'Forecasting tourism: A sine wave time series regression approach', *Journal of Travel Research*, Vol. XXXII, No. 2 (fall), pp. 58–60.

Choy, Dexter J. L. (1984a), 'Forecasting hotel industry performance'. *Tourism Management*, Vol. 6, No. 1 (March), pp. 4–7.

Choy, Dexter J. L. (1984b), 'Forecasting tourism revisited', *Tourism Management*, Vol. 5, No. 3 (September), pp. 171–176.

Clifton, Peter, Nguyen, Hai and Nutt, Susan (1992), *Market Research: Using Forecasting in Business*, Butterworth-Heinemann Ltd, xiv + 266 pp.

Coates, Joseph F. and Coates, Jennifer (1989), *What Futurists Believe*, Lomond Publications, xiii + 340 pp.

Cornish, Edward (1977), *The Study of the Future*, World Future Society, x + 307 pp.

Crouch, Geoffrey I. (1995), 'A meta-analysis of tourism demand', *Annals of Tourism Research*, Vol. 22, No. 1, pp. 103–118.

Crouch, Geoffrey I. (1994a), 'The study of international tourism demand: A survey of practice', *Journal of Travel Research*, Vol. XXII, No. 4 (Spring), pp. 41–55.

Crouch, Geoffrey I. (1994b), 'The study of international tourism demand: A review of findings', *Journal of Travel Research*, Vol. XXIII, No. 1 (summer), pp. 12–23.

Crouch, Geoffrey I. (1992), 'Effect of income and price on international tourism', *Annals of Tourism Research*, Vol. 19, pp. 643–664.

Crouch, Geoffrey I., Schultz, Lance and Valerio, Peter (1992), 'Marketing international tourism to Australia: a regression analysis, *Tourism Management*, Vol. 13, No. 2 (June), pp. 196–208.

Cunningham, Stephen (1991), *Data Analysis in Hotel & Catering Management*, Butterworth-Heinemann Ltd, vii + 204.

Dalkey, Norman C. (1969), *The Delphi Method: An Experimental Study of Group Opinion*, The Rand Corporation, ix + 79 pp.

Darnell, Adrian, Johnson, Peter and Thomas, Barry (1990), 'Beamish Museum – modelling visitor flows'. *Tourism Management*, Vol. 11, No. 3 (September), pp. 251–257.

di Benedetto, C. Anthony, and Bojanic, David C. (1993), 'Tourism area life cycle extensions', *Annals of Tourism Research*, Vol. 20, pp. 557–570.

Elkins, Randyl D. and Roberts, Randall S. (1987), 'Evaluating the human resource (employment) requirements and impacts of tourism developments', in J. R. Brent Ritchie and Charles R. Goeldner, eds, *Travel, Tourism, and Hospitality Research, A Handbook for Managers and Researchers*, John Wiley & Sons, pp. 403–411.

Faulkner, Bill and Valerio, Peter (1995), 'An integrative approach to tourism demand forecasting', *Tourism Management*, Vol. 16, No. 1 (February), pp. 29–37.

Florida Department of Commerce (1995), *Florida Visitor Study/1994*, 40 pp.

Frechtling, Douglas C. (1992), 'World marketing and economic research priorities for tourism', *Tourism Partnerships and Strategies: Merging Vision with New Realities, 23rd Annual Conference Proceedings*, Travel and Tourism Research Association, pp. 20–27.

Gardner, Everette S., Jr, (1992), 'How to monitor your forecasts'. *Lotus*, April, pp. 54–57.

Granger, C. W. J. (1989), *Forecasting in Business and Economics*, second edition, Academic Press, Inc., xii + 279 pp.

Holden, K., Peel, D. A. and Thompson, J. L. (1990), *Economic Forecasting: An Introduction*, Cambridge University Press, ix + 213 pp.

Holman, Richard L. (1993), 'Egypt hurt by drop in tourists', *The Wall Street Journal*, February 16.

Jarrett, Jeffrey (1991), *Business Forecasting Methods*, 2nd edition, Basil Blackwell Ltd, viii + 463 pp.

Jenkins, Darryl and Frechtling, Douglas C. (1991), 'World tourism model simulations for West Germany, 1990–93', *World Travel and Tourism Review: Indicators, Trends and Forecasts, Volume 1*, Donald E. Hawkins and J. R. Brent Ritchie, eds, C.A.B. International, pp. 83–90.

Johnston, J. (1972), *Econometric Methods*, 2nd edition, McGraw-Hill Book Company, x + 437 pp.

Jørgensen, Finn and Solvoll, Gisle (1996), 'Demand models for inclusive tour charter: the Norwegian case', *Tourism Management*, Vol. 17, No. 1 (February), pp. 17–24.

Kaynak, Erdener, Bloom, Jonathan and Leibold, Marius (1994), 'Using the Delphi technique to predict future tourism potential', *Marketing Intelligence & Planning*, Vol. 12, No. 7, pp. 18–29.

Kennedy, Peter (1987), *Guide to Econometrics*, 2nd edition, The MIT Press, Cambridge, MA, xii + 410 pp.

Kmenta, Jan (1971), *Elements of Econometrics*, The Macmillan Company, xiii + 655 pp.

Levenbach, Hans and Cleary, James P. (1981), *The Beginning Forecaster: The Forecasting Process Through Data Analysis*, Lifetime Learning Publications, xiii + 372 pp.

Lewis, C. D. (1982), *Industrial and Business Forecasting Methods*, Butterworths, p. 40, quoted in Witt and Witt (1992, p. 86).

Makridakis, Spyros G. (1990), *Forecasting, Planning and Strategy for the 21st Century*, The Free Press, x + 293 pp.

Makridakis, Spyros, Wheelwright, Steven C. and McGee, Victor E. (1983), *Forecasting: Methods and Applications*, 2nd edition, John Wiley & Sons, xviii + 926 pp.

Martin, Christine A. and Witt, Stephen F. (1989), 'Accuracy of econometric forecasts of tourism', *Annals of Tourism Research*, Vol. 16, pp. 407–428.

Middleton, Victor T. C. (1994), *Marketing in Travel and Tourism*, 2nd edition, Butterworth-Heinemann, 308 pp.

Miller, James J., McCahon, Cynthia S. and Miller, July L. (1991), 'Foodservice forecasting using simple mathematical models', *Hospitality Research Journal*, Vol. 15, No. 1, pp. 43–58.

Moeller, George H. and Shafer, Elwood L. (1994), 'The Delphi technique: A tool for long-range travel and tourism planning', in *Travel, Tourism, and Hospitality Research, A Handbook for Managers and Researchers*, 2nd edition (J. R. Brent Ritchie and Charles R. Goeldner, eds), John Wiley & Sons, pp. 473–480,

Moore, Thomas W. (1989), *Handbook of Business Forecasting*, Harper & Row, xvi + 313 pp.

Morley, Clive L. (1994), 'The use of CPI for tourism prices in demand modelling', *Tourism Management*, Vol. 15, No. 5, pp. 342–346.

Moutinho, Luiz and Witt, Stephen F. (1995), 'Forecasting the tourism environment using a consensus approach', *Journal of Travel Research*, Vol. XXXIII, No. 4 (spring), pp. 46–50.

Naisbitt, John (1994), *Global Paradox*, William Morrow and Company, 304 pp.

Pindyck, Robert S. and Rubinfeld, Daniel L. (1981), *Econometric Models and Economic Forecasts*, 2nd edition, McGraw-Hill Book Company, xxii + 630 pp.

Rao, Potluri and Miller, Roger LeRoy (1971), *Applied Econometrics*, Wadsworth Publishing Co., x + 235 pp.

Saunders, John A., Sharp, John A. and Witt, Stephen F. (1987), *Practical Business Forecasting*, Gower Publishing Company, xii + 340 pp.

Schulmeister, Stephan (1979), *Tourism and the Business Cycle*, Austrian Institute for Economic Research, 140 pp.

Sheldon, Pauline (1993), 'Forecasting tourism: Expenditures versus arrivals', *Journal of Travel Research*, Vol. XXII, No. 1 (summer), pp. 13–20.

Shim, Jae K., Siegel, Joel G. and Liew, C. J. (1994), *Strategic Business Forecasting*, Probus Publishing Company, viii + 333 pp.

Smeral, Egon (1988), 'Tourism demand, economic theory and econometrics: An integrated approach', *Journal of Travel Research*, Vol. XXVI, No. 4 (spring), pp. 38–43.

Smeral, Egon (1994), 'Economic models', in *Tourism Marketing and Management Handbook*, 2nd edition (Stephen F. Witt and Luiz Moutinho, eds), Prentice Hall, pp. 497–503.

Smeral, Egon and Witt, Stephen F. (1992), 'The impacts of Eastern Europe and 1992 on international tourism demand', *Tourism Management*, Vol. 13, No. 4 (December), pp. 368–376.

Smeral, Egon and Witt, Stephen (1995), 'Tourism Trends to 2005, a paper presented at the 30th Tourist Research Centre (TRC) Meeting, Venice, April 7–10, 1995', unpublished, 20 pp.

Smeral, Egon, Witt, Stephen F. and Witt, Christine A. (1992), 'Econometric forecasts: Tourism trends to 2000', *Annals of Tourism Research*, Vol. 19, pp. 450–466.

Smith, Stephen L. J. (1989), *Tourism Analysis, A Handbook*, Longman Scientific & Technical, xii + 312 pp.

Summary, Rebecca (1987), 'Estimation of tourism demand by multivariable regression analysis', *Tourism Management*, Vol. 8, No. 4, pp. 317–322.

Turner, Lindsay W., Kulendran, N. and Pergat, V. (1995), 'Forecasting New Zealand tourism demand with disaggregated data', *Tourism Economics*, Vol. 1, No. 1 (March) pp. 51–69.

United Nations and World Tourism Organization (1994), *Recommendations on Tourism Statistics*, United Nations Department for Economic and Social Information and Policy Analysis, New York, 1994, v + 77 pp.

Uysal, Muzaffer and Crompton, John L. (1985), 'An overview of approaches used to forecast tourism demand', *Journal of Travel Research*, Vol. XXIII, No. 4 (Spring), pp. 8–13.

van Doorn, Joseph W. M. (1982), 'Can futures research contribute to tourism policies', *Tourism Management*, Vol. 3, No. 3 (September), pp. 149–166.

van Doorn, Joseph W. M. (1984), 'Tourism forecasting and the policymaker', *Tourism Management*, Vol. 5, No. 1 (March), pp. 24–39.

Van Doren, Charles (1991), *A History of Knowledge Past, Present and Future*, Ballantine Books, xxv + 422 pp.

Vandaele, Walter (1983), *Applied Time Series and Box-Jenkins Models*, Academic Press, xii + 417 pp.

Witt, Stephen F. (1994), 'Econometric demand forecasting', in *Tourism Marketing and Management Handbook*, 2nd edition (Stephen F. Witt and Luiz Moutinho, eds), Prentice Hall, pp. 516–520.

Witt, Christine A. and Witt, Stephen F. (1990), 'Appraising an econometric forecasting model', *Journal of Travel Research*, Vol. XXVIII, No. 3 (winter), pp. 30–34.

Witt, Christine A. and Witt, Stephen F. (1992), 'Tourism forecasting: accuracy comparisons across aggregated/disaggregated data', unpublished paper, 8 pp.

Witt, Christine A. and Witt, Stephen F. (1994), 'Demand elasticities', in *Tourism Marketing and Management Handbook*, 2nd edition (Stephen F. Witt and Luiz Moutinho, eds), Prentice Hall, pp. 521–529.

Witt, Christine, Witt, Stephen F. and Wilson, Nick (1994), 'Forecasting international tourist flows', *Annals of Tourism Research*, Vol. 21, No. 3 pp. 612–628.

Witt, Stephen F. and Martin, Christine A. (1987), 'International tourism demand models – inclusion of marketing models', *Tourism Management*, Vol. 8, No. 1 (March), pp. 33–40.

Witt, Stephen F., Newbould, Gerald D. and Watkins, Alan J. (1992), 'Forecasting domestic tourism demand: Application to Las Vegas arrivals data', *Journal of Travel Research*, Vol. XXXI, No. 1 (summer), pp. 36–41.

Witt, Stephen F. and Witt, Christine A. (1995), 'Forecasting tourism demand: A review of empirical research', *International Journal of Forecasting*, Vol. 11, No. 3 (September), pp. 447–475.

Witt, Stephen F. and Witt, Christine A. (1992), *Modeling and Forecasting Demand in Tourism*, Academic Press, vii + 195 pp.

Witt, Stephen F. and Witt, Christine A. (1991), 'Tourism forecasting: Error magnitude, direction of change error, and trend change error', *Journal of Travel Research*, Vol. XXX, No. 2 (fall), pp. 26–33.

Witte, Robert S. (1989), *Statistics*, 3rd edition, Holt, Rinehart and Winston, xviii + 504 pp.

World Tourism Organization (1995a), *Concepts, Definitions and Classifications for Tourism Statistics: Technical Manual No. 1*, ii + 126 pp.

World Tourism Organization (1995b), *Collection of Tourism Expenditure Statistics: Technical Manual No. 2*, v + 104 pp.

World Tourism Organization (1995c), *Collection of Domestic Tourism Statistics: Technical Manual No. 3*, vi + 125 pp.

World Tourism Organization (1995d), *Collection and Compilation of Tourism Statistics: Technical Manual No. 4*, v + 149 pp.

World Tourism Organization (1995e), *A Satellite Account for Tourism*, v + 81 pp.

World Travel and Tourism Council (1995), *United States Travel & Tourism: A New Economic Perspective*, 16 pp.

Yong, Yeong Wee, Keng, Kau Ah and Leng, Tan Leng (1989), 'A Delphi forecast for the Singapore tourism industry: Future scenario and marketing implications', *International Marketing Review*, Vol. 6, No. 3, pp. 35–46.

Index